CHAINED BIRDS

a true crime memoir

CARLA CONTI

WILDBLUE
PRESS

WildBluePress.com

Chained Birds published by:
WILDBLUE PRESS
P.O. Box 102440
Denver, Colorado 80250

WILDBLUE PRESS is registered at the U.S. Patent and Trademark Offices.

Hardback:978-1-964730-31-8
Paperback: 978-1-964730-32-5
Ebook: 978-1-964730-30-1

CHAINED BIRDS

CONTENTS

AUTHOR'S NOTE

This is a work of nonfiction. Certain names and places have been changed for the privacy and protection of some story participants. Any resemblance to actual persons, living or dead, or real events is absolutely true.

DEDICATION

For the afflicted

PREFACE

The genesis of this book belongs to Mother Nature and impulse. It stems from an overnight snowfall that lingered on a cold, dreary winter day in 2011 and the whim of an abused inmate in a federal prison in the middle of nowhere Pennsylvania.

This book exists because a convict once threw a snowball at a prison guard and hit him in the face.

Picture a writer's or investigator's *murder board*, a giant bulletin board covered with paper fragments from a years-old case that haunts its creator. The board takes up half of a wall. It holds photos of inmates nicknamed Okie, Arson, T-Rex, and Rey, plus pictures of high-security prisons like Atwater, Allenwood, Big Sandy, Lewisburg, and Coleman II. It features a Hells Angels biker patch, the meth-lab RV from the TV series *Breaking Bad*, and 1950s mug shots of Boston mobster Whitey Bulger. Tacked to the middle is a pictorial primer on jailhouse tattoos and their meanings, flanked by a list of the major federal prison gangs and their foot soldier clans. Geographic references are interspersed, including a bus schedule from Florida to California that meanders through Pittsburgh and an article about the closure of a seedy motel near Stockton.

At the far-left end of the board is a crude drawing of a snowball on scrap paper, indistinguishable from a planet or an orange, except I know what it is because I've lived with the nuclear fallout from this snowball for too many years. Picture a red string tied around the thumbtack that holds the snowball sketch in place and extends across the board to the pushpin holding up the last item on the right: a book cover mock-up featuring a black and white bird illustration. A thousand stoplights and crossroads traverse this strand of string—too many for a murder board—but the A-to-B of its trajectory is indisputable.

That snowball, thrown in a momentary act of defiance at a barbaric correctional officer, set off a chain reaction that caused a prison guard-orchestrated stabbing, felony charges and a criminal case, two penitentiary gang hit orders, and is now linked to the closure of one of the most heinous and violent experimental prison programs in the country.

Were it not for that packed ball of slush and frozen water vapor, the specific atrocities revealed in this book would have remained buried. No snowball, no *Chained Birds*. No klieg lights. No new infotainment tale of our broken prison and criminal justice systems.

But there was a snowball, which led to *United States v. Kevin Sanders* and much more than I bargained for as part of the defense team. And if I learned anything worth sharing from this decade-long, somber odyssey, it's this: The first step to redress is exposure.

PROLOGUE
THE FALLEN

JUNE 20, 2008

On the first day of summer, in the middle of a California heatwave, 22-year-old correctional officer Jose Rivera kissed his girlfriend goodbye in their Chowchilla apartment and drove 28 miles north for his shift at Atwater Prison.

He was still in his probationary year with the Bureau of Prisons (BOP), having started his career at Atwater the previous August. He'd come to the job after four years in the Navy, including two tours in Iraq. But he really wanted to work for the California Highway Patrol, and he was biding his time at Atwater while waiting to learn the status of his state application.

Rivera lived and worked not far from where he grew up, in a small, modest home surrounded by miles of fruit orchards and row crops. He was the middle of five children and still very protective of his siblings and mother. As an A student in high school, he used to run interference with bullies who dared to mess with his family, and his softspokenness belied a man who pursued the courage of his convictions. All the Riveras lived within 10 minutes of each other, and after nearly three years away from them in Iraq, Rivera never wanted to leave the San Joaquin Valley again.

Assignments at Atwater high-security pen rotated, and today, Rivera was scheduled as the Unit Officer for housing Unit 5A. In a better world of record-keeping, Officer Rivera might have logged into the prison computer system to see that a troublesome inmate had arrived last night, someone flagged as a potential threat to the unit or staff. But this new transferee, James Guerrero, was conspicuously missing from that Posted Picture File or PPF list. Neither the prison he came from nor the Atwater intake team added him to the database despite his recent assaults on officers and a documented suspicion that he was responsible for killing a correctional officer in Guam in 1987.

However, staff protocol for checking the PPF was also lax, and Rivera had only looked at the list a handful of times in his ten months at Atwater. This was by no means unusual. Most staff did not check for updated PPFs because the policy was murky.

The point is Rivera showed up for his shift at Atwater unaware that on his unit, a new Guamanian inmate with a history of violence against officers was celling with a fellow Guamanian, who was serving life for murder.

Unfortunately, Rivera was also not privy to a prescient conversation between his colleagues the night before about the two inmates from Guam.

—

Guerrero, 43, arrived at Atwater the day before as a disciplinary transferee from the Coleman II federal prison in Florida. His intake screening revealed his recent staff assaults and the suspected killing of the correctional officer in Guam 20 years earlier. The record showed Guerrero was serving a life sentence under the "three-strikes" law for armed bank robbery.

Unit Manager Marie Orozco initially assigned Guerrero a cell in her Unit 2B. But at intake, Guerrero, for an undocumented reason, complained and said he wouldn't cell with anyone in that unit. A solution, however, was found by a Special Investigative Services (SIS) officer who convinced Guerrero to cell with another Guamanian in a unit that housed fellow Asian and Pacific Islanders.

A different SIS Lieutenant, Jesse Estrada, approached Orozco at dinner to tell her of the change, and her first reaction was, "You're going to put him in with another killer?"

This other killer and Guerrero's new cellmate was Jose Sablan, age 40, who was serving life for a murder he committed in Guam, plus additional years for attempted murder and felony escape.

After reconsidering the circumstances, Orozco argued with her colleague that she believed Guerrero belonged, at least initially, in the Special Housing Unit (SHU)/solitary confinement and not in general population. Lt. Estrada pushed back and said Guerrero needed the programming available in "gen pop" and that Guerrero's assignment to cell with Sablan in Unit 5A would stand.

Orozco relented. "Okay, if that's what you're going to do—we'll be lucky if he doesn't end up killing somebody before the night is out."

No one was killed that night. In fact, the night was uneventful, and it turned out that new cellies Guerrero and Sablan knew each other from their incarcerated days in Guam.

—

Officer Rivera's Friday morning shift in Unit 5A was also uneventful. The 10 a.m. official headcount was routine, and, as was typical during a heat wave, morning recreation was significantly more popular. By early afternoon, when the temperature had reached 100 degrees, inmates preferred congregating inside the air conditioning.

Perhaps as a welcoming gesture for the newly arrived Guerrero—or just because it was any other day in Atwater—the Asian and Pacific Islanders on the lower tier of Unit 5A were getting drunk on a fresh batch of prison wine.

Atwater's recipe for homebrewed alcohol involved holdover fruit from inmate meals and sugar "cooked" out of carbonated soft drinks sold at the commissary. The cooking and fermenting were achieved with a "stinger," a rigged heating element crafted of metal and an electrical outlet. The distilled liquid was then funneled back into the plastic soda bottles and dispersed throughout the prison, traded for favors, sold for books of stamps, or as payment for gambling debts.

Prison wine was so abundant in Atwater that correctional officers (COs) who came across the ingredients, a stinger, or the end product sometimes disposed of the contraband without even writing up a disciplinary report. Similarly, when officers discovered intoxicated inmates, they usually locked them in their cells to "sleep it off." An incident report was not always filed.

As Officer Rivera's 3:30 p.m. headcount approached, he "called count" and started securing the unit's first floor. After each inmate returned to his bunk, Rivera locked his cell door.

At 3:20 p.m., Rivera approached a group of Asian and Pacific Islanders on the first floor. He engaged them in brief conversation, and inmates Sablan and Guerrero were noticeably intoxicated. The group broke up as inmates headed to their cells for the count, and the two Guamanians made their way to the unit's upper tier and cell 223.

After securing the lower level, Officer Rivera climbed the stairs and began the second-floor lockdown. At 3:23 p.m., he reached cell 223, where Sablan and Guerrero stood outside. As Rivera attempted to lock them in, Sablan pulled an icepick-type shank from his pocket and stabbed Rivera in the torso. The officer ran, with both inmates in pursuit, and Rivera made it to the upper tier stairwell before Sablan stabbed him in the shoulder. The injured Rivera staggered down the steps and bought himself a few seconds by head-butting Sablan midway on the stairs. At 3:24 p.m., at the bottom of the stairwell, Rivera pressed the panic button on his body alarm and prayed someone would reach him in time.

However, the catastrophic problem was that Rivera, as the unit manager for that day, was the only officer with a key to Unit 5A's front door.

At this point, Guerrero had caught up to Rivera on the first floor and tackled him to the ground, holding him by his legs as Sablan mounted the officer and stabbed him over and over. Rivera received eight more thrusts with the ice pick before a female secretary from a unit office arrived on the scene—but she had no front door key. The secretary, who shouted at the inmates to no avail, was quickly followed by a female unit manager who requested radio assistance and also had no front door key. Outside responding staff arrived at the unit but couldn't get in.

Neither female staff was armed with any nonlethal weapons, and they watched helplessly as Sablan continued stabbing Rivera until finally, at 3:25 p.m., the compound officer arrived with the unit door key. Agonized staff rushed inside to the bloody scene and subdued both inmates.

In those excruciating two minutes, while waiting for help, Rivera was stabbed a total of 28 times in the torso, head, and neck. Officers attempted CPR measures and then rushed him on a gurney to Health Services. Life-saving measures continued until an ambulance arrived, but Officer Rivera was pronounced dead at the local hospital. The cause of death was two puncture wounds to his heart.

As expected, Rivera's brutal murder hit his family and the Atwater prison staff hard. Thirty-two correctional officers from FCI Dublin outside San Fransisco and Victorville, 300 miles away, came to Atwater to relieve Rivera's colleagues who attended his memorial service. Some attendees heard Rivera's girlfriend say that the day after he was killed, his acceptance letter to the California Highway Patrol Academy had come in the mail.

The Bureau of Prisons had not lost an officer in the line of duty in 11 years. Not since April 3, 1997, when Scott Williams, Senior Officer Specialist at USP Lompoc, was fatally stabbed in the neck by a prisoner while routinely escorting inmates from the chow hall back to their cells.

Atwater's high-security inmate population of 1,123 went into a three-month lockdown, and there were immediate calls by the correctional officers' union for increased staffing and protective gear like stab-resistant vests, pepper spray, batons, and tasers. Like almost every other federal penitentiary, Atwater was chronically understaffed, and Rivera should have had a second officer with him to manage the 100 inmates in Unit 5A.

The BOP released few details about Rivera's death and spent the next nine months investigating every abject failure that led to the tragedy. Officials learned that Sablan's eight-inch icepick-shaped shank had been fashioned from stainless steel rods stolen from the kitchen's industrial dishwasher. Conveyor belt parts from this same dishwasher were used to make weapons in a hostage-taking episode the previous fall. In that incident, an officer in Unit 5A was held at knife-point by inmates protesting the fact that gangs were controlling cell assignments and collecting a "tax" on them. After negotiations, the officer was released with only minor injuries.

But in the wake of Rivera's death — and long before the Bureau made its report public the following summer — it was under increasing pressure to act, to do something. Within a month of the murder, the BOP had classified inmates Sablan and Guerrero as being "unable to rehabilitate." This dovetailed perfectly with an announcement at the end of October 2008 that the Bureau would be creating a new Special Management Unit (SMU) for the most violent and problematic prisoners throughout the federal system. The idea was to house the "worst of the worst" inmates in one place to make the open-compound prisons safer. Plans were drawn up to convert the oldest federal prison in the country into a much more restrictive institution, where the most troublesome would be locked down nearly 24 hours a day under austere conditions.

In February 2009, the United States Penitentiary (USP) Lewisburg, in Central Pennsylvania, began receiving its first inmates for the new SMU program. By the time the Bureau of Prisons released its 21-page *Board of Inquiry Report* into Rivera's death in June 2009 — which cited understaffing, prison wine, dishwasher-made weapons, and the dysfunctional key policy as major factors in his murder — the bed space for Lewisburg's experimental SMU program was already full.

EPIGRAPH

"The truth is rarely pure and never simple."
   — Oscar Wilde

PART I

OLD PRISON JOKE

How many prison guards does it take to throw a handcuffed inmate down a flight of stairs?

None. He fell.

CHAPTER 1
A SNOWBALL IN HELL

FEBRUARY 2011, LEWISBURG SMU G BLOCK RECREATION, 9:35 A.M.

Twenty-seven-year-old Steven "Oakie" Tremblay, a tall, lean suitcase bomb builder from Oklahoma, was into his fifth set of burpees when the outside metal door to his recreation cage clanged open. He stopped mid-pushup, his hands pressed into slush from overnight snow, to see who was in the sallyport, the secure vestibule with its own locked entry and exit that led directly into the 8-foot by 20-foot rec cage that Oakie thought would be his alone for an hour. He tightened and then relaxed to see the CO had removed the handcuffs of Spider, a recent dropout of the Aryan Resistance Movement, or ARM.

Spider's drop-out status rendered him an acceptable rec partner for Oakie, who had to be separated from all white supremacist gang members because he stubbornly refused to join them. This defiance did not sit well with Casper, the leader of the Aryan Brotherhood, and if any member of the AB or their foot soldiers were to encounter Oakie, they'd have to deliver a beat-down message or worse. When Spider was still an ARM lackey—denoted by a pair of Hitler SS lightning bolts tattooed on the base of his shaved head—he'd once mistakenly identified Oakie as a fellow "Peckerwood" associate due to Oakie's blond goatee and blue eyes. The two had been enclosed in rec cages directly across from one another when Spider looked Oakie up and down, nodded, and said, "Sup, Wood?"

"I'm not your fucking Peckerwood homeboy," Oakie spit out in disgust.

Now, with handcuffs removed and the rusted sallyport door locked behind him, Spider sized up Oakie the same way, but all he said this time was, "Sup?" Oakie ignored him while resuming his burpee repetitions. Spider began jogging in a small snow-packed circle, careful to stay on his side of the rec cage, a middle unit of five attached in a row on a concrete pad. The pair exercised in silence, inhaling and exhaling misty clouds into the morning air, like the others up and down their row and in the tier of cages across the frozen walkway, two, or sometimes four-to-six men to a cage. Muffled banter and loud exchanges carried on around them, with some inmates in the middle acting as messengers for end-to-end conversations. All of them had gotten up at 5 a.m. to ensure they were included on the day's rec sheet because this was the only hour of the day they were allowed outside their tiny, decrepit cells.

Just over 1,000 SMU inmates were locked down nearly 24/7, except for three showers and five hours of recreation each week. This deleterious housing was a key SMU feature designed to motivate the gangbangers, murderers, and lifers with nothing to lose to undertake the four-phase program and earn greater freedoms. If they stayed out of trouble and weren't sent back to Phase I on a CO's whim, they could make it out of Lewisburg in two years and rejoin an open compound prison.

Spider broke the silence again, this time with some gossip about his former gang. "The AB's setting up a hunger strike, you know," he told Oakie, adding that now that he's no longer ARM, he won't have to starve himself. Oakie grunted, unimpressed, and said between lunges, "They've been threatening that for months."

It was no secret that the AB leadership in Z Block was trying to orchestrate the strike to protest a smorgasbord of SMU conditions, ranging from the small to the deadly. There was the shrink-wrapped crap food and disallowed staples like personal radios and basic additional toiletries, and then there were the roach and mice-infested cells. But mostly, it was the double-bunking with non-compatible cellmates in those revolting cells, originally designed for just one person, that was behind the strike.

Specifically, it was the prison's policy of cuffing inmates in their cells before transporting them anywhere that kept the prisoners on edge and afraid for their lives. Before leaving for rec, a shower, or rare use of a computer for legal purposes, an inmate had to place his arms behind him and through the food slot in his door to be cuffed before being escorted. It was the same when he returned—cuffs were only removed once inside his cell, and he extended his wrists through the food slot. This perilous policy left the cuffed inmate at the complete mercy of his uncuffed cellie, who may or may not have murder on his mind and a shank.

All those violent personalities on top of one another nearly 24 hours a day culminated in more inmate-on-inmate stabbings and suicide attempts than even the local press was aware of. Two inmates had already been killed in their cuffs by their cellmates since the SMU opened, and one inmate, who'd asked for psychology services but was denied, hung himself with bed sheets tied to his cell window bars and died in the hospital five days later.

—

The hour outside flew by despite no real conversation between Oakie and Spider. As rec officers approached the sallyports up and down the tier, the two inmates finished their cardio routines, their gray sweatpants and sweatshirts fully drenched with perspiration and ground slush. Oakie stood in front of the sallyport, poised as the first one out, as a portly officer with a familiar limp in his left leg drew near and turned the key into the first lock. Oakie's heart returned to racing, and he staggered back against the cage wall, instantly triggered. He tried to cover by telling Spider, "Nah, man, you go," as he slumped toward the ground and struggled to breathe. Oakie's fast-blinking eyes had not deceived him—the fat officer with the bum leg was his abuser from Big Sandy: Dennis MacDonald.

In a flash, Oakie was back at his previous prison, wearing paper clothes and tied to a gurney in a basement interrogation room, while a female officer electrocuted his testicles under MacDonald's orders. MacDonald had laughed and said, "I'm turning you into a girl." And then his forehead was doused with a burning solvent. That had been six months ago, and now MacDonald was here in Lewisburg, where Oakie thought he'd just heard someone address him as Captain: a transfer *and* a promotion. Oakie couldn't believe it.

On impulse, Oakie scooped up two handfuls of snow and packed it, unnoticed, into a ball as he waited for his turn to pass through the sallyport. Before he could be cuffed, and just as MacDonald recognized who he was, Oakie hurled the snowball at the captain, and it landed on his face. The ambush caught MacDonald off guard, and he fell to the ground, where Oakie repeatedly kicked him in the groin as inmates cheered him on.

Other officers rushed in to rescue MacDonald, and Oakie was pepper-sprayed and subdued, face-planted on the snowy concrete. Out of breath and with pink wet cheeks, MacDonald cuffed Oakie, bent closer, and whispered, "You think you can escape me, boy, with another transfer? You'll never leave this place unless it's in a box." Then the captain looked around for dramatic effect and said in front of many witnesses, "Who around here can I put you in a cage with?"

CHAPTER 2
THE CHAMELEON

MARCH 2011, LEWISBURG SMU INTAKE

Kevin Sanders hadn't stepped foot outside the razor wire of United States Penitentiary (USP) Allenwood in seven years—not since he'd arrived from California on a ten-year gun charge. But on this drizzly late winter morning, "Chico Blanco," or just "Chico," as he'd been known until 20 minutes ago, had exited Allenwood in a brown jumpsuit and blue slip-on "bus shoes," aptly named for what came next. With handcuffs chained to his waist and his ankles shackled, Kevin boarded a long, white prison bus with bars across the windows and no other passengers.

One of two armed correctional officers motioned for him to take a seat, and Kevin picked a middle bench, sliding easily to the window despite the belly chain linked to his handcuffs. He'd created this maneuverability by exhaling and tightening his muscles when the torso chain had been applied, resulting in some wiggle room when he relaxed.

Of Kevin's many regrets and wishes throughout his 36 years, the one foremost on his mind now was that the bus ride to Lewisburg Prison was only 20 minutes long. His ears popped as the bus descended southward from the scenic ridges of the Appalachian Mountains, and Route 15 gave way to what most would consider duller views. But not to Kevin. The gray landscape, dormant grass, and lifeless trees of a Central Pennsylvania winter not quite finished were a wonderous sight for someone who'd been in prison most of his adult life. For a lackluster 10 miles, he cherished each passing car, gas station, liquor store, roadside house, and especially the occasional glimpse of the Susquehanna River's west branch.

The middle of Pennsylvania was home to one of the country's highest concentrations of prisons and jails, easing the burden on the federal Bureau of Prisons to find Kevin a new home. Lewisburg's Special Management Unit, only 13 miles from Allenwood, was the easy transfer choice, but only after Kevin's prison record was cherrypicked to make him qualify.

What had been problematic, and therefore not presented as evidence in his SMU referral hearing, was a glowing report he'd received two months prior on his job duties. Kevin had been given an excellent work performance rating for picking up trash around Allenwood's compound, and it earned him a meager bonus. He'd been cited as "dependable" with a "can-do attitude" who volunteered for extra work—hardly the profile of an out-of-control, impossible-to-manage, murderous inmate the SMU was designed for.

So, to make it work, officials reached back a year and a half into Kevin's history to highlight two incident reports. One vague report said he'd assaulted another inmate and possessed a dangerous weapon. The other report said Kevin was seen "chasing another inmate while wielding an unknown item." The other inmate, it was noted, had "no known injuries."

Besides these two old reports, Kevin's testimony that he was no longer in "good standing" with the Montañistas and feared for his life helped tick that last box for SMU designation. This confession that he'd once belonged to a gang—not remotely close to being a newsflash inside

Allenwood—was prescriptive, nonetheless. Qualifications met, check, check, and check.

Like everyone else throughout the federal prison system, Kevin had heard about the violence and conditions at Lewisburg, which had supplanted the supermax at ADX in Florence, Colorado, as the new worst pen to do time. But he'd had no power to fight the SMU designation and advocate for placement elsewhere, such as at USP Canaan, a maximum-security prison in the Pocono Mountains that would have been a two-hour bus ride away. By the time of his SMU hearing, Kevin had been drained and life-starved from a month in solitary confinement, or "protective custody"— the only solution to keep a Montañista from killing him. And even after the hearing, Kevin had had to wait two more weeks for that day's bus transfer, where every highway billboard, warehouse, and factory was a sight to behold.

With less than two miles to go, the white prison bus exited the divided freeway for a rural road heading west. The setting was abruptly pastoral, dotted with shiny dome-topped silos, farmhouses with red outbuildings and acres of inactive cropland. Large, flat, harvested cornfields ran up to the road's edge, defined by an endless line of old-timey utility poles. Kevin committed it all to memory, for these scenes of Americana would be the first things he'd sketch after settling into his new cell with his drawing paper, art supplies, and other belongings.

The bus passed neither person nor vehicle as the heavenly stretch of road continued after one more turn and on through the decorative iron gates of Lewisburg prison, where a last mile of tended grounds and old-growth trees welcomed its visitors. Kevin found those last few tranquil miles affirming and took them as a sign. Despite everything he'd heard about Lewisburg's SMU, this prison couldn't possibly be as bad as the lonely, soul-sucking hell of solitary confinement.

"Clothes off!" yelled one of two intake officers in Lewisburg's screening room, as if he were addressing a dozen new inmates instead of just one. "You know the routine," he barked, and Kevin complied, shedding his jumpsuit, holding out his hands, turning them over, sticking them in his mouth, and pulling wide to show off his gums. "Feet!" directed the officer as Kevin lifted each one to show the bottoms. Then, lastly, the nadir of strip search humiliation: "Bend over and spread 'em!" and Kevin parted both butt cheeks while being ordered to "Cough!" and "Lift up your sack!" True to form, the correctional officer inspected from a distance, not wanting to go anywhere near this inmate's junk.

While he was naked, Kevin was weighed, his height measured, and his tattoos were photographed to corroborate his profile in the BOP's central database. He was still Caucasian and 5 feet 11 inches tall, weighed 189 pounds, and listed as having brown eyes and hair on his closely shaved head. He sported a dark mustache and matching forked beard down to his collarbone with a small soul patch of hair under his lower lip.

Kevin's face was relatively free of tattoos compared to his body. A small, inked tear drop appeared under the outward corner of his left eye, and under the far corner of his other eye was a small spider web—the universal sign for doing time. A larger spider web began at his neckline and gave way to a mosaic of slate-gray images that covered his front and back torso, arms, and legs. Tattoos of jesters, jokers, clowns, and a dozen variations of skulls fought for skin space alongside the body ink of a gremlin holding a pistol, a python's head with fangs, a couple of female heads attached to voluptuous breasts, and so on.

But the most notable ink marking for the intake officers was the large three-peaked mountain image across Kevin's chest that was the unmistakable symbol of the Montañistas. The COs also photographed the back of Kevin's legs because his left calf was tatted with the letter "V," and his right calf was inked with the letter "L." He'd gotten these initials as a teenager in Central California after joining the Valley Locos, a small street gang of mostly Hispanics with a few whites. It was the VL, all those years ago, which had nicknamed him "Chico Blanco" (meaning *white boy)*—a moniker he'd resurrected in Allenwood when it came time to choose his protective "car" or gang.

"Clothes on!" yelled the CO, who nodded toward a fresh pile of prison-issued boxers, t-shirt, khaki uniform, and black boots. While he dressed, the second officer pulled Kevin's possessions from the black garbage bag he'd brought from Allenwood and placed them on a nearby table. With every item that came out of the bag, the officer said either "Nope," "No," or "Not allowed." The discard pile included his charcoal and color sketch pencils and half ream of blank paper, his MP3 player, black digital watch, sunglasses, Nike tennis shoes, sweatpants and shirt, and personal toiletries— all of which he'd purchased from Allenwood's commissary with money earned from his cleanup job, or bartered for new tattoos applied with his homemade tat gun. The only thing he was allowed to keep was his Bible.

"What the fuck, man?" Kevin asked incredulously. "Language!" said the officer who'd conducted the strip search, and he threw a Lewisburg SMU handbook on the table where Kevin was seated. "You're Level 1, inmate Sanders, study up. SIS is on its way for your debrief."

Generally, after the strip search and photos, new inmates would be sent on for medical and psych evaluations, but Kevin was a special case. SIS, or Special Investigative Services, needed to know why he'd been transferred from Allenwood so they could document which groups or gangs

Kevin couldn't come into contact with. The word "debrief" meant Kevin was expected to renounce his former gang, so he'd have to repeat for new ears the entire drama that brought him to this moment.

While he waited, he leafed through the handbook and found the section describing the SMU Levels. There were four, and at Level 1, he was allowed few personal possessions and one phone call a month, which would bother him more if he had anyone to call. But the more Kevin read, the more disheartened he became, especially when he realized he'd be locked in a cell nearly 24/7. No prison yard. No chow hall. No TV or radio. Rec on only five days. A shower three times a week. It looked like workbooks and programming were the only outlets here and the only means toward regaining his possessions and greater freedoms. The handbook said the SMU program could last 18 months to two years. But he only had three years left on his sentence, which probably meant he was stuck in this fresh hellscape until he could book a halfway house near the end.

QUAY HEARING

"Says here you ran the yard at Allenwood for the Montañistas," said the pot-bellied Special Investigative Agent introduced to Kevin as Captain MacDonald. Kevin shrugged.

"What's a white guy like you doing running a Hispanic gang's prison yard?" MacDonald pressed. Kevin offered another shrug. He didn't feel like explaining that he'd fallen in with the Montañistas because he speaks fluent Spanish and that they were the first ones who'd courted him. He'd needed the protection of some car (gang), so that was that.

"I'm not really a Montañista," Kevin said, "I just hung with them."

MacDonald shared a skeptical look with his colleague, a Special Investigative Supervisor, Lieutenant Lippit. She wore her dirty blond hair in a ponytail and clicked her pink fingernails repeatedly on the Formica tabletop.

"Um hm. That mountain tat on your chest says otherwise," Lippit said, taking notes on a legal pad. Both officials appeared not much older than Kevin, maybe in their early 40s.

It's true. Kevin had risen through the Montañista ranks to second-in-command behind shot-caller Lorenzo Cruz, a.k.a. "Rey." It was Kevin's job to keep their yard as drama-free as possible by steering his people clear of whites, blacks, and rival Hispanics. He'd also managed the gang's influx of smuggled-in cell phones, cigarettes, and drugs, although the drugs were strictly a financial commodity because the Montañistas prohibited drug use within its car. Kevin enforced a long list of "household policies" that included learning American Sign Language and Braille (for covert communications) and rules about weapons (always have them on your person) and boots (always have them on your feet). He had also ensured new recruits got welcome packages of toiletries, a radio, a courtesy shank, and commissary snacks that every Montañista contributed toward, and that all the foot soldiers complied with their mandatory workouts. It was an enviable post overseeing the yard and day-to-day operations, with benefits to match—until it wasn't.

"I don't want nothing to do with the Montañistas anymore," Kevin told them. "And I can't be around them. Write that down on your yellow pad." Lt. Lippit glared at him.

"Your month in the hole. Tell us about that," MacDonald said.

"Six weeks," Kevin corrected, then laid out the events that earned him this transfer.

Rey had been in the hole as a disciplinary measure, he told them, and the shot-caller was worried about getting replaced as leader. So he devised an outlandish, evil scheme for getting out. Rey reasoned that if one of his foot soldiers perpetrated a violent attack, Allenwood officials would be forced to let Rey out to control his people, and Rey would remain top dog.

"I got a kite telling me to hit Mamba in the yard," Kevin explained as Lt. Lippit wrote down his story. Both SIS officers were overly familiar with kites: clandestine messages written on small pieces of paper with tiny print, tightly rolled smaller than a cigarette. They were often hidden inside a baggie in an inmate's orifice until they could be passed along. "And Mamba is my best friend, so I said, fuck that.

"Mamba was *short*—he'd be out in less than a year— and I couldn't see sending my best friend back home busted up like that. It wasn't right."

"And so you refused the hit order," MacDonald said, but it was more of a question.

"Yeah, and then I was in the hat. You know how it works … I went to the top of the BNL." Kevin's placement on the Bad News List forced him to disavow the Montañistas and ask Allenwood officers for protective custody to stay alive. And now Kevin's separation status was Lewisburg's problem.

"So now your keep-aways are *all* the Hispanics and the Blacks, obviously. You got any problem being around whites?" MacDonald asked.

"Nah," Kevin shook his head.

MacDonald sat back in his chair, crossed his arms over his ample belly, and said to Lt. Lippit, "Let's put him in G-Block. See which white inmates need cellies."

The Lieutenant clicked her nails a few times as if deep in thought. "I believe Inmate Keys is in need of a cellmate," she snickered, squaring her eyes on Kevin. MacDonald cracked a smile, and the two SIS agents shared a look that Kevin instinctively knew meant only one thing: *trouble.*

CHAPTER 3
THUNDERDOMES

Inmate Mark Keys, a 43-year-old Las Vegas casino robber, a.k.a. "Arson," was ready for a new cellie. For three weeks, he'd enjoyed taking a dump in his parking-space-sized cell without another human hovering nearby. But after two days with no one to talk to except during that one hour of rec, Arson decided the isolation was worse. Lucky for him, that changed when Kevin Sanders got bussed in from Allenwood, trying to stay one step ahead of the Montañistas.

By the time Kevin had arrived, the hunger strike was over, but that didn't stop COs from using the strike as a pretext to rearrange the housing of an especially irritating inmate. Kevin's introduction to G-Block began with the deployment of two use-of-force teams outside a nearby cell because one inmate inside refused to submit to hand restraints and accept a new cell assignment. Ten officers in protective gear, padded vests, and helmets with face shields had gathered, and foam projectiles were fired through the food slot to get the inmate to comply. When the officers finally subdued and shackled the inmate and carried him down the hallway, he was heard proclaiming, "I'm not on the food strike! Check the cameras! I've been taking my meals since Monday!" To which one of the COs replied that they were moving him to a cell with another hunger striker where the water would be turned off.

"You're gonna have to kill me in here!" the inmate said. "I ain't going for none of this shit—mail me out in a box, man!"

Kevin bristled at the drama that he now assumed pervaded every federal prison. But at least he was compatible with his new cellie—as long as Kevin didn't cross him. Arson—not nicknamed for anything related to fire, but because he was a hot head with a short fuse—was agreeable enough. He was shorter and thinner than Kevin and a few years older, and his most prominent feature was a giant swastika tattooed on his bald forehead. Inked across his chest, amid a collage of other tattoos, were the letters NLR, standing for Nazi Low Rider.

Arson was ambitious, Kevin learned, and wanted to gain favor with Casper, T-Rex, and the Aryan Brotherhood (AB) crew confined largely to Z Block. Arson took a liking to his new cellmate and began vouching for Kevin, telling anyone who'd listen that Kevin was no longer a Montañista and could be trusted in the white power circle. This was fine with Kevin, who, once again, needed the protection of some car, and the AB, with its foot soldier acronyms, was his only option.

One month after his arrival, on a chilly April morning, Arson and Kevin prepared for another rec session with the usual non-invasive, nowhere-near-their-genitalia pat-down and scan with a hand-held metal detector. They would rec together, this much was certain, but the final number of men in a cage, possibly as many as six, was anyone's guess.

Officer Willis ran rec that morning, and one by one, COs, under Willis's direction, escorted each inmate, cuffed behind their back, from the holding area to their designated pen. There was a rhythm and flow to the marching routine that ended at the sallyport, where, once inside, cuffs were removed, and the inmate could open the door to the actual rec cage. The process repeated, with Willis and other officers returning to the holding room for another inmate to place somewhere among the double row of cages. On and on it went until all the cages were full, and then the reverse happened when the hour was up.

Arson was ahead of Kevin in the lineup and taken to a cage occupied by two unfamiliar faces that were definitely not white. The pair knew each other and congregated in the corner, and Arson thought they might have spoken Spanish. The rec officer brought Kevin to the cage last, but as he passed through the sallyport, he sensed something was off. Arson's face was slightly twisted, and his hyper-alert eyes stared at the rec cage occupants 20 feet away.

When Kevin got a good look at the other two men, bile rose in his throat, and he broke out in a cold sweat. "What the fuck, man! That's Rey!" he whispered to Arson. "That's fucking Rey from Allenwood!"

"Fuck you talking about, homie?" said Arson. "Shot-caller Rey?"

"The fuck is he doing here?" Kevin could not fathom the situation. He was supposed to be kept away from *all* Montañistas. How could this happen? How could they make him share space with the one Montañista who'd issued a kill order against him?

Kevin turned toward the walkway, gripped the chain-link, and yelled, "Hey! Hey," in an officer's direction. But Arson yanked his shirt backward and whispered, "Nah, man, it's too late now. We gotta rumble."

"But we ain't got no knives ..."

"They might not either," Arson whispered. "And we gotta hit them before they hit us."

Kevin knew this was true. And he was suddenly grateful to be celling with a guy who had his back, even if Arson was a little too eager to go into battle. Arson had agreed with

Kevin's decision not to hit Mamba and thought Rey was a piece of shit for trying to get out of the hole that way. So here was Arson, ready to pay his respects to his new cellmate, and Kevin could hardly pass on it. And before he knew it, Arson was charging across the cage, hollering, "Let's get these mother-fucking 'Nistas!"

Arson landed the first set of punches with right hooks to Rey's head and upper body. Then Arson held Rey in place by his T-shirt while Kevin rapidly struck him with both fists in the head and face. Rey's associate grabbed Kevin by the waist to pull him off of Rey, and he eventually dropped to his knees while maintaining an iron grip on Kevin's legs. Kevin started punching the associate to free himself but couldn't break his grasp even after several elbow thrusts to his back. Arson, meanwhile, was making mincemeat of Rey's face.

The mele lasted 57 seconds before officers arrived, radioed for backup, and the inmates disengaged. No one got sliced or needed serious medical attention because the Montañistas didn't have a shank, making Kevin both the unluckiest and luckiest inmate in recreation that morning.

Though little blood was spilled, Arson was pleased because it was a proper beat-down. The AB might not have been watching, but word would spread about their heroic effort and that Arson had landed the first blows. Plus, it would put to rest any nagging doubts about Kevin's allegiance to his former car. Kevin was one of them now.

JULY 2011, LEWISBURG SMU Z BLOCK RECREATION, 9:50 A.M. MONDAY

Atsá Biyáázh, a.k.a. Little Eagle, a 44-year-old serial bank robber from Texas, was among the first wave of Z Block inmates taken out for recreation that morning. His separatee status was simple—there wasn't anyone he couldn't be around—yet he would still rec with the same Sureño gang dropout he celled with. Nothing ever changed.

Sometimes, when they were racked in for count and had to stand bedside and state their inmate name and number, Little Eagle would shout proudly in Navajo, "Atsá Biyáázh yinishyé, 'Ats'oos Dine'e nishłį, Totsohnii báshíshchíín..." Translation: I am called Little Eagle, I am The Feather People (his mother's clan), born for Big Water (his father's clan) ... but he could never get to his maternal and paternal grandparent clans because a CO would cut him off. "Knock it off, Chase!" they'd say. "You're getting another 400!"

Little Eagle would relent, revert to English, and state his birth name, Westin Chase, and inmate number. Depending on the CO, he'd sometimes get hit with a 400-level infraction like loss of visitation privileges, which didn't matter because his mother and sister would never make the trip from Texas for a lame onsite video visit. Even if they took away his commissary for 30 days, it was always worth it to hear his Navajo name and mother's clan spoken out loud.

Little Eagle had asked to cell with another Native American, but there were only a few of them among the SMU's thousand or so inmates, and his request was either ignored or not possible, he guessed.

It so happened that Lewisburg's most famous current inmate, Leonard Peltier, was an American Indian. But Peltier, 67, was considered such a security threat that officials kept him isolated. Little Eagle had known Peltier at Leavenworth, where they'd developed a deep bond. But Peltier's high-risk status at Lewisburg meant the Sioux native rarely crossed paths with anyone other than prison officials.

Peltier was serving two life sentences for the 1975 murder of two FBI agents at South Dakota's Pine Ridge Indian Reservation. But Peltier, a political activist with a checkered past, always claimed he wasn't at the shootout that resulted in the agents' deaths. Indeed, the case against him was very thin, and his trial was tainted with fabricated evidence and the perjured testimony of multiple witnesses who said the FBI terrorized them into lying.

Over the years, Peltier's so-called wrongful conviction status was championed by a myriad of civil rights supporters, including Jesse Jackson, Nelson Mandela, and the Dalai Lama, plus a host of advocacy groups like the National Lawyers Guild, American Association of Jurists, and others. A prominent judge and law enforcement figure involved in his case even joined the chorus for his clemency, and the "Free Leonard Peltier" movement spawned sympathetic films and books about the defacto political prisoner ... none of which did him any good behind the bars of Lewisburg's SMU.

—

As Little Eagle considered the banality of it all, he noticed a new Z Block face in an officer's grip, a white boy being taken to the cage directly across from his.

"Hey! Where'd you come from?" Little Eagle asked. The Caucasian, wearing long, baggy white shorts and a gray knit cap despite the weather, looked over his shoulder and said, "G Block."

"Any Natives over there in G, or any that come with you?"

The white boy was uncuffed through a slot in the sallyport and, once inside the larger pen, walked to the end to continue conversing. He poked his fingers through the chain-link and said, "Nah, no Natives in G. Haven't seen any ..."

The American Indian nodded. "I'm Little Eagle."

"I'm Kevin."

At this point, Officer Shemp, who was running rec, was placing a shorter inmate in long, baggy orange shorts and a matching gray knit cap into Kevin's cage.

"Who's that?" Little Eagle asked.

"My cellie, Arson," Kevin said.

Arson joined Kevin at the far end, and the two discussed something in low voices. "This is Little Eagle," Kevin told his cellmate, and Little Eagle nodded.

"Hey," Arson said.

And then Little Eagle wanted to know, "Why'd they send you two from G Block?"

But before Kevin could answer, a hush swept across the range as a CO started escorting a known troublemaker down the sidewalk. It was that mental case Steven Tremblay, a.k.a. Oakie, who'd been flooding Z Block with his toilet water, barking out his window, and keeping everyone up at night with his constant banging. Oakie had stabbed someone a few days ago, and since then, he'd rec'ced alone. But as the CO who gripped Oakie's arm passed the few remaining empty cages, time stopped as each inmate watched to see where Oakie would be placed.

Oakie's escort stopped in front of the rec pen directly across from Little Eagle, who saw his new friend grow agitated. "Hey man, don't do this," Kevin told the CO. "That dude's no good. Don't put him in here." Little Eagle watched Kevin make stern eye contact with the officer and then back and forth cutting motions under his chin with a flat hand. The officer ignored him and turned Oakie over to Officer Shemp, who fingered his keys to let him into the sallyport. Kevin repeated himself, telling Shemp, "No man, don't put him in here, don't do it."

"This is Tremblay's assigned cage," Shemp said. "This is where he's rec'cing." Oakie struggled against the officer's grip and kicked the sallyport door before he was shoved inside.

Once the three were locked inside the cage, Officer Shemp did not return to the holding room to retrieve more inmates but instead stood outside that cage with his hand on the *duces*—his belt radio alarm. Arson extended his hand in a goodwill gesture to Oakie, who rebuffed it with a slap, prompting Kevin to tell the troublemaker, "Stay in the corner, then. Stay the fuck away from us."

After a minute or so, as Oakie kept to himself on the opposite end of the cage, Shemp disappeared and resumed his rec officer duties. But Oakie wasn't content to stay in the corner, and he started aggressively pacing the length of the cell.

And that's when the yelling started.

"Get that nutcase! Get that motherfucker!" were some of the first chants that echoed from the windows of Z Block's upper tier, where the Aryan Brotherhood was housed. "Oakie's no good, man! Get that guy!" The commotion drew more faces to the windows with more yelling and spread to every AB associate up and down the rows of recreational cages. "Fuck him, man," "Fuck that dude," was the growing refrain, and when one distant voice from the third-floor window proclaimed, "He's got an apple on his head!" it wasn't a statement but an order.

Arson moved on Oakie first, pinning Oakie to a corner and making stabbing motions to his head and torso. Kevin joined in, made similar stabbing motions, and threw in a few knee thrusts for good measure. While Oakie was getting stabbed up, every convict with a sharpened plastic weapon pushed them through the fence onto the grass because a strip search would absolutely follow the drama playing out in the three-man cage.

The 30-second assault only stopped when CO Shemp and one other officer came running toward the cage. "Okay, guys, that's good. That's enough," Shemp said, with his hand on the duces, but this time he pressed the alarm. "He's had enough."

Arson and Kevin retreated as officers responded to the alarm. Oakie, who was bleeding from his head and chest, had endured it all without calling for help or slumping to the ground. He exited through the sallyport to the safety of the walkway while Kevin and Arson were ordered to drop their weapons. One knife fell to the middle of the cage.

A medical team and a half dozen officers responded, and one of the COs quipped, "There's Oakie, making friends everywhere he goes." Lt. Lippit, her ponytail swinging, joined the scene, and Oakie was placed on a stretcher. She leaned in close and told him, "That's what you get for hitting MacDonald." He responded by coughing up blood.

A confused officer, CO Hazel, looked at the pale, bleeding victim and quietly asked, "Why'd she say that?"

CHAPTER 4
THE ATTORNEY

MAY 2012, U.S. DISTRICT COURT, PENNSYLVANIA'S MIDDLE DISTRICT

On a humid, mid-summer morning of typical commuter traffic, 47-year-old Scott Powell was zigging around buses, tractors, and law-abiding drivers to reach the U.S. District Court on time. He'd only been given an hour's notice that he had a new client and wasted precious minutes looking for a clean shirt and tie.

For 18 years, Scott had built up a law practice in North Central Pennsylvania, defending drug dealers, pimps, money launderers, pervs, and a supporting cast of outlaws. But business was slow, and more and more, he relied on these random courthouse calls saying it was his turn again to play public defender for someone who couldn't afford an attorney. For the first time, he was a month behind on paying his alimony, and the $125-an-hour defender rate was a lifeline. Back when the program started, it only paid $40 per hour, and very few of the region's attorneys wanted to sign on.

Scott's appointment today would mark a first: his client was an inmate from Lewisburg—he wasn't told the charge—and Scott was a little worried that he knew nothing about federal prison or its inhabitants. But he had tried cases in state court, so that would have to do.

Scott raced from a parking spot inside the federal building, up the elevator, and into the overly-lit sterile courtroom. He was 10 minutes late for the arraignment but had missed nothing. The 60-something part-time magistrate judge, Archibald Smith, smiled at Scott on his way in, and a clerk handed him a copy of an indictment.

"Morning Scott. How are you?"

"Great Arch, and yourself?"

Scott took a bench seat next to another court-appointed attorney he knew, Frank Davis, who whispered, "That's your guy on the right. Mine's the little guy with the swastika."

Across the room sat a pair of heavily tattooed Caucasians in orange jumpsuits, their wrists and ankles shackled. Two armed federal marshals stood between them and an exit door. Scott thought his client looked a little like the actor Vin Diesel (if he were tatted up) and was glad not to be representing the Nazi—although, who knew what ink markings were under his client's clothes.

Scott scanned the indictment that a grand jury had just handed down. The two inmates were charged with assaulting a third prisoner in a recreational cage *ten months ago*, and this time lag stunk to high Heaven.

"Why the fuck did it take them so long to bring charges?" Scott whispered to Frank, who said, "No idea. I'm wondering the same."

The judge called the proceeding to order. He advised both inmates of their Fifth Amendment right not to incriminate themselves and explained they would each have a taxpayer-funded attorney appointed at no cost. Introductions were made, and then Judge Smith read aloud the charges against the pair:

Count One — Assault with a Dangerous Weapon. Specifically sharpened plastic objects, with intent to do bodily harm and without justification or excuse.

Count Two — Assault Resulting in Serious Bodily Injury.

Count Three — Possession of a Prohibited Object. Specifically, 5 ½ inch long plastic shanks with "string handles." (Scott wrote a "?" next to that in his document's margin.)

"The statutory maximum for these felonies is a 25-year prison term," the judge added. "Do you understand?" Each prisoner said they did.

"All right. Before you confer with your counsel and enter your pleas, Assistant United States Attorney Neil Galloway—who represents the government and is bringing these charges—has a video to show the court. Some of us are going to step inside the jury room to see it."

The marshals led the defendants into the adjacent room, followed by the judge and stenographer. Just before the attorneys filed in, Galloway, the tall, silver-haired prosecutor, took Scott and Frank aside.

"We're offering five years. It's a good deal, considering they could get another ten if they don't plead."

Their clients could risk getting ten more years (on top of what they were already serving) if they went before a jury and lost. Or they could plead guilty now, save the government the trouble and expense of a trial, and take five years. This was a typical exchange in the federal court system in which 97% of all cases ended in a plea deal.

"Let's see the video," Scott said, and Frank agreed.

Galloway stood at a TV monitor. "Can we dim the lights? This is about three minutes long."

A grainy, silent video appeared on the screen. It was captured by a surveillance camera in the corner of the rec cage and showed a top-down view of Kevin Sanders, Mark Keys, and the victim, Steven Tremblay, inside the 10-foot by 20-foot chain-link pen.

The video began with the victim taking a lap from one end to the other but sticking to his side of the cage. Then, at the 12-second mark, inmate Keys attacked, forced him into the corner, and inmate Sanders joined the fight. The two assailants threw some punches, but mostly, they made stabbing motions, over and over, as the victim crouched lower in the corner. Scott tried but lost count of the knife thrusts. There were dozens, he thought.

At the 45-second mark, two officers appeared outside the cage, and Sanders and Keys stepped away. The victim gathered himself, walked to the sallyport, shook the door until it was opened, and stepped out of the cage without assistance. But Scott noted from the indictment that he spent three days in the hospital with a punctured lung and other injuries.

The rest of the video showed a growing officer presence and inmates returning to their workouts in nearby cages. Inmates Sanders and Keys conferred in the corner under the camera, then paced around the cage and were finally led out. At the 3-minute 13-second mark, one officer entered the cage and picked up something off the concrete floor. Then, the video was over.

Fuck me, Scott thought as he exhaled with a long blink. He turned to Frank, who wore the same look of defeat. Both attorneys prepared to huddle with their clients when Kevin Sanders stood up and shouted, "Play the tape from the beginning! Where's the rest of the tape?"

—

Scott, confused and intrigued, had just a few minutes to talk to his client before the arraignment wrapped. Back in the courtroom, he addressed his client in low tones, trying to keep their conversation away from his co-defendant and the federal marshals.

"What do you mean by the rest of the tape?"

"Man, I tried to tell the cop, 'No, don't bring that guy in here.' I was shaking my head and made motions like this," he said, waving his flat hand back and forth under his chin, a common signal for cease and desist.

"Did the officer see you make this motion?"

"Of course. But it was the cops who set it up from the beginning. Them and the AB. ..."

"AB?"

"Aryan Brotherhood." His client's voice was so low Scott could barely hear him. He looked around and whispered to his attorney, "There's a witness. There's this guy who watched the whole thing, who saw me waving off the cop. He'll talk, he'll tell you ... but the beginning part of that videotape will show it plain as day."

CHAPTER 5
THE BIG HOUSE

SUMMER 2012, THE BIG HOUSE

Wednesdays were visitation days at USP Lewisburg, and as many times as he could after the arraignment, Scott drove over an hour each way from his lake cottage near Wilkes-Barre to see his client. Kevin was getting screwed by the system and seemed to want to hold these prison bastards accountable. So Scott could not, in good conscience, urge Kevin to plead out his case. If his underdog client wanted to take it all the way, Scott was his man. Fate had brought them together for a reason.

Scott was used to long commutes to the other courthouses and jails, and this one was particularly scenic. He listened to Rush Limbaugh on AM Radio as his 2008 black Passat glided along a forested two-lane highway that cut through the edge of a state park and skirted Pennsylvania game lands. He encountered only rural and light industrial terrain, nothing urban or scary that would require the presence of his licensed .38 caliber semi-automatic in the glove box. Still, it was nice knowing the gun was there because one never knew.

The Big House, as it was known to locals, was a storied institution built in 1932 that, over the decades, housed a roster of notorious organized crime leaders and associates. The list included: Al Capone, a.k.a. Scarface (Chicago's infamous Prohibition-era gangster), Whitey Bulger (at the time just a bank robber and years away from becoming Boston's crime boss), Jimmy Hoffa (Teamsters Union president probably killed and disposed of by the mob after his release), John Gotti (head of the Gambino Crime Family, served three years there for airline hijacking), and Henry Hill (mobster-turned-informant whose story became a book and then the film *Goodfellas*). This unique profile earned the red-brick prison another moniker, "Mafia Row," which harmonized with the imposing structure's Italian Renaissance style.

The prettiest part of the drive—the last two miles of corn fields, barns, and silos—struck Scott as an incredible juxtaposition when he passed through the iron gate of USP Lewisburg. Endless acres of breezy, productive, and verdant farmland prospered right next to a fortress of drab, cramped, and violent prison cells. He couldn't think of a more startling contrast.

Visitor parking was found past Heartbreak Ridge Road and just off Big House Circle and Henry Hill Drive. Scott thought whoever named these roads definitely deserved some props.

—

"ID." "Jacket off." "Belt off." "Arms out." "Lockers that way." The check-in, metal detection, and pat-down routine never varied, including the disdain from officers who grunted their commands. But today, instead of seeing Kevin through a glass panel and talking by phone, they would have their first "contact visit" in a small private room that Scott had had to fight for.

Scott had missed several Wednesday visits in July after his father, Bill, had suffered a heart attack in Douglasville, and Scott had more or less moved into his childhood home during his dad's hospitalization and recovery. He worked remotely on his laptop and filed the first briefs in the case now assigned to a 70-year-old semi-retired judge out of Scranton.

Kevin told Scott two things that made the attorney think they stood a decent chance of an acquittal. One, Kevin said that if he hadn't joined in the fight to help Arson, Arson would have turned his knife on Kevin per the universal gang code of conduct. Kevin would have been stabbed up right there in the cage, possibly killed. Two, Kevin said he did not have a knife and only used his knees and made stabbing motions with his fists to make it appear legitimate to Arson and the AB watching from the third floor of Z Block.

Between those two things and the "wave off" that Kevin said he made to the CO bringing Trembley to the sallyport, there was enough reasonable doubt mixed with extenuating circumstances for a jury to consider.

Scott was expecting a confidential hand-delivered letter from Kevin today, hence the reason for the private room. Scott had gotten a surprise call from Kevin's brother Martin, explaining that Kevin had written a 25-page highly sensitive letter detailing events that led up to the rec cage assault. The letter stated why it happened and named corrupt officials and gang leaders in their roles. But the letter had been taken by COs and not returned, and Kevin had been harassed and punished all summer because of it. His brother said Kevin had duplicated the letter and kept it safe with an inmate friend, the friend who had called his brother to get a message to Scott. COs had denied Kevin's every request to call his attorney, and prison officials returned some letters Kevin wrote to Scott without explanation.

After waiting a few minutes, Kevin appeared with a three-man escort, cuffed behind his back. One of the officers carried Kevin's green folder of legal documents and correspondence that Scott had mailed him. When he was uncuffed and they had the room alone, Kevin asked, "Hey Scott, how's your dad? I hope he's doing better this week."

"He is, actually, thanks for asking. His housekeeper has him up, moving around more than he wants, and she's cooking his favorite foods, only without butter and salt, and sneaking in more vegetables. He's got it pretty good … How are they treating you?"

"I get visits every week by the shakedown squad, sometimes more. My cellie got tired of the games these cops been playin' with me 'cause he's affected too. We almost came to blows … but I got a new cellie now."

"That's good," said Scott. "I did hear from your brother, so I'm aware of how they keep moving you to different cells, take your property, strip you, and x-ray you … he said they make you wear paper clothes?"

"It's all part of them head games. They're just mad I'm going on the record with their bullshit. Ain't nothin' they can do about it in the end."

Kevin opened his green legal folder and removed a sealed envelope addressed to Scott with large block letters stating LEGAL MAIL. "Slide this in your file," he said, nodding at Scott's brown accordion legal folder he was allowed to bring in along with a yellow legal pad and pen. "So you know the first version of this letter was stolen on orders of Captain MacDonald?"

"Okay."

"I'll tell you what else was stolen. The printed email you sent me, talking about locating that former Lewisburg SIS officer who goes around testifying at trials. That wasn't in my legal papers when I got my property back."

Scott exhaled. "Fuck. Well, okay … speaking of that guy, I've asked the judge for money so we can hire him to testify about the gang structure here, the rules, how you had to assist Mark Keys in the rec cage—everything, so that you don't have to do it on the stand. I'm also asking for money to hire an investigator."

Kevin nodded. "What's this judge like?"

"Old. Ornery. But he did grant our continuance because of my Dad's heart attack ... I should ask for another one because the fucking BOP can't even give us a working copy of the rec cage fight on CD. Neither I nor Keys' attorney can get the video to play—it's in some kind of proprietary format."

Kevin nodded, processing every word. "And what about the rest of the video?"

"Yeah. Well, right now, the prosecutor's office is saying that's all there is. But I'm working on it."

The two talked more about the type of defense Scott would like to pursue and how the victim Trembley's mental state could be used to their advantage. Kevin said he'd heard that Tremblay was suing the BOP for the injuries he sustained in the assault, and Scott confirmed this was true. Scott was keeping tabs on the civil suit, he said, but he didn't tell his client how much this could complicate their case.

As their time came to a close, Kevin pulled a piece of paper from his green folder and slid it across to his attorney. It was a beautiful drawing of a woman's hands locked in prayer, holding a rosary, and in the corner, in delicate calligraphy, it read, "In Loving Memory of Joanne."

At one of their previous visits, they had talked about their families, including Scott's twin sister and their mother, Joanne, who had died the previous year. Like her daughter, Joanne was a devout Catholic, and now, seeing this drawing touched Scott in an unexpected way.

"This is amazing," Scott said. "I didn't know you could draw like this."

"There's a lot you don't know about me, Scott," Kevin said, grinning. "I thought your Dad might like to have it. Maybe it'll make him feel better."

Scott swallowed and couldn't find the words to express what this gesture meant to him, but smiled and said again, "This is really amazing. Thank you." Scott turned and knocked on the door, and three escorting officers appeared. The room was so small that they asked Scott to step out while they double-cuffed his client. As Kevin was being led away, one of the officers looked at the prayer drawing on the table and said, "What's this?"

Before Scott could answer, the CO snatched it with one hand and crinkled it in both. "This is contraband," he said and walked away with the nicest gift anyone had given Scott in a long time.

CHAPTER 6
THE CLIENT

EARLY FALL 2012

It was a mixed blessing that Scott's solo practice was drying up because he had little energy for anything but *The United States v. Kevin Sanders*. He now lived and worked out of the Powell family vacation house on the shore of Shawnee Lake, a small cottage his Dad stopped going to after his mom died and his lovely sister didn't have time to visit. In his divorce, Scott had lost the stately Victorian with a home office that he and his ex-wife had painstakingly restored, as well as custody of their daughter Ashley. But the 13-year-old came out on some weekends for grilled burgers and movies they'd pick up from Redbox. In a nanosecond, they had gone from reading all the *Harry Potter* books together to watching gore and slasher films that Scott feigned enthusiasm for because that's what she was into now. Sitting next to her and sharing popcorn, he'd endured the likes of *The Human Centipede*, *Transylmania*, *Halloween II*, *The Bleeding House*, a *Hellraisers* sequel, and more. *What parents do for their kids*, he thought.

Scott had transformed one of the cottage's small bedrooms into an office with a slab of butcher block counter, two sawhorses, a chair, and a filing cabinet. His computer faced a poorly insulated window that looked out onto the lake, and for now, this was his happy-enough place. His case files were carefully organized, including all of Kevin's letters (that he'd received). The most explosive letter was, of course, the one Kevin had secretly given him, and Scott did not feel entirely comfortable having it in his possession. Most of the pages were devoted to the origins of prison gangs as Kevin understood them, their structures, and mafia-like hierarchies. He explained the general rules and consequences for breaking them and how each gang disciplined their own members who got out of line—so that a rival gang couldn't do it first, and also because that was standard gang protocol.

But unlike in his other letters, in this one, Kevin named *names*. He identified three prison officials who were in on the set-up to place Tremblay into his rec cage, and he named the Aryan Brotherhood shot-caller who issued the hit order on the victim. And, in this letter, Kevin expanded on why he believed Tremblay ended up in his rec cage that day. They had already established that the AB wanted Tremblay taken out because he'd been disrupting Z Block with his psychotic behavior, like flooding his cell with toilet water so that his feces dribbled down into the cell below him—the cell of high-ranking gang member T-Rex.

But there was another reason for the assault that had nothing to do with the AB and everything to do with a foul captain who'd been embarrassed in front of inmates months earlier when Tremblay hit him in the face with a snowball. Kevin hadn't witnessed it, but all the inmates knew the story of how, after Captain MacDonald fell to the ground, Tremblay kicked him in the nuts, and MacDonald vowed revenge. And specific revenge—"Who around here can I put you in a cage with?" is what some of the inmates heard.

Kevin said MacDonald's desire for revenge is why he ignored the crafting of plastic shanks from overhead fluorescent light covers in Z Block. "He knew about it and let it slide," Kevin wrote. And then once Tremblay's rec cage assignment was ordered by MacDonald and carried out by two other corrupt officers, "They knew the rules and what would happen," his letter said. "They do it all the time. That's why those cages are called *Thunderdomes*."

Some of Kevin's blistering allegations had no direct bearing on the case but were important descriptions of Lewisburg's living hell all the same. "Cops making inmates suck dick" in the basement, where there are no security cameras, struck Scott as particularly vile.

He wasn't sure if he could prove anything in that radioactive letter that now formed the basis of their case. But Scott also knew the judge would never allow him to put the Bureau of Prisons on trial per se. He was overwhelmed with information and the task before him, and he reminded himself to breathe while popping Advil for lower back pain that wasn't getting any better.

Scott filed a motion to dismiss Kevin's case based solely on the missing part of the videotape, calling it intentional destruction of exculpatory evidence. A month later, the government's reply brief dealt an unexpected blow: Lewisburg Prison's videotape database self-erased every 14 days, and any video that wasn't retained was irretrievable now.

The prosecutor argued that even if a video section showed Kevin making a signal not to put Tremblay into the rec cage, "the officer didn't see it. Apparently, the signal was so subtle it was unobservable." But also, Galloway added, Kevin's subsequent actions invalidated any prior alleged signal anyway.

Typically, motions to dismiss were routinely denied, but the judge ordered a hearing and scheduled it for the week before Thanksgiving.

The attorney for Kevin's co-defendant and cellmate saw the writing on the wall and convinced Mark Keys, a.k.a. Arson, to take the five-year plea deal. Scott knew he now owed his client the same thoughtful analysis, so he made copies of the pertinent pages to mail to Kevin and typed a cover letter.

—

Dear Kevin,
Please find enclosed a lot of bad news. Don't give up. I will be filing a motion for a continuance later today and I am going to try to talk my friend Lucy Sandberg, a fellow criminal defense lawyer, to come down with me and go over this plea agreement. Not that I think you should sign it. But calculating federal sentencing guidelines is not my strong suit. It is hers. I will be down just as soon as I can.
Yours very truly,
Scott Powell, J.D., P.C.

—

"Hey doll, I have a favor to ask," was Scott's message to Lucia Sanderg's voicemail. Lucy was a partner at a large law firm with political connections, and often took on pro bono cases with her employer's approval. She was a few years older than Scott but looked ten years younger, and with her petite runner's body, blond hair, and dark blue eyes, she was always a favorite of presiding judges. Her firm benefited from the professional connections she cultivated while representing the indigent, and any defendant who drew her card usually won the lottery.

And sadly, for Scott, she was just out of reach romantically.

After a brief affair while he was going through his divorce, she decided it was unprofessional to be sleeping with anyone who might one day appear in her courtroom. With her firm's backing, she had her eye on a judgeship, and her mind was made up. Scott had disagreed vehemently but respected her decision, and he counted her among his most trusted colleagues and friends.

Two years ago, she represented a Lewisburg inmate who repeatedly kicked his cellmate in the head while his cellmate was cuffed behind his back, resulting in permanent brain damage. Lucy's client had preemptively struck his cellie—a known danger to everyone—because the deranged cellie kept threatening to kill him. Her client was charged with assault resulting in serious bodily injury and pled guilty. At his sentencing, Lucy argued that her client hadn't wanted to be in that position but did what he had to do to save his own life. Both the prosecutor and judge agreed her client acted out of fear and that the victim "had asked for it." Still, Lucy's defendant got an additional three years on top of his already lengthy sentence.

Lucy met Scott in the prison parking lot, and they went through the check-in and security routine together. He didn't think he imagined that the officers were a little less gruff this time, and possibly even used actual sentences. Once the three were inside the small legal visitation room, Scott made the introduction that Kevin was expecting.

"So Kevin," Lucy said. "I understand your charges and the plea deal offered … and please know that Scott hasn't violated any attorney-client privileges with you, that he and I have only talked about readily available facts and generalities."

"Miss Sandberg, that's okay. If Scott's vouching for you, I trust you."

Scott pulled a sheet from his folder, the prosecutor's five-year plea agreement, and placed it in front of his client. Lucy tapped it with her finger and said, "The thing about this is, it's a known outcome. It's five years. I know it doesn't seem right under the circumstances, but if a jury finds you guilty, you could get a higher sentence. Probably not the 25-year max, but maybe as much as ten. All judges have some discretion in sentencing, and I know your judge—he's not inclined to be lenient."

Kevin took this in and asked Scott what he thought.

"I can't make this decision, Kevin. The odds are not in our favor ..."

"Ninety-five percent of federal cases are pleaded out," Lucy interjected. "And of the five percent that go to trial, fewer than one percent of defendants win their cases."

They all sat in silence for what seemed like a long time. Then Kevin reached for Scott's pen and wrote in big block letters at the bottom of the page NO WAY. He flipped the page around, and Lucy looked at it skeptically. "Well, okay then. I wish you the best of luck." She smiled as she knocked for a CO escort so she could make a court appearance in Williamsport.

"Listen, Kevin," Scott said. "I appreciate the confidence you have in me but let me give you some more bad news before you decide. I didn't put this in my letter, but the judge denied our request to fund the Lewisburg expert witness I tracked down. *And* he won't pay for an investigator."

Kevin, deflated, sunk his head on the table.

"So why don't you sit on this for a day or two, and we can talk about it next time I come back. I'll print off another copy ..."

"Nah," Kevin cut him off. " Don't need to. Let's do this."

"I really think you should take some time ..."

"Fuck 'em," Kevin said. "Let's do this."

Scott nodded pensively. "Okay. Fuck 'em." And then he added, "Well, in that case, I do have an idea to raise money for our expert witness."

CHAPTER 7
THE DINERS CLUB

" And I'm telling you, we're not Baby Boomers. We're Generation *Jones*," Leroy said with a mouthful of apple cider cream pie. "Look it up. Did you watch *Leave It to Beaver* or *The Brady Bunch*? Were you into Bob Dylan or Bruce Springsteen? *The Graduate* or *Saturday Night Fever*?"

"I like Bob Dylan," said Eric, who dug his fork into the same pie plate and then the Dutch apple crumb cake to compare.

"I loved *The Graduate*," Scott's sister Pam added, reaching for a bite of the shared apple upside-down cake. She offered a bite to her husband, Russ, who protested but then gave in.

"It's not what you like. It's what you identify with, idiots," Leroy wiped the cream from the corner of his mouth and pushed the empty plate away from him. "Goddamn, that was good."

Gordo held up his iPhone and lectured the eight of us crammed into a diner booth on the street level of The Orchard Inn. "Gen Jones, born between 1955 and 1964, is an anonymous generation wedged between Baby Boomers and Generation X, defined by a sense of competitiveness—'keeping up with the Joneses,'—and a sense of yearning or craving, as in 'Jonesing for' something."

"No shit," said Scott, grabbing a fresh glazed apple fritter from a pile that was dwindling fast.

"Never heard of it," Brad added.

"Makes sense," I said, wedged between the two. "But I've always felt more like a Gen Xer anyway. Hey, I call the last fritter!" I groaned and sunk back into the booth with my first warm bite of the diner's signature pastry. "God, I've missed these."

I had missed these people, too. It was our 30th high school reunion, and I hadn't seen any of them since the 25th class gathering. And I couldn't make some informal get-togethers in between because I'd been in Switzerland for the last three years. My husband Jim, our teenage boys, and I had returned to Philadelphia that summer from Jim's whirlwind expat assignment, and we were still settling back into American life. Finally, with a weekend all to myself, there was nowhere else I'd rather be but in that diner, kicking off the reunion with my Douglas High besties and some well-deserved carbs.

We called ourselves The Diners Club—not just because we always met up there when we came into town—but also because years ago, Leroy had wanted to pay his portion with his fancy Diners Club International charge card and was told in no uncertain terms that they didn't split checks, and they had no idea what the hell kind of card that was and wouldn't take it.

Douglas County, in Northeast Pennsylvania's Susquehanna Valley, was still the fairyland of covered bridges and heirloom apples of my childhood. Likewise, Douglasville (*so many* Douglases, named for a Revolutionary War general) had changed little since my youth. Main Street was just as vibrant, with many of the same clothing and jewelry shops, the hardware store, and the duplex movie theater still in business, but now with new retail neighbors like a cupcake boutique, craft distillery, and microbrewery.

The two landmarks that book-ended our town were also thriving. On the west side Douglas University, formerly Douglas College, now folded into the state system of higher education, had tripled its enrollment from its small liberal arts days. And the apple processing plant on the east end still employed several hundred, churning out applesauce, apple butter, cider, and pie fillings. Modern-day Douglas County had more industry and a burgeoning healthcare network than it did back in the day, leading to a significant DU matriculation that had chosen to stay and raise families. When we went to school, the have-nots whose kids qualified for free lunches had fewer options. Some earned a modest living mining anthracite in the regional, not-yet abandoned coal mines. For others, the only work they could get was in the orchards at harvest time.

Gordo and Leroy had driven in from Pittsburgh together, and Brad, my high school boyfriend, had come in from North Jersey. Pam and Russ drove from Harrisburg, and Eric had come the farthest. He'd flown in from Wisconsin, and Scott had picked him up at the Scranton airport. All four of them were staying with Pam's and Scott's dad in the twins' childhood home, while the rest of us had rooms at The Orchard Inn. I'd booked a block of rooms a year ago because this was the first weekend of Apple Fest. The carnival that celebrated all things apple was a long-time tradition that predated even us, and we still called it Apple Fest even though it was rebranded the Apple and Arts Festival as it drew larger and larger crowds.

Wisely, the spouses—except for Pam and Russ, who were married class sweethearts—declined to attend because we were insufferable with our inflated, long-winded stories about our teenage selves. We did idiotic things when our frontal lobes weren't quite developed, and we loved hearing those exploits repeated and overblown. The time, during senior sketch week, when the basketball team had donned high heels and appeared behind the auditorium curtain with only their legs showing for a best-legs contest, and Leroy had stuck up his two middle fingers under the curtain to flip off the entire rest of the school—and never got caught because none of his teammates would rat him out. Eric, before he became a model adult citizen, streaked with the rear of his pants down across the JV football field. And who could forget when Brad, Leroy, Gordo, and Scott snuck into my cheerleading camp dorm with a case of Schlitz and then had to hide out under our beds until they could make their escape in the wee hours?

But we also cared about our current selves and stayed in touch by email and Facebook. As a waitress came by with more coffee, the eight of us started going around the table for everyone's personal and family updates.

We'd all seen the summer Facebook photos of Scott and Gordo skydiving in the western part of the state. It was Gordo's second time, and he wasn't sure Scott would go through with it after the training session. But when they reached 14,500 feet, Scott wanted to be the first one out with his instructor in their tandem jump. After a minute of freefall at 120 miles an hour, Scott's instructor deployed their joint parachute, and Scott could see Pittsburgh and Cleveland below him as he floated toward the target field. It was the most exhilarating five minutes of his life.

"I really just wanted to see if I could jump out the door," he told us. "And I did."

"And you did," his sister echoed.

"And you didn't even shit your pants," Gordo said, laughing.

"No, but I fucked up my back when I landed," Scott said, who winced as he tried to get comfortable against the booth's upholstery.

"Never would I ever," I declared, reaching for the water pitcher. I refilled my glass and casually topped off Brad's.

He smiled and didn't know I'd been watching him grip his hands under the table so tight that his knuckles were white. We all pretended not to notice his unsteady gait and trembling fork and understood he was going through a rough patch, to say the least. Only Gordo and I knew Brad had called Scott for help after a particularly bad bender in September. Brad had lost his keys, wallet, and phone and didn't know where he was when he came to. But he knew his friend was an attorney in Wilkes Barre, PA, and a call to information had gotten routed from Scott's old work phone to his cell phone, and Scott had come to the rescue. Brad's wife, Susan, was supposedly making ultimatums over his drinking, yet they were still married. I thought about Brad behind the wheel of their minivan and wondered if she let him drive their home-schooled kids to soccer practice.

"Carla, your *Swiss Family Conti* blog was *amazing*," Pam beamed. "I wanted to go everywhere you did, all those European capitals ... " and then she reached across the table and grabbed my wrist, pulling my arm toward her. "Oh my Gosh!" she said. "Russ, look at this!" My cheeks flushed as everyone stared at my silver, diamond-encrusted watch. "Anniversary gift from Jim," I swallowed. "We got it in Lucerne."

I immediately second-guessed what I'd worn and should have thought to dial it down a notch. I'd gotten into the habit of dressing better in Europe, and that day, I'd worn some of my staples—the Prada leather handbag, my Dior heeled boots, a silk scarf circled loosely over my sweater, and, of course, my beloved Longines watch. I spent the rest of the morning tugging on my sleeve to cover it.

Scott rescued me by regaling the table with his current court case, a federal prisoner accused of stabbing someone, but it was almost like self-defense, he said. He was learning all about prison gangs like the Aryan Brotherhood and said the judge had it in for him. "There's no way we'll get a fair trial."

I rolled my eyes because I knew what was coming. I'd already heard of this inmate, Kevin Sanders, three times. Starting in the summer, Scott had brought him up in our email exchanges, telling me what a talented artist he was, that he was just trying to survive a corrupt system and hellish environment, that I should write a book about him, blah blah blah. Scott even suggested I read the book *The Hot House: Life Inside Leavenworth Prison. Uhm, no thank you*, I wanted to say.

"I told Carla this case would make a great true crime book," Scott declared.

"And I told you I can't do it justice. You need to call the local newspaper."

"You're a crime reporter, for Christ's sake!"

"A million years ago, I was, Scotty," I said, giving him the stink eye. I wanted to tell him that even if the subject matter interested me—which it absolutely did not—I didn't have the time. I wanted to say these things, but he already seemed hurt.

"Look, I know you think I'm 'wasting my talents,'" I said dramatically, using finger quotes. "But this just isn't how I want to spend my time."

"Scotty!" his sister said. "You did *not* say that to Carla!"

"I'm afraid those were his exact words, Pam. You know how unfiltered he is." This, plus Pam throwing her napkin at him, drew some laughter and eased the moment.

Thankfully, I didn't hear any more about it over the weekend.

CHAPTER 8
THE JOURNALIST

EARLY NOVEMBER 2012, SHAWNEE LAKE

A few weeks after our reunion, I found myself driving two hours north again on I-476, this time to answer what I could only describe to my husband as a distress call. Days before, I'd received a FedEx envelope from Scott with some bizarre contents. It contained a 10-page letter in printed block handwriting I didn't recognize, a professional letter from a retired prison official, and two letters from Scott. His first letter to me, handwritten and back-dated by a week, read:

—

Dear Carla,

I need your help. This is about my client Kevin Sanders. I am trying to set up a website to raise money for his defense. I need to hire an expert witness (his letter enclosed) and I petitioned the court for $10k but only got $1.5k. So I have to raise the rest myself.

Turns out my college buddy is now a marketing VP at Twitter and will tweet out a website with Kevin's story—IF I can get one made. This is where you come in. Kevin has written the narrative for the website but it is way too long. Will you please edit it? When you're done with it, burn it. I don't want anything in Kevin's handwriting floating around.

You're getting this because we go way back.

Much Love,

Scott

—

Scott's second letter was typed on his legal stationery and dated two days prior:

—

Dear Carla,

Per our conversation, you have agreed to assist in Kevin's defense by editing his statement. I am enclosing one dollar, your requested fee.

By accepting this engagement letter, you are considered part of Kevin's defense team. The information being disclosed to you is covered under the attorney-client privilege and cannot be discussed or distributed outside our little circle. In the event that you are ever questioned about this, kindly invoke client privilege and do not disclose any information absent written consent by my client, myself, or a court order.

Best Regards,

Scott Powell, J.D., P.C.

—

What the what? I didn't know which letter irritated me more, and there was no dollar bill to be found. I had half a mind to ignore everything else in that envelope and try to get out of Scott's mess for good. But he was clearly desperate, and

I felt bad, so I leafed through the 10-page prisoner letter, calculating how much time it would take me to whittle down his horror story into something suitable for a website.

I emailed Scott a simple response: "Got your packet. We should talk. What's your cabin's address?"

—

I had gone to elementary school and junior high with most of The Diners Club but hadn't met Scott until 9th grade French. He and his sister Pam and a handful of others (as happened every year) had enrolled in Douglas High after attending the town's Catholic school, which only went through eighth grade. Our parents, however, ran in the same social circle, and, in fact, our mothers were the best of friends. Even though our families lived in the same section of Douglasville and our parents played Pinochle or Bridge once or twice a month, I never hung out with either Scott or Pam until they came to the high school.

My maiden name was Parello, and theirs was Powell, so I ended up sitting in front of Scott in French class. I was rocking my braces and a short, failed Dorothy Hamill hairstyle because my brown curly locks refused to conform.

I remembered Scott as a lanky kid with kind eyes and wavy hair parted in the middle like all the other boys. He was a shy newcomer who often read boring magazines like *U.S. News and World Report* while a teacher lectured. We'd struck up a friendship based on doling out juvenile romance advice to each other. He was trying to "go with" a cute blond with long, fantastically straight hair, and after I got my braces off and learned how to use a blow dryer, I was trying to get the attention of a sophomore track star.

One day in French class, when Scott was called upon to conjugate a verb, and he shrugged in silence, I called him out on his bullshit. "I don't know who you think you're fooling, pretending to be dumb all the time," I said … or something like that. The truth was I never remembered the conversation that Scott insisted took place and which apparently had made quite the impression.

Earlier in the year, when my father passed away in Florida, Scott had lent a more sympathetic ear than most because he and Pam had just lost their mother the year before. My dad had died a horrible death from an atypical kind of Parkinson's, and I'd spent our last few months in Switzerland, flying back and forth to Orlando to support my mother and brother. I'd watched my poor father wither away into feebleness and eventually not be able to recognize me, and outside of my family, only Scott knew those details. My mother was incredibly touched to receive Scott's sympathy card along with The Diners Club flowers that Pam had arranged for the funeral.

—

My BMW SUV bounced along a gravel road on the south side of Shawnee Lake dotted with small clapboard cottages on tiny lots. Scott said to look for the green one, and I pulled up next to a mini A-frame, the color of lime Jello. He stood in his doorway smiling, and we hugged hello. That's when I knew something was really wrong. He needed a shower, but worse, he'd gotten so much thinner in just a few weeks. His stubbly face was gaunt, and he carried himself stiffly as he led the way inside. He immediately started picking up clothes, magazines, mugs, and what looked like case files strewn about. "Sorry," he said. "I lost the cleaning lady in the divorce, too."

"Don't worry about it," I said. "It's just me."

He excused himself to change from stale sweatpants into something else, and I started poking around his kitchen. The sink was piled high with dirty dishes, which also littered the countertop, and I opened the fridge to find nothing of substance: just cans of beer, a Chinese food container, some olives, and condiments.

"Hey, can I use your bathroom?" I hollered down the hall and then made a beeline for his medicine cabinet. A few minutes later, I came out shaking a bottle of Vicodin like a rattle.

"What's going on, Scott?" I said, more judgment than concern in my voice. He opened his hands like he wanted me to throw him the bottle. "Don't mind if I do," he said, but I just set it down on a smidge of empty surface.

It wasn't even noon, and I could see he'd poured himself a Stoli and ginger ale because of the container evidence on the coffee table. He motioned for me to join him on his back deck that overlooked the lake—by far the cottage's best feature—and I grabbed my coat and followed. Despite the November chill, the deck was pleasantly warm, with the sun beating down. We sat facing the water in a pair of Adirondacks, but it took him a long time to ease into his seat.

"Okay, so you have back problems," I said, unleashing my detective skills. "How much Vicodin are you taking?"

"It's a herniated disk. And they're just painkillers, Car."

"But this script is your Dad's, from, like, three years ago."

"Yeah, I know. I'm out."

I put my hands over my face and breathed in and out. "This," I said, wagging my finger up and down at his frail frame, "is not sustainable. What is your plan?"

"Surgery. But I can't get it done until January."

"Because ..."

"Because I have a big hearing coming up with no expert witness ..."

Again, with the expert witness, I thought. "So, get it postponed."

"I've already had two continuances. You don't understand."

He was right; I didn't understand. But what good would he be to his client in that hearing performing in what would surely be a worse condition than this? I tried explaining from a layperson's point of view, and it seemed to resonate.

"Or," he perked up and grinned, "maybe I can file a motion to continue based on the availability of my *new investigator.*"

I sighed. "Whatever it takes," I said, not knowing what I'd just signed up for, but only that I wanted to help a friend.

—

We spent some time talking about his case, the judge, the prosecutor, and how unfair, in his opinion, the whole system was for defendants in federal court. After he showered, at my polite suggestion, we continued our conversation over grilled Reubens at Skee's Sandwich Shop. I tried to lighten the mood with a joke about his "burn the letter" business regarding his client's ten-page narrative.

"A bit dramatic, no?" I said. "It struck me as very cloak-and-dagger … or should I say, cloak-and-shank?"

"Ha ha," he said, unamused. "It's no joke, Car. You don't fuck with the Aryan Brotherhood. When you're done with the letter, burn it."

Jesus, I thought. *Okay.* I insisted we stop by the Acme on our way back to stock his fridge, to which he responded appreciatively, "Yes, ma'am."

We put groceries away and washed the dishes by hand. He dried them and tried not to show how tired he was. When we finished, I suggested he take a nap. I said I had a few files I wanted to look at and that I'd let myself out. He didn't hesitate to take me up on the offer.

As the sun started to dip over the western edge of Shawnee Lake, I installed a program I found online onto Scott's PC, that would allow me to turn the rec cage assault video into something we could view. I spent more time watching and rewatching the video than it took me to reformat it, burn two copies on CD, and email it to myself.

The video was brutal, but I watched it with a certain level of detachment, maybe because there was no sound or maybe because I'd already heard about it. Was it much worse than a YouTube video of a bar fight where everyone walks away at the end? What would a jury think of this, I wondered.

I did, though, notice something odd about Kevin just before the fight started 13 seconds into the video. At the 10- and 11-second marks, Kevin, with his back to the surveillance camera, reached into the back of his white baggy shorts. I went frame by frame over that video section again and again to try and make sense of it. It was a subtle gesture, and whether he was retrieving an object or doing something else, I couldn't say.

I left the CDs on Scott's now-tidy coffee table with a note. "You owe me a dollar," it said with a smiley face.

CHAPTER 9
PERFORMANCE ART

JANUARY 2013, DOUGLAS COUNTY PRISON

Over the prosecutor's objections, Scott had gotten his hearing on intentional destruction of the videotape postponed until January. He'd had back surgery right after Thanksgiving and then mended in Douglasville at his dad's house with the help of his father's housekeeper. Scott caught some stolen glances between the two senior citizens and suspected she was much more than just a cleaning lady.

I didn't know how to help my friend prepare for the hearing—I was really just a sounding board for his theories and strategy. While I'd covered criminal trials as a police beat reporter in my early career, I didn't feel like a productive member of anyone's defense team, despite a piece of paper saying so. I did, however, know how to build a website and was a fast and concise writer, so I spent my time around the holidays putting together the *FreeKevinSanders.com* blog that asked for donations by PayPal.

Our publicity would come from a viral Tweet by one of Scott's fraternity brothers, who was a big executive now at Twitter. The weekend before he'd rescued Brad from his bender, Scott had flown out to the Midwest to his Big 10 undergrad school for a football game with his frat boys. He discussed his dilemma with the Twitter guy, who had nearly a million followers, and the guy assured Scott he would help.

"His tweet will say something like, 'take a look at this, this sounds wrong, do something if you're interested,'" Scott explained in a letter to Kevin. And he told me, "I believed him when he said he would help. If not, we're fucked."

The whole point of the website was to get enough donations to pay for the expert witness, the retired Lewisburg SIS officer, whom Scott wanted to explain the prison gang world to the jury. The witness's $10,000 fee seemed outrageous to me, but Scott said his $175 per hour was the going rate for someone good. "I consider that reasonable when I pay orthopedic surgeons $2,000 for a one-hour depo," he added. This was a highly sought-after expert who testified around the country, "and when he's on the stand, defendants win cases they're not supposed to."

This expensive witness agreed to clear his calendar for the second week of May, the new trial date, and so raising the cash in time seemed doable. When I felt the website was polished and complete, I was to give the word, and the tweet would go out. By New Year's Eve, the site was live, and Scott said he would reach out to his Twitter executive friend.

—

Scott expected the hearing to last at least a couple of days, so in January, I booked a nice room with a flexible check-out using Jim's hotel points a few blocks away from the district court. And because Pennsylvania was in a deep freeze with high temps only in the teens, I brought the warmest coat I owned—my black, mid-length, sheared beaver fur with a hood. I didn't really think a PETA nut would douse me with a bucket of red dye, but I stayed on high alert just the same.

The night before the hearing, Scott and I met at the Douglas County Prison, where Kevin Sanders had been moved so he could appear in court the next day. Scott wanted to go over his testimony again, and it was my first opportunity to meet the man I felt I already knew based on what he'd written for the website.

We left our coats behind and crossed the frigid parking lot for my first-ever jailhouse scan. After we entered, Scott introduced me as his investigator, and the friendly DCP officers invited us to sit on "the throne"—a bulky metal detection box with a seating ledge. Scott had brought one of his spare suits for Kevin to wear tomorrow and handed it to a CO who scanned it separately.

Kevin was already waiting in a private visitation room with no guard or cuffs. He and Scott embraced immediately, and then he gently shook my hand. "Kevin, meet Carla, our defense tech whiz and investigator extraordinaire."

"Uhm, that's a bit much," I said with an awkward smile.

We sat around a table, and Scott explained the lineup for tomorrow's hearing. The prosecutor would start with a handful of COs, and then Scott would put Kevin and Little Eagle on the stand to talk about what happened before the rec cage fight—events that could have been seen on the video if prison officials had kept it or had not purposely deleted it, as Scott would argue.

Scott then wondered about Kevin's transport to the courthouse, 50 minutes away, and he ducked out to talk to the warden or someone to make sure everything was lined up.

When we were alone, Kevin smiled at me with kind eyes and said, "You must be really good friends with Scott to come up here and do this. I can't thank you enough for the website and everything you're doing." He shook his head and looked at the floor like he was humbled that I would leave the comfort of my conventional life, with children almost grown, for a front-row seat to this legal thriller.

"I'm happy to help," I smiled back.

"So you drove up here from Philadelphia?"

"Uh-huh," I said.

"Is it nice?"

"A lot of it is," I laughed.

"So you're a writer?"

"Well, once upon a time, I used to write for a living, so …"

"Are you gonna write a book about me?"

"Oh," I said, taken aback and not willing to admit I was considering Scott's initial bait. "I don't know about that. For now, I'm just focused on the website and helping Scotty with the case."

"Scott-eee," he grinned, and I laughed, knowing I would never hear the end of that.

"If you do write a book, I can tell you all kinds of stories. Not just this case stuff, but everyday living-in-prison stuff."

He stood. "Like, this is what our workouts are," and he dropped to the floor for a quick pushup, followed by a leap in the air, then dropped again for another pushup, then lept in the air. He repeated these burpees three more times, and my eyes widened with each one. *Holy shit!* I thought.

But the show continued. He demonstrated how he could evade a CO's body search by hiding contraband in various open crevices, like under an armpit or behind a knee, and then moving it elsewhere when told to show hands or stretch limbs. He used our pen as a pretend prohibited item and maneuvered it with a magician's smooth sleight of hand.

Pleased with his performance, Kevin took a seat. And then, when Scott returned, I must have still looked stunned because he said, "Everything okay in here?"

"Uh-huh," I fake-smiled. I couldn't wait to tell him later what he missed.

CHAPTER 10
HEARING DAY 1

JANUARY 2013, MONDAY

The William J. Nealon Federal Building in downtown Scranton was a sprawling structure that housed a U.S. District Court, a post office, and some other government offices. It was originally built in 1930 in the Art Deco style and then expanded in 1991 to double its size. Its thoughtful restoration and quality of the new annex—with a granite and limestone exterior to match the old courthouse—kept the building a historical landmark. The interior of the original structure was even more impressive with its intricate plaster accents, marble floors, bronze doors, and wood-paneled courtrooms.

Courtroom No. 1, where we were headed, was one of the two original courtrooms on the 4th floor. It was incredibly regal and nearly took my breath away when I stepped inside. It featured tall, rich oak wainscoting, raised wood panels, layered crown molding, and a delicately carved frieze behind the judge's bench. But the pièce de résistance, also behind the judge's seat, was the original 1931 colorful folk-art mural titled "Justice with Peace and Prosperity." The courtroom could have been a movie set, it was that spectacular.

As a lover of architecture, history, and performance art, entry to this building and Courtroom No. 1—plus last night's histrionics—had already been worth the drive.

Presiding over *The United States v. Kevin Sanders* was semi-retired judge Harold Anderson. Appointed to the bench by Bush I in 1991, he'd recently earned "senior status" at age 70. As long as Judge Anderson kept a 25% caseload, he was entitled to this form of semi-retirement for the rest of his life, complete with full office staff and the chambers of his choice. As a Lackawanna County native who'd spent 20 years commuting to federal courthouses in Harrisburg and Williamsport, choosing to gavel and rule in Scranton for his remaining days had been an obvious move.

The hearing began at precisely 1 p.m. Judge Anderson, bald and bespectacled, had a reputation for running his courtroom like a drill sergeant. He wasted no time laying the ground rules and getting Scott and Prosecutor Galloway to agree to a witness list—including which of them had to be sequestered—and more.

Kevin, swimming in the dark suit from Scott's heavier days, sat at the defense table next to Scott. I took a place behind them on the first spectator bench, with a pile of empty legal pads and extra pens at my side for copious note-taking.

—

Galloway's first witness was a technician with Lewisburg's Special Investigative Supervisor (SIS) office. Tech Officer Ehrlich was the official who obtained and transferred a copy of the rec cage assault video to a CD, something he said he'd done at least 50 times before in other cases. Lewisburg's video system, he said, had about 500 cameras and was digital now; any reference to "videotape" was outdated. At this point, Galloway played the three-minute video on a monitor for the court. The judge gave nothing away as he watched, arms folded across his robe.

When it was over, the prosecutor asked the tech how he had chosen which part of that incident to preserve on CD.

"Basically, I like to grab a minute or two before the incident happens, up through when the inmates leave the area," he said.

"In a case like this," said Galloway, "would you go back and get video from the time the inmates left their particular cells and were walked down to the cage?"

"No. That wasn't necessary," the tech said.

Then Galloway got SIS Ehrlich to explain how the video system self-erased every two weeks because the computer server couldn't store more data than that. Galloway asked, "At any time during that 14-day period, did anybody come to you and ask for more video or say there was something important not shown on the CD you prepared?"

"No, sir."

"No further questions, Your Honor."

———

Scott began his cross-exam by asking the technician how he came to be the one who made the video CD. The tech answered that it could have been anyone in the SIS office, it just happened to be him.

"Did anyone tell you to do it?" Scott asked.

"No."

"Did you do it on your own?"

"Yes, sir."

"How did you hear about the incident?"

"It was an assistance call."

"So you took it upon yourself to go retrieve the video?"

"Yes, sir."

"Are there any other copies that showed more of what happened and were edited?"

"Sir, I don't know. That's the only copy I know of, the only copy I made."

"To whom did you turn it over?" Scott asked.

But the judge interrupted. "For the sake of clarity, Mr. Powell, are you talking about the disk?"

"I'm talking about ..."

"But I need to understand," the judge continued. "I want to try to understand. You are going to have to be more precise in your questions. As I understood, he downloaded this from the system and burned the disk. You are going to have to be more precise in what you're talking about here. I'm not sure he understands you. So be precise in your questions."

"Let me withdraw that question and go back for just a minute," Scott said. "You testified that you like to start copying videos at least a minute before that incident occurs. Right? That's your practice?"

"Minute or two. It depends on the situation."

"Would you agree with me that there isn't a minute before on this video, that the fight starts within seconds?"

"Well, you saw what I just saw. It's Kevin Sanders with his hand in his buttocks heading right towards Tremblay."

"I understand that. What happens in the minute before?"

The judge interrupted again. "Well, I think that misstates the facts, Mr. Powell. I saw the video, and I can interpret that for myself. That's not the relevant inquiry, I don't think. I think you were making the relevant inquiry, which is why did he cut anything off, if he cut anything off."

"Understood," Scott said, and then turning to the witness once more, asked, "So, to the best of your knowledge, you do not know what kind of computer server system is at Lewisburg?"

"Top of my head, no, I can't answer that question."

"To the best of your knowledge, do you not know whether Lewisburg uses the Vicon Collector system?"

Judge Anderson interjected. "He's answered it. Come on, Mr. Powell. You know, I don't want to be at this excessively."

"Okay, one more question. Could anybody else, in the 14 days before it self-erased, have copied the entire incident if they wanted to?"

"They could have, until it was automatically deleted from the server."

—

Galloway, on redirect, asked the tech, "So if you would have looked at any video that was available prior to the incident itself, is it fair to say nothing was going on?"

"No, sir, nothing was going on."

The judge allowed Scott a brief recross. "I don't mean to beat you up. I don't. But who would be the person at Lewisburg who knows the most about how your server system works?"

"Objection, Your Honor," said Galloway. "Relevance. Who cares?"

Judge Anderson said, "Hold it. Stop it. What system are you talking about, Mr. Powell? You have to be precise because we're talking about a lot of stuff. We're talking about burning a CD. We're talking about storage. We're talking about everything else …"

And on it went into the weeds of the judge's need for clarification, computer operating systems, software, and details that got Scott nowhere. He finished his recross with this exchange. "While you were watching the video on the server preparing to copy it to CD, did you watch to the point where Kevin Sanders entered the cage?"

"No, sir."

"And you were never asked to?"

"No, sir."

"Okay, no further questions."

—

Several exhibits were introduced, including the typed incident report, medical reports of all three inmates, and a photocopy of two plastic shanks that officers said were recovered from the scene.

Correctional Officer Howard, one of the last responding officers to the rec cage fight, took the stand, and Scott asked him about gang-issued hit orders at Lewisburg.

"Gang hits are put out at almost every federal institution in this Bureau," the CO said.

"If you were putting an inmate into a rec cage," said Scott, "and the inmates inside the cage said, 'don't do it,' what would you do?"

"I would return the inmate to his cell."

"You wouldn't put him in?"

"No."

He then asked the officer if Tremblay did something that offended a high-ranking white gang member, would Tremblay be in danger?

"If he disrespected a high-ranking gang member? Could be."

But Scott's greater point was made by getting the CO to admit there was no "hole or segregated safe spot in the SMU" for inmates to go to if they felt threatened.

Galloway had no questions for the witness, so the court issued a brief recess. I huddled with Scott and Kevin and did not dare say that, so far, I thought Scott was barely treading water.

CHAPTER 11
HEARING DAY 1 CONTINUED

JANUARY 2013, MONDAY

"Call your next witness," the judge said to Scott.

"Call Kevin Sanders," Scott said.

Kevin took the stand in his ill-fitting suit and was asked to bring his microphone closer as he recounted for the court the events preceding the rec cage assault.

He explained how, as he was being escorted to the rec cage, a Native American engaged him in conversation. Kevin was placed in the cage first, he said, then his cellie Mark Keys came in, and then the range got quiet as an officer escorted Steven Tremblay down the walkway and turned him over to CO Shemp, who put him into Kevin's and Mark's cage.

"I tell the officer directly, no man, don't put him in here, don't put him in the cage."

"Officer Shemp?"

"Yeah, Officer Shemp, the one who was running rec that day."

"Why did you say not to put him in the cage?"

"Because there's going to be a problem. That Tremblay dude is an issue—he's been flooding the tier, jumping other white people, creating problems on Z Block.

"So for him to be put in our cage, we have to get involved in a conflict now, and I don't want to be involved."

Scott pivoted and got into Kevin's background as a Montañista, the hit order that was put out on him at Allenwood—because Kevin refused to assault his best friend—which was the event that led to his transfer to Lewisburg. This segued into Kevin getting put into a rec cage at Lewisburg with the one Montañista who wanted him dead.

"And you specifically told them you were not a Montañista and could not be with Montañistas?"

"I specifically let it be known I'm not a Montañista, that I don't rec with Montañistas, that there will be problems."

Scott's direct exam of Kevin veered into the topic of Lewisburg's white power gangs and became lengthy, and the judge grew irritable. "Why do I need to know these people? Can't we move this along, Mr. Powell? I think the narrative is far afield. I mean, again, I get your essential argument for the purpose of the hearing. Let's all just take a step back and understand we're not at trial here. So let's move along," the judge said.

"Understood," Scott responded.

"This is not a jury trial," the judge added.

"Okay."

Scott resumed questioning Kevin about the current rec cage incident. Kevin testified that as the tension built and inmates' hollering grew louder, "I know something is going to happen, I can feel it." And so Kevin reached into his shoe and grabbed a "kite"—this was, he testified, a tightly rolled piece of paper with secretive information written in tiny lettering, about the size of a cigarette. Kites were how inmates passed messages to each other, and, like this one, often contained sensitive gang intelligence. It was Kevin's job to carry the kite, while it was his cellie Mark's job to carry the knife, he said.

Scott asked why Kevin retrieved the kite from his shoe.

"It has a lot of valuable information in it. As I reach into my shoe and grab that, I stick it in my ass."

The courtroom fell silent, and a few jaws dropped, including mine. Scott motioned for him to continue.

"And the fight just happens like that, everybody is yelling," Kevin continued. "It goes down. I secure the information, and we're engaged in combat."

"Did you ever have a weapon of any kind?" asked Scott.

"No, I didn't."

"Why did you have to get involved in the fight?"

"I had no choice. If I didn't even assist my cellie, then I would have been targeted for a hit, directly by him in the cage."

"Why?"

"That's how it is. The whites brought me into their community, gave me housing, gave me structure, and protected me, which the institution couldn't do. Now, if there is any altercation, I have to aid and assist them. If I don't, then I would have been directly stabbed up in that cage next."

The judge exhaled, exasperated, and said, "You're trying your case, Mr. Powell. You're opening the door to a potential problem here, to voluminous cross-examination by Mr. Galloway that is going to impair his right to a fair trial. Counsel, approach."

There was a long sidebar wherein I knew Scott was being reprimanded over legal issues I didn't understand. When he returned to the defense table, looking sullen and worn, Kevin and I exchanged a worried look.

—

It was Galloway's turn to cross-examine Kevin, and he started by saying two shanks had been found at the rec cage scene, "But you didn't have one?"

"No, I didn't."

"And you didn't pull a shank from the back of your pants?"

"No, I didn't. That ain't where we carry them. We carry them in the front of our boxers in the slit that's in the front. That's how come you never see Mark Keys reach into the back of his ass and grab a knife. I was kiestering a kite—hot information."

"What happened to the kite?"

"I kept it kiestered. They never took it to x-ray."

"Is it still there now?"

"No." Kevin looked at Galloway as if he'd lost his mind.

"What did you ultimately do with it?"

"Destroyed it, then I had to re-make it."

The prosecutor circled back to the events leading up to the fight after all three men were placed in the rec cage, particularly the inmate yelling coming from the top floor of Z Block.

"And you can't give me the name of one person who ordered the hit on Tremblay?"

"I could, but I want to invoke my Fifth Amendment right now."

"You don't have one pal," Galloway smirked. "You're testifying."

Kevin was quiet for a moment. "The higher-ups from us," he said. "The people who call the shots for the ..."

"I want names."

"The higher-ups."

"Give me a couple of names."

"I don't have all their names specifically."

"Give me a couple names."

"Trevor Rexton."

"That's one. Who else?"

"That's the only one I can give you right now."

Galloway took a step back and thought for a moment. "So as soon as this incident was over, you immediately told somebody, hey, make sure you hang on to the video because hey, I'm trying to wave him off. Right?"

"No. I had no opportunity to speak with nobody about it."

"But the FBI came out and investigated the next day. You could have told the agent, hey, take a look at the video, right?"

"The FBI didn't try to talk to us for a month."

"Did you ask your staff rep at your disciplinary hearing to hang on to the videotape or to take a look at the video?"

"No."

"You didn't tell the disciplinary hearing officer to save the video?"

"No."

"You didn't tell anybody to save the video, because it will show I'm motioning to somebody?"

"By my knowledge, any type of crime, you usually save the whole video. You walk into a bank and you rob a bank, you show them walking into the bank, you just don't show them pulling the gun."

—

It was 2:50 p.m., and the judge was dismayed that each lawyer still had more witnesses to present. The hearing would clearly have to continue the next day. Galloway said he thought he could get through his witnesses fairly quickly, but the judge said, "Nothing has been short thus far."

"I realize that," Galloway said.

"That would astonish me," the judge continued. "We're moving at the speed of a glacier here." After a brief recess, Judge Anderson returned to the bench and called for the day's last witness.

"We call Westin Chase, Your Honor," said Scott.

A tall, fit Native American, with long, flowing black hair, appeared in an orange jumpsuit. A U.S. marshal removed his handcuffs, and he took the stand. The courtroom deputy stood before him and said, "Raise your right hand."

"I'm a Navajo, that's not my way."

"I'll say, do you swear or do you *affirm*," the deputy said, and Westin Chase agreed to the latter.

"Sir," Scott began, "are you also an inmate at USP Lewisburg?"

The judge interjected. "Can we stipulate that for the purpose of the witness's testimony, that he was an inmate at this time, that he was present, that he was proximate to the incident, and then we'll move to the incident? Is that acceptable, Mr. Galloway?"

"Thank you, judge," Galloway said.

"All right," the judge said, motioning for Scott to continue.

"Did you see what happened with Kevin Sanders and Inmate Tremblay?"

"Yes."

"Can you tell me?"

Westin Chase explained that the morning of the incident, he noticed a new inmate being escorted to a rec cage, and they engaged in conversation. "It was Mr. Sanders, this gentleman here," Chase said, pointing to Kevin.

Westin described their conversation and then said he saw Mr. Sanders' cellmate, Mark Keys, get put into the cage. Then it got quiet when Inmate Tremblay, a known troublemaker, was escorted down the walkway, he explained. And at that point, Mr. Sanders "was trying to say, like, don't put Tremblay in here. You know, trying to give stern eye contact, body language to the CO." As he said this, Chase was moving his flat hand back and forth under his chin.

Scott said, "Let me stop you. You are making a motion with your hand that is kind of like someone cutting their head off?"

Chase kept demonstrating the motion, moving his hand back and forth near his neck, and said, "No, no, no. Like no, no, no, don't put him in here."

"Describing it for the record, your hand is flat, you're waving it under your chin?"

"Like no, no. This guy, don't … hey, don't put him in here."

"All right. Did you see what happened after my client did that?"

"Rec Officer Shemp was determined to put Inmate Tremblay in the sallyport, and Mr. Sanders went over and started talking to the officer, but the officer put him in the sallyport anyway."

"Did you hear anything?"

"I could hear Mr. Sanders say like, hey, no, you know, this guy shouldn't be in here."

"What happened next?"

"Rec Officer Shemp put him in there. He stood there for a minute and put his hand on his thing like he was expecting something to happen from the beginning."

"You are putting your hand on your hip."

"Okay. He has like a radio. On that radio, there is some kind of little button that they push, right? So he was standing there for, I would say, a minute. So I knew already something is happening."

—

On cross-examination, Prosecutor Galloway queued up the video so Chase could point out where he was standing. He was just visible in the rec cage across from where the incident occurred.

"What happens when an inmate tells a correctional officer, hey, don't put me in there?"

"Sometimes they put them in there anyway because they want to see something happen to that guy," Chase said.

"Oh, okay. Well, what does an officer do if he doesn't put an inmate into the cage under that circumstance?"

"He takes him back to his cell."

The video played on the monitor, and Chase narrated part of it. "I'm standing right here," he said, pointing.

"That's you watching it?"

"Yeah." When they got to the end of the video, Chase said, "And right here, here comes Shemp, and he said, 'All right guys, that's enough, that's enough, he's had enough.' But that's not what they usually do. They yell out, 'Stop! Stop! Stop! Get down on the ground!' But that's not how he was doing it. It's like he wasn't excited about it. Like he knew it was going to happen, and he wasn't really trying to stop it."

Galloway paused and then questioned Chase about the yelling coming from Z Block's top tier. "Who was yelling to get Tremblay?"

"High-ranking members of a gang."

"Who were they? I want names."

"T-Rex."

"Who?"

"T-Rex."

"Who's that?"

"He's one of the big guys."

"What's his full name?"

"I don't know his full name?"

"Was he the only one yelling?"

"No, there were others, but I don't know their names. I could hear other people in the cages saying to get him, too. This Tremblay guy would throw feces on people, spit on them, disrespect a lot of people. There's a lot of people mad at this guy. I think the officer put that guy …"

"Objection," Galloway cut off the witness who was answering his own question. "Speculation, Your Honor."

"All right," the judge said. "We'll stop the answer there. Mr. Powell, any additional questions?"

"No, Your Honor, thank you."

"All right, you may step down," the judge said to Chase. "And we'll pick this up at 10:00 a.m. tomorrow. That concludes the hearing for today."

CHAPTER 12
RECAP AND RECON

The Marshal Service led Kevin out for transport back to the Douglas County Prison. It was too early for dinner but not for drinks, so Scott and I fought the bitter headwinds for a pub across the street. We unloaded our coats and gear at a four-top in the corner and gave a waitress our order.

"*Oof,*" I exhaled. "Rough day at the office, honey?"

"Fuck," he said, rubbing his forehead between his eyes.

"Shit, that wasn't even a day, that was only three hours," I said.

"What do you think so far?" he asked.

"Oy. I think you're doing the best with what you've got. But if the main issue is the missing part of the video, I can see the judge finding that technician credible." This disappointed him, but he nodded.

"Speaking of the judge, what have you done to make him hate you? Is he like that with everyone?"

"I honestly don't know. I never had him before. But my friend Lucy's been in his courtroom many times, and I never heard her complain."

I waited until the waitress dropped off my glass of Pinot Noir and Scott's Labatt Pilsner to ask, "What did he say to you at sidebar?"

"Oh my God ... both Neil and Anderson attacked me for raising the self-defense issue. I said it was relevant to the motion. Neil said it didn't matter if there was a wave off, that it didn't justify what happened."

"I kept hearing the judge say, *Says you. Says you* ..." I said.

"Yep," Scott took a sip of his beer. "Anderson told me I *crossed a fine line* and had just previewed my case for Neil, and didn't that make Neil happy? In his infinite wisdom, His Honor stopped me to spare Kevin his constitutional rights."

I wasn't sure what to make of that, except I knew Scott was giving his all to a case that his opposing counsel and the judge probably wished had been pleaded out.

"Did Neil Galloway really ask if Kevin still had a kite in his butt?"

We laughed almost to the point of spit-takes, and then I asked, "There's no way he could have stored a shank in his ass, right?"

Scott shook his head, still laughing. "No way. Kevin drew me a sketch showing how they keep their shanks tied to a string in the front. They hang right there next to their genitalia, and the cops never want to pat them down there."

I shook my head and had another sip of wine. "And what's up with his 'I want names! I want names!' WTF?"

Scott turned serious. "I don't know what game Neil's playing, but that kind of shit can get Kevin killed. It's not like Neil will prosecute T-Rex for hollering out a window. I don't know what the fuck he's doing."

"T-Rex. Kevin mentioned him in one or two letters."

"Trevor Rexton. Promoted to Lewisburg AB shot-caller after Casper got transferred. And believe me, they all fucking know who he is, including the judge."

Scott had a 40-minute drive back to his lime green Jello cottage for some much-needed rest and prep for the next day. I finished my wine, and Scott left half his beer on the table. He walked me to my hotel in the stinging cold and hugged me goodbye as we parted ways.

—

After getting cozy in my sweatpants and ordering room service, I used Scott's login to the federal court document database, otherwise known as PACER, and searched for Trevor Rexton, a.k.a. T-Rex. Several civil suits popped up.

In the oldest suit, Rexton sued the Bureau of Prisons when he'd been at USP Victorville, saying officials wouldn't properly treat his Hepatitis C. A judge dismissed that case partly because he eventually got the medical treatment he was seeking.

A second civil suit filed by Rexton alleged "excessive use of force" when Lewisburg COs purposely transported him in a pair of handcuffs too small for his large frame. According to the record, the double cuffing was instituted for any suspected AB gang member after several of them (not Rexton) assaulted correctional officers right after the SMU had opened. In his complaint, Rexton said the COs refused to use the "big boy" cuffs on him, which resulted in cuts, open wounds, numbness, pins and needles, loss of dexterity, and permanent nerve damage. He was transported four times a day this way for a year, which constituted "torture," he said, and he had to receive ongoing treatment with ointment, bandages, and warm compresses. The suit was eventually dismissed. Interestingly, to me, it was Judge Harold Anderson who heard that case and agreed Rexton's cuffs were warranted due to his history and penchant for violence.

The third suit I found, on the surface, seemed like a nuisance suit, the kind brought by a "serial filer" with access to a jailhouse lawyer. Rexton's complaint involved his punishment following an assault he committed in a Z Block rec cage *two weeks after* Kevin's rec cage fight. But digging deeper into the suit left me stunned and a little queasy.

Rexton's supporting documents called his rec cage assault an "attempted murder," and Rexton didn't even dispute it. The record stated that Rexton and another inmate stabbed a fellow prisoner 78 times in the chest, neck, abdomen, and upper and lower back with sharpened metal objects. The victim had been able to pull himself into the sallyport, and two bloody metal shanks with orange material wrapped around their handles were found just outside the fence.

The victim quickly fell into a state of non-response to verbal and pain stimuli and was rushed to a hospital. He suffered a punctured lung, a ruptured aorta, a ruptured chest artery, and a sliced trachea, all causing massive internal bleeding and blood loss. He spent many hours in surgery and remained intubated in critical condition. (The unnamed victim survived, according to a recently filed appeal.)

The prison reports were prepared by officers who witnessed the stabbing, plus those who saw it play out on video. There were several mentions of the video, and all references discussed action occurring right before Rexton and the other inmate jumped their victim from behind. None of the notes involving the video mentioned anything about a visual of the inmates being put into the cage. I guessed that possibly, probably, the video of that incident was captured in the same way as Kevin's, with the video beginning only seconds before the attack.

The reports also noted that when officers responded to the scene, "All inmates were ordered to lay on the ground," which they eventually did. It wasn't clear if the video captured that or not. Regardless, this was a documented deviation from the way Kevin's rec cage assault had ended, with Officer Shemp saying, "Okay, guys, that's good. That's enough. He's had enough."

I sighed. The video of Rexton's assault was probably something we could ask for, but we'd run the risk of it only helping the prosecutor if that video started like Kevin's, mere seconds before the assault. And the part at the end where the inmates were ordered to lay on the ground—it's not like we could cherry-pick that segment for our benefit only. But what did I know? I emailed Scott a link to the case with my junior analysis.

At Rexton's disciplinary hearing, he declined to speak in case he was prosecuted, but he was never charged. Instead, he received, among other things, a loss of commissary, phone, and visiting privileges for four years, the basis for that civil suit. The records showed he was initially convicted of methamphetamine drug trafficking and gun charges in California a decade ago, and he'd gotten additional time for an attempted murder right after he was imprisoned. Already in his late 50s, Rexton was essentially a lifer since he'd be 108 years old on his projected release date. I assumed the BOP and FBI didn't want to waste their time bringing new charges against someone who was already going to die in prison. And I wondered if he would die in the supermax at ADX in Florence, Colorado, where he was transferred six months after Kevin's rec cage fight.

I recognized several names from that civil suit and supporting documents—names of COs who either testified at Kevin's hearing or were on the government's witness list and would be taking the stand.

And the most prominent name I identified was, again, the judge in the case—Harold Anderson.

CHAPTER 13
HEARING DAY 2

JANUARY 2013, TUESDAY

T he hearing came to order on time the next day at 10:00
a.m. Seven Lewisburg correctional officers and an
FBI agent were lined up to testify. Judge Anderson asked
the lawyers to agree on who should be called and in what
order to avoid duplicative testimony. Scott and Galloway
conferred briefly, and then the prosecutor said, "I don't
think we can, Your Honor."

"No, we can't," said Scott.

"You can't agree? Well, that was the old college try,
wasn't it? That was about eight seconds."

Galloway pushed back. "I'm not going to stipulate to
something that's not true. I'm sorry."

"I'm not casting aspersions," the judge said. "I'm only
venting …" They all agreed to allow Galloway to take the
lead on examining the COs, and Scott sat down as the first
witness was called, Officer Crone.

Crone was the CO who set up the rec roster the morning
of the assault, and Galloway asked him to describe the
conversations he had with the three inmates involved. Crone
said he first went to Sanders' and Keys' cell and spoke only
to Inmate Sanders through the cell window.

"I explained to Sanders that I was going to put Inmate Tremblay in their recreation cage and asked if there was any problem. Inmate Sanders said no, there's no problem, I get along with everybody. I then went across the hall and spoke to Inmate Tremblay and asked him if it was okay to rec with Inmates Sanders and Keys, and he assured me yes, I have no problem with that."

"LIAR," Kevin wrote in large letters on a legal pad Scott had given him.

Crone said he checked the rec and shower sheets and a computer program to see if any of the three inmates had a "keep-away" status from each other, and they didn't.

Galloway asked, "Did you have occasion to talk to Inmates Sanders and Keys after Tremblay was stabbed that day?"

"Yes ... I went down to the cell and spoke with Sanders. I said something to the effect of, look, if you have a problem with somebody, just let me know, it saves a lot of paperwork."

Kevin underlined LIAR twice after that remark.

"What was his response?"

"I believe Inmate Sanders inquired as to how Inmate Tremblay was, and I said, not good. He also said, 'I bet he doesn't kick on that door tonight,' which surprised me. I didn't know. Apparently, there was an issue the night before where Inmate Tremblay kicked the door. He told me it's up to the individual races to take care of their own."

"Excuse me. Who said that?"

"Inmate Sanders said that, to police their own ranks to prevent trouble with other races or groups."

On cross-exam, Scott asked Officer Crone if he vividly recalled his conversation with his client. "Is it possible that you are mistaken in what you recall?"

"No, I am not mistaken."

"If Mr. Sanders would say you approached him and said do you rec with *whites*, and he said yes ..."

The judge interrupted. "He recounted his conversation. What are you doing? He said he got it right the first time. So are you going to read it back to him? Is that what you are doing?"

"Well …"

"No, that's not what you are going to do. Keep going."

"Nothing further, Your Honor."

—

Officer Johnson took the stand next and stated he was the CO who had actually escorted Steven Tremblay to the rec pen that morning but didn't have the keys to let him into the sallyport. He had done this after taking Tremblay to medical for a doctor's visit.

"Did you see any indication from inmate Sanders here not to put Tremblay in the cage?"

"I don't recall."

"Did you happen to stand there while Tremblay was being put in the pen with your finger or thumb on your deuces getting ready to push?"

"No. I am very busy. So, I'm sure I dropped him off and took off to get the next inmate. So no."

"No further questions."

Before Scott got up from his chair for his cross-exam, Kevin wrote on Scott's legal pad, "LIAR." Scott nodded and approached the witness.

"And you didn't see my client make a motion with his hand under his chin to indicate not to put Tremblay in the cage?"

"Objection, Your Honor. Asked and Answered."

"Sustained. Move on, Mr. Powell."

Scott continued. "And you couldn't open the sallyport because it takes a special key?"

"It took a set of keys that I didn't have, yes."

"And Officer Shemp had those keys, correct?" Scott asked.

"Yes. But other officers had those keys as well."

"Okay. Do you know who opened the sallyport door that day?"

"No."

"But Shemp could have?"

"It's possible, yes."

With no more questions for CO Johnson, the judge called for the next witness.

—

Officer Jamie Shemp was the next to be sworn in and take the witness stand. Shemp testified to his background and long employment at Lewisburg and said he was the officer running recreation that day. Galloway asked if he was the officer who put Tremblay into the rec cage, and he replied, "I did not put him in."

Kevin jerked in his seat, leaned over to Scott, and whispered, "That's a lie."

"Okay, who put him in? Do you know?"

"I don't know that."

"When Tremblay was put in, were you standing there?"

"No."

"Did you ever see Sanders waving you off or waving somebody off as far as putting Tremblay in the cage?"

"No, sir."

"Assuming you had seen that, what would you have done?"

"I would have not put him in."

"Why?"

"Because if I feel there's imminent violence, I surely do not want to see it happen."

Galloway recounted the prior testimony by Kevin Sanders and Westin Chase, where each of them had said Kevin waved off Shemp, but that Shemp had put Tremblay in the cage anyway and then stood there with his hand on his body alarm, waiting for something to occur. "Did that happen?"

"No, sir."

Shemp said he only came to the cage when some unknown officer called for assistance to end the fight.

On cross-exam, Shemp never veered from his story. He told Scott any number of officers could have put Tremblay into that cage, and he didn't know who it was.

"Did you hear anything when you were in the yard?" Scott asked.

"I'm not sure exactly what you're looking for."

"Did you hear any hit orders coming down from the third tier?"

"No, sir."

"Did you hear anybody yelling 'Get him!'?"

"No, sir, I don't recollect that. Not to my knowledge."

"To clarify your answer, are you saying you don't know whether that happened on this day or it didn't happen on this day?"

"I can't say, no. I don't remember anyone saying, 'Get him.'"

"No further questions," Scott said.

—

After a short recess, the prosecutor told the court that the next two officers to testify participated in the disciplinary hearing process for the assailants, a routine procedure after a rec cage assault like this.

CO Chambers was the disciplinary hearing officer who drafted both hearing reports for inmates Sanders and Keys.

The five-page document from Kevin's hearing was entered as an exhibit, and Galloway asked him to read a portion.

"Sanders testified that he did stab Tremblay with a sharpened weapon. He testified that the DHO has been around long enough to know how things work in prison. He stated Tremblay was a nuisance to other inmates."

"Did Inmate Sanders give you any indication that it was self-defense on his part?"

"No, not during the hearing."

"Did he give you any indication that he told them, hey, don't put me in the pen with this guy, because there's going to be problems or anything?"

"No."

Then Galloway asked Officer Chambers to read from Mark Keys's hearing report. "Keys testified that he did stab Tremblay with a sharpened weapon during the incident. He testified that Tremblay is a problem for other inmates. And he also stated that he was the lead on this and his cellmate Sanders only had his back."

"Did he give any indication that he said, gee, don't put me in this rec pen with this guy?"

"He did make a comment to the effect that they shouldn't have been in the same cage."

"Okay, nothing further."

Scott had just one question on cross. "Did you read my client his Miranda rights at that hearing?"

"Read him his Miranda rights? No."

"No further questions, Your Honor."

—

CO Gwyn was next on the stand. He was the staff representative for both inmates at their joint disciplinary hearing.

Galloway asked, "Did either of them give you any indication that, hey, we were defending ourselves in this stabbing?"

"No. I knew nothing about … I had never seen the video. I was just there as a staff rep. As far as the statement that they shouldn't have been put in the rec cage with inmate Tremblay, they never made that statement to me."

"Did one of the two inmates in the hearing take the lead?"

"Yes."

"Who?"

"Mr. Keys."

"Why do you say that?"

"When they were in the holding cages waiting to go into their DHO hearing, Mr. Keys told Mr. Sanders, 'Hey, don't worry about it, I'll do most of the talking.' And he did most of the talking in the hearing."

Scott had just one question for this witness. "Do you know whether or not inmates Sanders or Keys thought they were going to be prosecuted at the time of the hearing?"

"I have no idea if they thought they would be prosecuted."

CHAPTER 14
HEARING DAY 2 CONCLUSION

JANUARY 2013, TUESDAY

We broke for a one-hour lunch. Kevin was returned to a holding cell by a U.S. marshal and given a paper sack with a baloney sandwich, a bag of chips, an apple, and a bottle of water. Scott and I headed to a deli across the street for a surprising gourmet meal. I delighted in an order of gnocchi with butternut squash and maple sauce while Scott picked at a plate of Chicken Francese.

"Of course, they're going to lie," Scott said. "Not all of them, but enough of them."

Then he said to me, "Thoughts?"

"Well … is it problematic that Kevin admitted to stabbing Tremblay in his disciplinary hearing? I don't see you trying to refute that. Why did he say it?"

"First of all," Scott said, taking a bite. "They didn't read him his rights and tell him that anything he said could be used against him if they prosecuted. Second, he and Keys were told the FBI *wasn't* going to prosecute, so he didn't think the hearing mattered."

"Do you have proof that the FBI initially declined to prosecute?"

"Just Kevin's word. There is a CO who supposedly told him that, but the CO has transferred out, and he'd probably lie about it if I could get him subpoenaed, which Anderson and Galloway would fight me on, and we know how that would go. So, to answer your question, I don't have anything written to back it up."

We talked about the pitfalls of the Rexton video I emailed him about last night, and he thought it was too risky to go after it. "But that is some ace detective work, Mrs. Conti. You really could have been an investigator, you know."

"Awe, shucks," I batted my eyelashes, pretending to be flattered.

"By the way, Kevin says T-Rex slit that guy's throat for a one-way ticket to ADX, where inmates get their own cells with a shower and TV."

"Jesus," I said with a mouthful of gnocchi.

"That's how bad things are at Lewisburg," he said.

—

After lunch, the court was told there were only three more witnesses. A tall, imposing Special Investigative Services technician, Officer Walters, took the stand.

The prosecutor had only one quick topic for the officer. "Did you send Keys and Sanders to another part of the institution on a mission to take care of Tremblay in July 2011?"

"No, sir."

"No further questions," Galloway finished.

Scott's first question on cross-exam was, "Do you work under SIA Captain Dennis MacDonald?"

"That's correct."

"Was there ever a time when you or Captain MacDonald received some kind of written communication from Kevin Sanders asking for a meeting with you and MacDonald?"

"I'm not sure I understand your question."

Scott repeated it.

"Not that I recall."

"What does SAC stand for?"

"SAC? "Soldiers of Aryan Culture."

"Are they a white gang?"

"Yes, sir."

"And do you know what AB stands for?"

"Aryan Brotherhood."

"Do you know what NLR stands for?"

"Nazi Low Riders."

"Was there an occasion when there was a conflict between the SAC and AB?"

"Yes."

"In fact, didn't the AB put a hit out on the head of the SAC?"

"Not that I'm aware of."

"What was the problem then?"

"Objection. Relevance," said Galloway.

"I'll give him a little bit of latitude on this," the judge said.

Scott continued. "Do you recall ever meeting with my client, Mark Keys, and Captain MacDonald in G Block regarding transferring Sanders and Keys to Z Block?"

"Yes."

"Tell me about that."

"If I remember correctly, there were several NLRs and SACs in that unit, and we just needed to split them up for officer safety."

"Officer safety? So it was a purely random act, moving Sanders and Keys ... not so they could broker a peace between the AB and SAC?"

"Not that I'm aware of. The moving is done on a daily basis."

"Do you recall why you were in the basement of G Block talking to these particular guys on that day?"

"I don't recall."

"No further questions."

—

The next witness to appear was Special Investigative Supervisor Lt. Deborah Lippit, a petite officer with sandy brown hair and dark nail polish. She testified that an SIS investigation wasn't necessary for the rec cage fight because they had video of it. She had written one of the many officer memos of the assault and referred the case to the FBI the same day.

In questioning her, Galloway focused on several exhibits, beginning with the medical reports of the three inmates created right after the assault. He had her read from Kevin Sanders' and Mark Keys' reports, citing neither inmate sustained injuries.

"And on the second page of Mr. Tremblay's health service record, it shows he received, oh, in excess of 40 stab wounds. Is that correct?"

"Yes," she said.

Galloway asked her to look at exhibit 10. "Were you the one who recovered the shanks in this case?"

"I believe Mr. Shemp recovered one of them, and then I recovered the other one."

"What did Mr. Shemp do with the one he recovered?"

"He handed it to me."

"So you ultimately got both shanks in this case?"

"Yes."

"And there are Xeroxed copies of those shanks, correct?"

"Yes."

"No further questions, Your Honor."

Scott introduced himself to Lt. Lippit and then asked, "Why, among all the cases that take place at Lewisburg in the course of a year, why was this one selected for referral to the FBI and prosecution?"

"There was serious bodily injury sustained. There were weapons involved," she said.

"Isn't it true that this case was referred to the FBI and selected for prosecution because a civil suit had been brought against the Bureau of Prisons by Steven Tremblay, for the injuries he received in the rec cage assault?"

"That doesn't make sense to me. But I have no idea. That doesn't sound logical."

"But you, yourself, are a defendant in this case, aren't you?"

The judge intervened. "How does that relate to the motion? How does that have anything to do with this motion? We're not at trial."

"Okay …" Scott pivoted with one last question for Lt. Lippit. "Did you say to Mr. Tremblay after he left the rec cage, this is what you get for hitting …"

"No," she answered quickly.

"No further questions, thanks."

"You may step down, ma'am," said the court.

—

The hearing's last witness was FBI Special Agent Brenner. Under questioning by Scott, he testified that he was notified the day of the assault that it had been "a serious incident" and went to Lewisburg the next morning. Brenner said he saw the same video that the court saw and no other versions that showed inmates being led into the cage.

"At some point, did you make a determination as to whether or not to pursue prosecution?"

"Right off the bat, yes."

"What was that determination?"

"The fact that the defendants were positively identified. Three people in a cell. One taken out with injuries. Two taken out reportedly with shanks. Both of them were relatively short-timers, one on the cusp of getting out. Our three criteria—the severity of the incident, the amount of time the players have left to serve, and the quality of the identification—we were strong on all three bases."

"So your position was that you would prosecute from the very beginning?"

"That's correct, sir."

"Did you ever indicate to anybody at Lewisburg that you were not going to prosecute?"

"Never, sir."

"The bloody clothing that was retrieved from inmates Sanders and Keys, was that taken into evidence?"

"Not by us, sir."

"Did you ever notify SIS that the evidence, the bloody clothing, could be returned to the inmates?"

The judge interrupted. "How is this helping on this particular motion?"

"Well, my client was under the impression that no charges were being filed."

"You're going to have to focus your inquiry," the judge said. "This is a specific pretrial motion on a very limited basis. This is not an adventure in discovery, nor is it a preliminary hearing."

"Understood. No further questions."

Galloway, on cross-exam, asked the agent to look at Exhibit Number 3, the agent's memo from two days after the assault. "Any indication on there that the case was declined in any way?"

"No, sir. There's a notation on the bottom, an 'open and assign' from my supervisor."

"That means opened and assigned?"

"Correct."

"Take a look at Exhibit 4. You indicated you tried to interview the two defendants. Is that correct?"

"Yes, sir."

"Did they give any indication, hey, look, there is more video, or we were trying to defend ourselves, or we had to do this, or it was a necessity? Any indication whatsoever?"

"No, sir. Both inmates declined to be interviewed."

"Let's turn to Exhibit 6, a copy of which I have provided to the Court and defense counsel. Is this a document you received during the investigation?"

"Yes, sir."

"Would you describe it?"

"It appears to be a letter."

"Would you read the highlighted portions?"

"My dad died in March. Then my mother October 30th. On top of all that, I stabbed some lame 45 times."

"Who was this letter written by?"

"Mr. Keys."

—

Scott, on redirect, asked the agent how he got the letter, and he responded Officer Walters gave it to him. It had come to Walters's attention through the typical mail and phone call monitoring the prison conducted, particularly for any gang members. Keys had written the letter to his sister.

"Agent Brenner. Your attempt to interview my client and Mark Keys, you did that on August 15th. Correct?"

"Yes, sir, you are correct."

"And isn't it correct, from the testimony we've heard, that the video had already been erased by that time?"

"Apparently, sir, yes."

"No further questions."

—

Before adjourning, Judge Anderson said he would rule promptly after both sides submitted post-hearing briefs.

"All rise," the courtroom deputy said, and a U.S. marshal collected Kevin for a return to Lewisburg Prison. He and Scott hugged, and Kevin shook my hand. "I'll be in touch, buddy," Scott assured him.

Scott and I, both drained, had the same idea to decompress at the pub across the street. As we gathered our things, Scott said, "Jackson!" at a rotund man in suspenders with a long white beard, mustache, and ponytail, walking toward us. They exchanged a hand hug, and Scott lit up. "You came," he smiled.

"I was in the neighborhood," Scott's friend said, extending his hand to me. "You must be Carla." He held my gaze with twinkling eyes, and my hand, tiny in comparison, was lost in his substantial grip.

"I'm Jack Bear."

CHAPTER 15
THE VOLUNTEER

JANUARY 2013, TUESDAY, SCRANTON ALE HOUSE, 5:00 P.M.

"Well, my friend, I feel for you, drawing Anderson in the great judicial lottery of life," Jack said. We settled into a booth, and Jack, with permission, ordered us all old-fashioneds. "If it weren't for bad luck, your boy would have no luck at all."

I didn't know it, but Scott emailed Jack this week for case advice and tips on handling the judge. They told me a story about how they'd tried a federal case together eight years before, representing a pair of crack cocaine dealers, and Jack's client had fired him. They lost their cases.

We were famished and started with two plates of BBQ wings. Scott and I shared one, while Jack, with a napkin tucked into his shirt collar, enjoyed the other. Jack was 12 years older than we were and had been taking on court-appointed cases in Pennsylvania's Middle District that much longer than Scott.

"Lewisburg's SMU is a scandal and a travesty," he said, licking his lips. "It houses too many people under the worst conditions. The world would be better off if it were shut down and used to store nuclear waste."

Jack told Scott he admired the principled stand he was taking with the case and that "my offer of support still stands to show these assholes that you're not alone. Some of us will not back away from a moral line in the sand." I looked at Scott with wide, hopeful eyes at what I thought was happening.

"Appointed or not, paid or not, I'm available to help a brother, even if it comes to sitting in the courtroom with you—that would piss off Anderson, right?"

I covered my mouth in joyous surprise as Scott hugged his friend. "Jackson, you don't know what this means. I'm tired of fighting these bastards all by myself." And then he looked at me apologetically. "Not that Carla hasn't been a great paralegal and investigator, but she hasn't passed the bar yet," he smiled. "And I knew your newspaper reporting skills would come in handy."

I started to respond, but Jack declared, "A reporter? Good God, a liberal! As if the case wasn't complicated enough!" We howled with laughter, and then Jack looked at me over his glasses. "And she wants to write a book, no less."

"Well … *maybe*," I said. "I might write a book …"

"She's writing a book," Scott said.

Over burgers dripping with gooey toppings, Jack said he'd read every blog post on the *Free Kevin Sanders* website. He found it truly compelling, and Kevin's story was another reason he offered to help. But he had concerns about the crowd-funding aspect, telling us this could present a problem regarding indigency and court-appointment rules. This was news to me, and Scott said he'd look into it.

Then, we discussed the likely outcome of the hearing. "Anderson won't dismiss," Jack said flatly, and I sensed Scott knew this was true. "So let's focus on the trial.

"Check with Kevin about me sitting second chair. If he's good with it, I'll come to your house and look at the file. I'll buy you lunch."

The website had been finished for weeks, but Scott's Twitter friend hadn't come through yet with the promised viral tweet. But because I had some basic search engine optimization skills—I'd been tinkering with websites since Microsoft *FrontPage* and FTP uploads—*FreeKevinSanders.com* had reached a small audience. This translated into meager donations of $385 so far.

Judging from the comment section, the readers were mostly sympathetic to Kevin's portrayal. They were drawn to his story, beginning with his abusive childhood at the hands of an alcoholic mother and an outlaw-biker father, who ran a Hells Angels chapter out of his body shop. Kevin grew up in Central California amid a hotbed of Hispanic and Mexican street gangs, and the relatively innocuous 31st Street Gang became a family substitute. As a youth, he turned to petty crimes and drugs, was in and out of juvenile detention, and then in prison as a young man. While his father taught Kevin how to airbrush designs on the hoods of muscle cars and Harley fenders, he also taught him how to cook meth.

One of the blog installments described a scene that could have come from the trendy *Breaking Bad* TV series. Kevin's meth-lab-in-a-camper was raided by officers from the Alcohol, Tobacco, and Firearms Bureau, who discovered among the illegal drug-making contents a sawed-off shotgun. Criminal charges were boiled down to one—a felon in possession of a weapon, which earned Kevin his ten years in the feds.

I concluded his profile by saying Kevin had been clean for eight years and was now fighting unjust charges. If a jury acquitted him because they agreed he had no choice but to participate in the rec cage fight, he could go free in two years and create a productive life for himself on the outside.

What I didn't mention in Kevin's backstory was the mysterious falling out between father and son that led ATF officers to raid the camper and discover the shotgun. According to Scott, it was Kevin's father who turned him into federal agents.

"Does that make sense to you?" I asked Scott. "That his father would turn him in because he was 'jealous' of the money Kevin was making?"

Scott shrugged. "All I know is what Kevin told me."

—

The week after the hearing, Jack filed his pro bono appearance on his laptop, sitting fireside at Camp Walleye, his Pocono hunting and fishing cabin. He'd settled into his favorite overstuffed chair after checking in back home with his wife Betsy ("she who must be obeyed") and feeding the dogs. "We're off to the races," he emailed us. "I'm very much looking forward to this. Nothing upsets the forces of oppression more than knowing a couple of wildmen will try a case because they believe in it and for the joy of the battle."

I opened my inbox the next day to find a wildly off-color email from Jack of the Benny Hill variety. I was among two dozen recipients, including Scott, treated to a joke that asked, "What causes the most auto accidents?" A half dozen photos of buxom and scantily clad women in high heels, crossing or standing roadside appeared below, followed by the answer: "Yep, you guessed it. Inappropriate footwear!!!"

A few days later, another one came with the subject line "Beach Fails," and it was a photo series of men and women at the beach stuffed into bathing suits too small or ill-fitting. "OMG!" I emailed Scott. "WTF?"

"Sorry, Carla," he said. "You found your way onto his friends list. Careful though. A former federal prosecutor is on this list." As were at least ten other attorneys.

"Can you tell him this is what Facebook is for?"

"Jackson Bear shuns all social media. He says it's a 'narcissistic waste of time.'"

"Well, he's not wrong ..." I said. Rather than hurt his feelings, I created an email forwarding rule that automatically dumped those messages into a "Stupid Jack Emails" folder.

—

While Scott and Jack worked on the post-hearing brief, I continued researching Lewisburg prison conditions and looking for anything that might help our case. I'd already found local newspaper articles that I'd referenced on the website, plus a 2011 article by a professor at Bucknell University, a private liberal arts college in Lewisburg, titled, *"Security here is not safe": violence, punishment, and space in the contemporary US penitentiary.* On the blog, I cited Professor Karen Morin's scathing piece, which revealed the inhumane and murderous conditions brought about by inmates in near-total lockdown in tiny cells, often with violent cellmates.

But the mother lode of secrets and atrocities was found via the online court database PACER, hidden inside thousands of electronically filed pages, waiting to be mined by someone with patience and the right keywords.

I found a slew of civil cases, some just recently filed, that stemmed from incidents that happened around the same time as Kevin's rec cage assault. An inmate named Jasper Rivera filed suit against the Bureau of Prisons for getting stabbed 15 times in a Z Block rec cage by a prisoner he was supposed to have a "keep-away" status with. Rivera alleged that both he and his attacker told the rec officer "to keep us apart," which was ignored, and that COs didn't intervene immediately. Rivera had been rushed to the hospital in critical condition.

One inmate claimed an eye injury and denial of medical care after a use-of-force team attacked him in his cell and that Lewisburg officers "have been setting people up to get hurt." The suit stated that COs "are retaliating against me." Captain Dennis MacDonald was listed as one of those defendants.

Another inmate claimed he was held down by one CO and forced to perform a sex act on another officer while a third one watched.

Inmate Ronnie Wiggins filed suit against the BOP for getting stabbed in a Z Block rec cage. Wiggins, a former Dirty White Boys leader who had to be kept away from all white gangs because he'd stabbed a DWB at another prison, spent two years in Lewisburg without incident until he was transferred to Z Block. Once in Z Bloc, his suit stated, he was put into a rec cage with five other inmates—bypassing other empty rec cages—and not given a choice to decline rec. Four of the five in the cage were DWB members, and Wiggins was immediately attacked by one of them, stabbed 22 times with a metal knife. He required surgery for his severe injuries and spent one week in the hospital. The complaint stated that COs failed to find his assailant's weapon via a pat search or hand-held metal detector and that they did not honor his separation requirements. Wiggins also said officers failed to respond to the stabbing in a timely manner.

I discovered a particularly hideous punishment Lewisburg COs allegedly doled out, called "four-pointing," in the unsettling case of Sebastian Richardson. In his suit, Richardson said he was "four-pointed" for refusing a hostile cellie known as "The Prophet," who had attacked over 20 former cellmates.

Richardson said his punishment first began with officers taking him to a laundry area, where they stripped him, put him in paper clothes, and then applied *ambulatory* restraints—chains and shackles so tight he screamed in pain, bled, and had difficulty breathing. COs placed him in a cell with someone similarly restrained and left the cell window open. It was February, and he was restrained like that for a week.

The suit said that eating and drinking in those restraints was nearly impossible, and worst still was the hygiene aspect of trying to use the bathroom—COs were supposed to offer bathroom breaks every two hours where one handcuff would be undone, but those bathroom breaks were regularly denied.

At the end of the week, when Richardson still refused to be celled with The Prophet, officers moved him to a basement room where they "four-pointed" him. Four-pointing was described as placing an inmate on a bedframe, then restraining his hands separately overhead with metal shackles attached to either the bed frame or the wall. The inmate's legs were shackled similarly to the foot of the bed frame. With limbs stretched out in that manner, the inmate's ability to move was completely restricted.

Richardson said he asked for water and a urinal and was denied both. As a result, he urinated on himself and was left in soiled paper clothing in a room where, again, a CO opened a window. He was kept that way for eight hours and then put back into the ambulatory restraints, where he remained for two weeks. COs then unshackled him for two hours so he could shower—the first he'd had in weeks—and then they started the restraint process over again when he still refused to cell with The Prophet.

Richardson's suit said he was kept in hard restraints for an entire month in the winter of 2011 in unsanitary and inhumane conditions, where his arms and hands became numb due to the tightness of the shackles, and he was denied medication to treat his mental illness and control his behavior. All of this occurred, said Richardson, as punishment for refusing a violent cellmate. During that time, Richardson said he had many rotating cellmates, also shackled in hard restraints, mainly because they, too, refused hostile cellies.

The Lewisburg cases were endless. Every time I searched with different keywords, more would crop up. Sprinkled among the three dozen suits I'd found so far were the names of many of the same Lewisburg officers linked to our case. But of everything I'd unearthed, Sebastian Richardson's suit was, by far, the most disturbing.

Many of the suits were filed by the same big law firms in Pittsburgh or Philadelphia or by state justice organizations. One shining star in this realm was The Lewisburg Prison Project, or LPP, a local non-profit offering inmates legal assistance and advocacy on confinement issues. After the Special Management Unit opened, the two-person staff received nearly 1,000 complaint letters yearly.

I reminded myself that these cases I'd found in PACER were the horrors I *knew* about because those inmates had the wherewithal or advocates to file in federal court. What about the inmates with no resources and cases that stayed buried?

It was depressing.

CHAPTER 16
PING PONG

WINTER 2013

S cott's post-hearing brief was a routine submission, but the government's response contained an ambush: Assistant United States Attorney (AUSA) Galloway objected to Kevin's use of a justification or duress defense and asked the court to strike that possibility.

Justification was an *affirmative defense*, with a lower standard of proof than beyond a reasonable doubt. There would also be more investigation, discovery, and trial prep for such a case, so Galloway objected. Federal courts, which typically didn't prohibit this strategy, had liberal discretion to strike it just the same.

"Defendant's alleged 'self-defense by proxy' is utter nonsense. Attacking someone from behind with shanks is not self-defense," Galloway wrote. His long reply brief returned to the kite in Kevin's shoe that he said he keistered. "How likely is it that someone would take a note from a relatively secure location like a shoe and 'stick it' in their 'ass' before commencing an assault? Not very."

Galloway reiterated his position that the video showed, just before the attack, Sanders reaching into the back of his pants with his left hand, removing something, transferring it to his right hand, then making stabbing motions with his right hand at Tremblay.

Ironically, argued Galloway, "the only one who could have claimed self-defense was the victim Tremblay if he could have gotten one of the shanks away from his assailants and used it on them."

Three weeks later, Judge Anderson rendered his decision on the video hearing: He denied Scott's motion to dismiss the indictment based on destroyed exculpatory evidence *and* said Scott could not use a justification defense. The judge agreed with everything Galloway argued in the hearing and in his follow-up brief.

—

Scott, undeterred, and with Jack's help, filed a motion to reconsider, referencing newer case law and saying that if justification had been the issue at the hearing, he would have put his client back on the stand to refute the claims of several officers. "While the Court may not have believed our witnesses, it has taken away Kevin Sanders' right to have his case decided by a jury of his peers."

Scott also said he would be filing a motion to retain the services of the expert witness (again) and attached the witness's impressive CV and fee schedule. He explained the witness would testify to the lawless nature of Lewisburg, including inmates getting stabbed in their cuffs and the enforcement of gang rules. The witness would say that his client was placed in a "kill or be killed situation" with no "hole" or segregated safe space to turn to.

Galloway, naturally, opposed the expert witness, launching a season of legal ping pong. With more back-and-forth briefs of support and opposition, extension requests, court orders, and clarifications, the docket had reached 85 filings.

The latest batch resulted in a rare moment of contrition by the judge. He reversed himself and agreed to hold a hearing on both issues—the justification defense and need for our expert witness. *Great, another hearing*, I thought.

SPRING 2013

Details from the January video hearing had spread to other federal prisons like a virus. An underground network of spies and cohorts passed along tidbits via letters and phone calls to gang members with skin in the game.

Scott received a letter from Kevin's cellmate Mark Keys, a.k.a. Arson, who was still at Lewisburg. It contained a warning to pass along to Kevin for trial. Arson stated that T-Rex (1,700 miles away at the supermax prison ADX Florence, in Colorado) was "NOT COOL that you said his name in open court … You said you had permission from everyone, right? No man, that's not how it is. Do not say anything about anyone ordering anything!"

"NEWS FLASH! It's not all about you Kevin! The fact is, we are hit. The quicker you accept that, the better off we will be. I take my hit on the chin like a man."

But then Arson said, "Look, I'm not your enemy. And I'll help you to a point," and he agreed to sign a statement saying, "To my knowledge, you were not armed with a knife. And if you did not help me, I would have got you for leaving me hanging! Have your attorney draw it up, and I will sign it."

It sounded very contrived, and I imagined Galloway would shred it to pieces if we tried to use it.

Arson's letter was followed by one from an inmate at Big Sandy in Kentucky, with a similar warning. This inmate, an AB associate, said Kevin needed "to keep all titles, names and acronyms out of things. THIS IS IMPERATIVE. We love him but are confused. He already knows about this, but just in case, I wanted to reach out before anything immoral happened by accident."

Interestingly, this pen pal indicated T-Rex (without naming him specifically) might want to testify, but that it would be for "him alone to say things," and that it was "all about the approach and can be done if coming from the person's mouth alone."

This not-so-cryptic point was confirmed in a third letter Scott received from T-Rex himself. Scott had written T-Rex about testifying at trial after the Big Sandy inmate opened the door.

> Dear Mr. Powell,
>
> I received your letter today regarding *United States v. Kevin Sanders.* I would do anything to help so long as it doesn't put any of my friends at risk. It's our belief the feds are working on a new RICO case for alleged AB members. I have never admitted to membership and never will. I've got to talk to some of my friends here, but I wouldn't hold my breath. I love to travel, though dread the idea of Lewisburg!

T-Rex mentioned the Lewisburg stabbing that got him transferred to ADX Florence—"I got no problem admitting that cops set it up"—and said he wasn't indicted for it because he was doing 70 years and "they only charge those doing ten years or less it seems." He then listed the names of five suspected AB associates, "friends" of his in Z Block at the time of Kevin's assault, who might be able to help.

This seemed oddly generous and yet moot. How could any of them helpfully testify if they wouldn't admit to gang membership because AB leaders feared a government racketeering case would be brought against them?

T-Rex ended his letter with this: "Please tell Kevin if there's any way to help him and not hurt no one else, he's got that, and I send my love and respects."

Scott received one last curious letter that spring, this one from the rec cage victim Steven Tremblay. It was a short note, mailed from his new prison in Victorville, Calif., stating he wanted to talk to Scott, but that was all. It didn't hint at the topic. Jack weighed in quickly that we should ignore it. In the civil suit Tremblay filed (initially with help from The Lewisburg Prison Project), he accused both Mark Keys and Kevin of stabbing him. And because we were arguing Kevin had no knife, Jack said Tremblay was "a minefield best left alone."

—

In April, Scott arranged a legal visit at Lewisburg so Kevin and Jack could finally meet. Jack, who hadn't seen Kevin testify at the hearing, wanted to gauge what kind of witness Kevin would be. "Juries want to hear defendants talk and explain things," he said. "Maybe once in 33 years, I've won an acquittal *without* my client testifying—it's that rare. This ain't my first rodeo."

The meet-and-greet had gone well, and Jack agreed with Scott that having Kevin testify was key to winning the case. A few days later, a Lewisburg CO told Kevin, "You're spending too much time with your attorneys." And, within a week, Kevin found himself on a "Con Air" flight to USP Florence's high-security unit with a stopover at the federal transfer center in Oklahoma City.

Lewisburg officers wouldn't let Kevin call or write his attorneys, and when Scott found out, he was livid. "AUSA Galloway signed off on it," he texted me in our first-ever SMS text exchange.

Not only had Galloway signed off on the transfer, but so had the Lewisburg warden—a curious move considering Kevin was supposed to stay at Lewisburg through mid-May for an "SMU reassessment" per a letter from the BOP's regional director.

Jack was used to seeing authorities play these games, and he told us not to sweat it, that we would get Kevin back. In the meantime, he added, USP Florence would seem like a vacation compared to Lewisburg. The hearing was moved to July, and the judge ordered the U.S. Marshal Service to return Kevin to the district as soon as possible.

—

By the end of April, the *Free Kevin Sanders* website had only brought in $875. It was obvious we wouldn't get the viral tweet, and I told Scott I didn't know how else to promote it. We were already blasting it to our combined 130-some Facebook friends, and neither of us had the interest or bandwidth to try and figure out Twitter. Scott reached out to the expert witness to see if he'd cut his fee in half, but he wouldn't. I researched other experts who charged less, but Scott insisted we engage the retired Lewisburg SIS officer.

Then, Scott got a surprise email from his former girlfriend. Lucy, a courtroom fan favorite who'd appeared many times before Judge Anderson, had his ear, and she passed along an unofficial message: remove the donation feature from Kevin's website. It violated all kinds of rules. We also had to remove any mention of Judge Anderson's name. *And* we had to return all the donations. What a flipping pain in the ass that was.

A reluctant Scott said we should probably take down the website altogether. Jack agreed and, without saying *I told you so,* filed a new motion for the expert witness services.

CHAPTER 17
GET OFF THE POT

MAY 2013

I was having a moment.

Now that Jack had joined the case as a vastly superior helper, what was I doing besides keeping us organized and weighing in on random emails? I had no more website duties. The guys were on point for the hearing, digging into the case law that carried the benchmarks of justification we had to meet. I felt like a glorified Della Street to their collective Perry Mason.

But I couldn't deny I was amassing a vast amount of information much stranger than any fiction. What was I going to do with it? Was I writing a book or not?

Since Scott, Jack, and Kevin assumed I was writing the true crime story I was witnessing firsthand, I decided to embrace it. I created an author website and professional Facebook page and started drafting a nonfiction book proposal.

This was not *my* first rodeo with a book outline and pitch. I'd been down this road many years before with a true crime story in Jim's hometown that I'd gotten pretty close to publishing. The case centered on a 1970s love triangle murder that was reopened in the mid-1990s with the exhumation of the victim's body. It was a small-town scandal turned national sensation, and I had unique access to some of the main characters. My young boys and I spent an entire summer at my mother-in-law's house so I could attend the trial, and I churned out an enticing book proposal that landed me a New York literary agent. But after pitching it to some editors, my agent learned a seasoned true crime author with several titles to her name was writing her version of the story, and so I, an unpublished writer, was shit-out-of-luck.

I looked up my former agent and learned he had died. But there was a writer's conference in NYC in August, and if I finished the proposal quickly, I could pitch it to agents there.

Now that I was officially wearing a writer's hat, I asked Scott to ask Kevin for a description of his transfer and what life was like at those other prisons. He said he would on their next phone call, and a couple of weeks later, I got my first letter from Kevin mailed to Scott in a large envelope stamped LEGAL MAIL on the outside.

He started his letter by saying, "I'm still in awe over the idea of you and Jack there to help and to show the truth and evil of Lewisburg SMU. I just can't put into words how I'm lost in wonder of the love I have been shown."

THE TRANSFER ODYSSEY

Kevin had been given a week's notice that he was shipping out to Florence. His possessions were sent ahead of him, so he had nothing to do in his cell until the day of departure. He was awakened at 4:00 a.m., sent to R&D (receiving and dress out), and placed into handcuffs with a black box and belly chain with leg cuffs. He boarded a bus for Harrisburg, to be followed by a "Con Air" flight to Oklahoma City. Once at the airport, though, he was told the flight was canceled due to weather, and he was sent back to Lewisburg for another week in a cell without his possessions.

"I had a hard week of wonder, not knowing why, after eight months of me asking to be placed into a level 3 & 4 program, why they really wanted me moved." (Lewisburg inmates who'd completed the first two phases were sent to other prisons to finish the last two levels.) At least one Lewisburg officer told Kevin that he was being sent away because he was asking some COs to tell the truth about how his rec cage assault was set up—and also because his lawyer was so aggressively pursuing the case.

He shipped out for good on a Monday, "glad to finally be away from Lewisburg, but worried about what was next." He watched the Pennsylvania landscape grow smaller through the airplane window, and three and a half hours later, he landed at the Federal Transfer Center at Oklahoma City—a mostly pass-through hub for federal prisoners with its own airport. Kevin was taken to "the hole" on the 4th floor, where he sat for a week watching the planes come and go. He had "no phone, no store, could only write three letters a week," and he rec'ced alone in a cage for an hour a day.

One week later, Kevin flew to USP Florence-High with some men who were on their way to the supermax ADX Florence "for killing other inmates in other prisons." Once he arrived in Florence, he was x-rayed for weapons and put through another quay hearing to confirm his keep-aways. He spent his first week in a 4th tier cell watching the other ranges, which housed specific racial gang members. These groups included "a mix of Mexicans (Sureños, Paisas, and Latin Kings), D.C. Blacks, and whites like ARM (Aryan Resistance Movement)."

The first tier was reserved for "ex-gang members, sex offenders and 'soft' inmates or ones who did not fit in with others."

Kevin started getting used to being allowed to congregate with others outside of his cell for up to five hours a day. But he said most of their outdoor recreation time was cut short because there weren't enough officers. Often, a rec officer would have to respond to an incident on another unit due to a lack of staff. "Why a max high-security federal prison is understaffed, I have no idea," he wrote. When in his cell, he passed the time drawing on prison-issued envelopes and working out.

His time in Florence was up after two weeks when the marshals came to get him to enforce the writ of habeas corpus that would return him to Pennsylvania. But due to the complex formula of intrastate prisoner transport, Kevin's journey back was far from direct.

When he boarded his next Con Air flight, a marshal drew an X with a Sharpie on his hand. And when he landed at the Oklahoma Transfer Center, Kevin joined other inmates with black Xs on a bus, which took them to a county jail 45 minutes away. He was uncuffed, checked in, given a red uniform, and then surprised to be led to a large 32-bed dorm. "This was new to me. After all my years living in cells, I was happy to be around so many people."

He spent the next ten days in the open dorm and earned the guards' respect because he kept the rowdy inmates in line. He got them to clean up after themselves, keep quiet hours at night, and stop stealing food trays and disrespecting others. "The night before I was to leave, the officers was stopping by the unit and wishing me luck on my case and hoped I came back through."

Kevin was awakened at 4:00 a.m. again for a bus ride back to the transfer center and then a last Con Air flight to Pennsylvania. When he landed, two marshals drove him in a van to the Douglas County Prison (DCP), where Jack arranged for him to stay through the trial.

—

Two weeks later, Scott forwarded me a follow-up letter from Kevin. He'd written it from DCP and said the housing was, for the most part, good. It was certainly better than Lewisburg or Florence, but not as nice as the county jail in Colorado. Kevin liked being on a range with other inmates and only having four hours of lock-down throughout the day. He had access to real recreation like handball, basketball, and playing cards, and he was especially fond of his 19-year-old cellmate, whom he called "The Kid."

"I started to teach him about respect and better ways to live in a prison setting," Kevin wrote. "I showed him how to work out. I also showed the boy how to cook a few things with the items we could buy so we would have something good to eat in the evening."

But Kevin tried to impart a more powerful lesson about how "his life on the other side of the wall was more important. I started to open the youngster's eyes so he could have something better for himself."

One day, without warning, a DCP officer told Kevin to roll up his things because he was being sent to the hole. Kevin had no explanation for it. Maybe the warden just wanted to shake him down, or maybe there were connections between those COs and the ones at Lewisburg. So Kevin sat in the hole with no possessions, "just my thoughts and the anger of the games people play in these places."

The next night, he heard the hole range door open, and in walked The Kid, "telling the officer that he wants to live with Sanders and he don't want to go into any other cell but mine." The Kid's wish was granted, and as soon as he entered Kevin's cell, "he hugged me and said he'd just come to visit for a few days."

Kevin asked how he arranged this, and The Kid told him he got busted on purpose for smoking in his cell. In the process, he'd smuggled books, cigarettes, toiletries, and snacks for Kevin in his bedroll.

"Smoking and joking, we passed the next few days together in the hole until he left to go back to the block, leaving me with the few things that make life a little easier in the box. I just hope the youngster can see a better life for himself on the other side. If words have power, let mine move the boy."

Kevin's letter ended: "I sit here along a path that gets hard at times, but I come through with faith. Some choices are not the best, but I try."

Behind the last page of the letter was a breathtaking ink drawing of a predatory bird perched in a tree—an eagle, I thought. A link chain was attached to one of its legs, but the chain was broken. The other half of the severed chain was wrapped around a tree branch. The bird was essentially free, yet it sat there, staring into my soul, begging the question: Why don't you fly away?

Kevin signed his last name at the bottom, and on the other side, he wrote the title: *Chained Bird*.

CHAPTER 18
ANOTHER RODEO

JULY 2013

T he day before the hearing, I got an early check-in at a boutique inn a few miles from Scott's cottage. Scott, Jack, and I planned to meet with Kevin at the Douglas County Prison and then work at Scott's place to fine-tune the strategy for what was expected to be a short hearing.

The DCP officers were even more friendly than before. Jack shook hands with several he knew, and after taking turns on the metal-detecting throne, the three of us were welcomed into the main hall where Kevin was waiting. Scott had brought the same loose-fitting suit, and I had brought an art supply kit of colored pencils, charcoal, and a sketch pad, which the DCP officers said he could keep. But Kevin was busy with a much larger art project, and after a round of hugs, he showed us around the vestibule and corridor as a CO walked behind us.

When Kevin left the hole, he asked the warden if he could do some painting projects, pointing out the faded lettering on an overhead beam that once must have meant something. The warden took him up on the offer, and Kevin restored the saying with a delicate hand that read: *Respect is earned on both sides of these doors.* Kevin was permitted to repeat the task throughout the prison, and he proudly showed us the painted phrase nearest the prison entry.

As we turned a corner, an entire cinder-block wall set up with yellow metal scaffolding and buckets of paint came into view. It was a massive mural in progress of one of the county's red-covered bridges, partially filled in, with a forest background outlined against a blue sky. Kevin beamed as he showed it off, and we were all mesmerized.

—

We treated ourselves to an Italian lunch on the rear patio of my inn. The buzzing cicadas forecasted another hot day, but it was cool under an umbrella on the flagstone terrace surrounded by hemlocks and shady maples. We had gorgeous views of the Endless Mountains to the north and sipped iced tea. While the guys waited for their pasta and I for my eggplant parm, Jack revisited the website fund-raising fiasco.

"Anderson could have handled it much more bluntly," he said. "It could have been infinitely uglier. We could've been hit with a *Rule To Show Cause* and a short-notice hearing in Harrisburg with mandated attendance by all three of us. The best result in that case would've been a very severe ass-chewing."

The food arrived, and Jack continued. "Myself, I've got plenty of ass, and it gets chewed on fairly regularly, so I'm used to it, but most people find it unpleasant to be chomped on by a federal judge." I cast a side-eye at Scott, and he said, "Yeah, we get it."

"All I'm saying is, it was handled with grace and discretion, and we should recognize that."

Mid-way through lunch, Scott reached into his briefcase and threw a multi-page document onto the table. It was a grainy report of some sort, stapled in the corner, and looked like a copy of a copy of a copy, and then some.

"Pray tell, counselor, *was ist das*?" Jack said, looking up from his fettucine.

Scott said he'd found it in his mailbox in an envelope with no return address or note from the sender. It was a five-year-old BOP intelligence report stamped "DOJ Sensitive" and "FOIA Exempt" (Freedom of Information Act) from a federal pen out West, and I leafed through pages as Scott explained. The memo was a summary of a 2007 prison yard riot—The Aryan Brotherhood and Dirty White Boys versus the Skinheads and Soldiers of Aryan Culture—that threatened to spill over into an all-out racial war within the prison. The origin had to do with a white gangster disrespecting the leader of a Hispanic gang and a proposed solution of the whites disciplining the offender to keep the peace. Except the white gangster refused to submit to his beat down for the good of his gang and the prison.

I paused my lunch to keep flipping pages. The memo read like a thriller, detailing the brutality, decrees, and hierarchy of multiple prison gangs, as well as their codependency with prison officials.

"And guess who's listed as a 'validated member of the Aryan Brotherhood?'" Scott said.

I found the page that listed all 28 inmates who participated in the riot. "Trevor Rexton!" I said.

"A.k.a. T-Rex," he added.

"It also calls Rexton 'well respected' and said he tried to broker the peace, making everyone shake hands," I read.

But the relevancy to Kevin's case, said Scott, was the fact that two gang members refused to fight, and prison officials had to move them to another prison for their own safety due to the expected gang punishment.

"Ahh, reprisals," Jack nodded. "Just like our boy. We can use this to impeach anyone who says Kevin wasn't in danger."

"Exactly," said Scott.

"And you don't know who sent this?" I asked skeptically.

"My best guess is it came from a soldier or a soldier's girlfriend," Scott said. "But I swear, I don't know who it's from."

—

A breeze off Shawnee Lake helped make up for the lack of air-conditioning in Scott's cottage. The two guys huddled around case files stacked on a card table in the living room while I took over the couch and coffee table with a scanner I'd brought from home. I was going through a box of letters and documents not on PACER to copy for a cloud-stored database the three of us could share. Once in a while, I'd shift over to the table to help find something or take more notes.

Our first task was to meet a four-element test of justification as defined by a new Third Circuit Court of Appeals case, *United States v. Taylor*. It was a precedential case argued last year, which meant it was authoritative and set a precedent; if we met the four elements of *Taylor*, Judge Anderson would have to allow us to use the justification defense.

The elements as they pertained to our case were:

1. That Kevin was under an immediate, unlawful threat of death or serious bodily injury to himself;
2. That Kevin had a well-grounded, or reasonable, fear that the threat would be carried out if he did not commit the offense;
3. That Kevin had no reasonable lawful opportunity both to refuse to do the criminal act and also to avoid the threatened harm; and

4. That Kevin had not recklessly placed himself in a situation in which he would be forced to engage in criminal conduct.

Our second task was to convince the judge that our expert witness was necessary for Kevin to receive a fair trial. That in itself was an uphill battle due to the judge's previous position and references to unnecessary taxpayer costs. Scott had fronted $1,500 for the retired SIS officer to draft a proffer letter outlining his testimony, and his letter and CV would be submitted as exhibits tomorrow.

"If we succeed at this, Anderson's hands are tied, and he has to let us put on the defense, which means he has to approve your budget for the expert," Jack said.

—

The next morning, we returned to Courtroom No. 1 on the top floor of the William J. Nealon Federal Building as a trio of musketeers, fortified by Jack, who handled all the oral arguments, or as Judge Anderson put it, "carried the bullet" for the day.

Jack began by introducing the prison riot memo and the letter Mark Keys wrote to Kevin, saying, "To my knowledge, you were not armed with a knife. And if you did not help me, I would have got you for leaving me hanging! Have your attorney draw it up, and I will sign it."

If the memo surprised Galloway, he didn't show it. Both Galloway and the judge agreed the letter could be interpreted two different ways, and that it did not necessarily mean that Keys' statement was true.

Jack went through the four points of *Taylor*, offering proffers of testimony or evidence that met each one. These included: Little Eagle witnessing Kevin trying to keep the victim out of the rec cage; Kevin's own testimony that he had no choice but to participate in the fight; our expert witness—using the prison riot memo for context—would tell the jury that if Kevin hadn't participated, he would have been hit immediately in the cage or very soon after (expecting a serious assault or possible fatal injury) and; Mark Keys' letter.

Lastly, Jack argued that Kevin didn't even have a shank. There was an absence of fingerprint evidence, and nothing on the video showed Kevin either had or disposed of one. This went directly to the criminality of the act, Jack said.

The judge asked for clarification. "So he concedes an assault, but he doesn't concede an assault with a deadly weapon?"

"Bingo," said Jack.

Prosecutor Galloway interjected, saying it didn't matter if Sanders had a weapon or not, that he was charged in Count 1 with *aiding and abetting* an assault with a deadly weapon.

But Jack countered that it was also a defense argument that because Kevin didn't have a shank, he was vulnerable to Keys turning on him in the cage.

—

The hearing moved to the issue of the expert witness, and the judge wanted to know how our expert would help convey that our client believed he was in imminent danger of being stabbed by Keys for not taking out Steven Tremblay.

"Because I believe it's necessary for the jury to hear more than inmate testimony for the defense to be credible."

"You're not answering my question," the judge said. "Why can't Mr. Sanders establish the immediacy of the threat if he says that it's his perception that he was about to be stabbed by Mr. Keys? Isn't that enough? Why do you need an expert on that?"

"No, sir, it's absolutely not enough."

"Well, why? I want you to tell me why. Why, when Mr. Sanders is going to take the witness stand and say the same thing? How does your expert augment that?"

"May I have a moment, Your Honor?"

Jack conferred with Scott at the defense table, then returned to face the court and eloquently stated, "I believe our expert, because of his history and long experience working inside federal prisons, is a credible source that bolsters the defense. It's not inmate testimony, which can be dismissed by the prosecution as a bunch of prisoners trying to shade the truth or lying to protect each other. This is a person from the other side of the gray wall who's saying, yes, what this inmate is saying, is true."

Galloway was up next and had a counterargument for everything, going on almost as long as Jack. He closed with a trite observation. "It's clear they want the expert to come in and say, well, there's a different prison culture, and you know, we have to abide by their rules. Judge, these are individuals who haven't been able to live by the rules of civilized society. That's why they're in prison."

The judge was visibly tired of the arguments. We could see on his face that he wasn't able to rubber-stamp the prosecutor's position. And when he said, "The sands have somewhat shifted here, in the Court's view," we had a glimmer of hope things would break our way.

CHAPTER 19
HOPES AND DREAMS

AUGUST 2013

F ive days later, Judge Anderson split the baby, giving both sides a simultaneous win and loss.

"As predicted: yes on defense, no on expert," Jack emailed us from his iPhone when he read the decision.

"The Defendant has not convinced us that he is entitled to expend nearly $25,000 of the judiciary's resources for the appointment and services of an expert witness," the court order stated. As he foreshadowed in the hearing, the judge said an expert was not required to present "the well-known fact that gangs and gang violence are prevalent inside federal prisons including USP-Lewisburg." The retired SIS officer "shall not be appointed as an expert," he ruled.

We were all disappointed, but Scott wouldn't back down. He decided to interpret the decision literally and take the cost off the table. He reasoned he could pay the expert out of his own pocket, and Jack said the semantics should work. Because of the trial's date shuffling and the uncertainty of his appointment, the expert was no longer available in October but would be in December. So, Scott prepared an affidavit for the expert to sign, noting his availability to testify in December and saying, "With respect to my fee, Mr. Powell has agreed to pay it personally." Scott filed it with the court along with a motion for a continuance.

At the same time, the guys thought it wouldn't hurt to see if Galloway would agree to a plea of two years. Scott fired off an email to the prosecutor, and Galloway's response was curt. "No chance on a two-year deal."

———

After the hearing, I only tuned in to the bare minimum from the guys because I was scrambling to polish my book proposal, *Under Duress: The Inside Story of One Man's Fight Against Prison Gang Warfare and Corruption*, for the writer's conference. When I left for New York, my quest had a new urgency, so I began to dream about the impossible. I knew Scott had no money for an expert—he told our Diners Club he'd been cleaned out in the divorce—so I wondered if I could help.

It was a ridiculous notion, dependent upon several fantastical events lining up like a Royal Flush: That I, with my 45-page true crime proposal in hand, could: 1) interest an agent on the spot, 2) said agent could interest a publisher asap, 3) said publisher would offer me a book contract for a manuscript not yet written, 4) said contract would come with enough of a book advance to cover the cost of the expert witness.

Stranger things have happened in the publishing world, and I figured I had nothing to lose. But this was now no longer a lark. I felt some additional, solely-instigated pressure, which I shared with no one.

The pursuit seemed doomed from the start. As I unloaded my things at the hotel so the valet could take my car, I realized, in my rush to get out the door, I'd left behind my garment bag of killer outfits. I called Jim, nearly in tears. He agreed to leave work early and make the two-hour drive, white-knuckling it through the Lincoln Tunnel he despised because he knew how important this was to me.

We dined extravagantly in Midtown Manhattan and sipped too many overly-priced Vesper martinis. Before I got too buzzed to concentrate, I practiced over and over my two-minute elevator pitch on him for tomorrow's agent session. He was full of encouragement, giving me dangerous confidence, even if I needed his arm to make it back to the hotel. Very early the next morning, he slipped out quietly for his long drive to work but left a note behind that said, "Go get 'em, honey!"

—

The agent session was held in the hotel ballroom, and I milled about with other hopeful writers, rushing to line up in front of our top picks based on the genre they represented or some other criteria. Only three of the dozen in attendance represented true crime, making my list easy. Thanks to Jim, I was dressed for success in my navy Anne Klein belted pantsuit and turquoise paisley pumps, though I was stunned to see so many aspiring authors wearing nothing nicer than athletic wear and tennis shoes. But what mattered most was the material and delivery. It was nerve-wracking for everyone to boil down our books to a few meaningful, catchy phrases and try to hook these gatekeepers face-to-face.

I sat across a table from the first agent I pitched, who was also a literary lawyer, and he spent more than the allotted three minutes with me. But then he concluded, "I'm sorry, I don't see this as a book. It may make for a great newspaper or magazine piece, though."

The second agent I pitched said the premise was intriguing, but the trial hadn't happened yet, so there was no ending. And if my protagonist wasn't acquitted, the agent thought she'd have a hard time selling it to editors. She did invite me to reach out after the trial, but it would have to be with a full manuscript. Selling this kind of nonfiction on spec "isn't really a thing anymore," she said. "Unless you're writing *How to Lose Weight and Become a Millionaire by Investing in Watermelon*, you need to write the whole thing."

The third agent I pitched, a woman from a big agency in Washington state, said something similar. "Because the case hasn't been adjudicated yet, no publisher will offer on it. I suggest you circle back after the trial."

Suddenly, I wanted to be in comfy pants back up in my room.

I sprawled out on the king-size duvet and eight pillows and opened the email on my Blackberry. I hadn't checked it since morning, and an email thread from Scott and Jack made my heart sink—the judge had denied our request for the expert even though Scott wanted to pay his fee. And the court order had come with a stern, almost ballistic rebuke.

"The meandering course that defense counsel have traveled is wearying, vexatious, and approaching a level that may be sanctionable. The author of the instant Motion is telegraphing that this case has become such a cause *celebre* to him that he has lost sight of appropriate advocacy.

"Indeed, his offer to pay the proffered expert's fees out of his own pocket is both bizarre and astonishing. We urge counsel to reign in his emotions and concentrate on formulating an appropriate trial strategy for the Defendant. While this Court admires and respects zealous advocacy, we are being presented here with something that has crossed over the line separating that and obduracy."

I needed my dictionary for part of that scolding.

"Okay. We've been dealt a dirty card. Welcome to our world, Carla," Jack said. From that point forward, our main objective, he explained, was to create a record for an appeal and employ tactics to show the jury how antagonistic the judge was toward our side.

"A hostile judge equates to sympathy for a defendant being railroaded, we hope. From now on, it's 50% record, 50% theater, 0% law, which is personally my favorite situation."

Then he tried to cheer up Scott by asking, "You know what they call the lawyer who graduated last in his class?"

The answer was, "Your Honor."

CHAPTER 20
LAWYERS, GUNS AND MONEY

FALL 2013

In September, Scott arranged to pick up paper transcripts of the two hearings from the courthouse in Scranton, and he shared an elevator with a staffer from the Lewisburg Prison Project. The staffer asked him if he knew that Steven Tremblay, our rec cage assault victim, had been deposed by the government in his civil suit. "I don't have a copy or know how it went," the staffer said. "I just know that it happened."

This was news to us. Almost a year ago, in Tremblay's docket, there had been an order granting a motion to take his deposition. But nothing filed since then indicated it had been done. If it had gone by the book, and the deposition *had* occurred and *had* contained anything favorable for Kevin's case, the government was duty-bound to let Scott and Jack know it. This was a pre-trial discovery *Brady* rule established by the 1963 U.S. Supreme Court case *Brady v. Maryland*.

But after the elevator tipoff, Scott had zero confidence that AUSA Galloway and the AUSA who deposed Tremblay in Victorville Prison, California, were playing fair. The only way to know if they were withholding evidence was to see the depo transcript. "I can't help but think the civil and criminal heads of the Hydra might have met for a few moments," Scott said.

Beginning that day, Scott wrote a series of emails and letters to Galloway, Galloway's boss, the California court reporter, and others, asking for the deposition, and he got the run-around from everyone. I kept a detailed log of his many requests, their dates, the non-responses, unhelpful replies, and the circular logic that flowed. As a final push to get the transcript, Scott was prepared to pay the court reporter $585 for it, but first, a "party to the suit" had to authorize it—meaning the government to whom he'd sent numerous requests—and it never happened. At that point, we were a week away from trial.

—

More headwinds followed. Three problems surfaced when Galloway and Scott exchanged their witness lists. Two of ours had disappeared into the ether, and one would have to be flown in Con Air style and might not make it in time.

Little Eagle had been transferred to USP Florence-High, and there was possibly just enough time to get him flown back. The judge granted a writ for his return and said he should testify by video if he couldn't make it by trial.

Two Lewisburg officers were now no longer available. One was Officer Walters, who testified at the first hearing. Scott wanted him back on the stand to talk about prison gangs in general and to see if he still couldn't remember the meeting in G Block's basement that resulted in Kevin and Mark Keys getting moved to Z Block. According to a DOJ legal assistant, Walters had retired to New England. He wasn't a crucial witness, though, and we could live without him.

The bigger blow was the loss of Captain MacDonald. We knew MacDonald was a bad actor and had likely set up the rec cage hit as revenge for Tremblay's snowball incident. But that snowball story as Kevin knew it, was hearsay. He hadn't witnessed it, so we couldn't use it. Instead, what we wanted MacDonald for—what we *needed* him for now because we were denied our expert witness—was to be an authority on the prison gang world. MacDonald's position as a gang intelligence supervisor would make him credible with the jury, even if he had to be treated as a hostile witness.

But it didn't matter. Poof, he was gone. The DOJ legal assistant said he'd retired also, somewhere out West. "Is that the best the Bureau of Prisons can do?" Scott emailed the assistant. "They must be receiving a pension. Don't you have a home address and telephone number? Can the BOP fax me any information that confirms they've retired? Frankly, the BOP and I have trust issues. Please advise." She did not respond.

The three of us did our own online missing person searches, and nothing turned up. We were out of time anyway. It was the Friday before the Monday trial, and all we could focus on was a weekend of prep at Jack's Camp Walleye. I didn't know what accommodations awaited at the hunting and fishing cabin, so I booked a nearby hotel off the interstate. I didn't think the guys would mind. It would free them up to burp and fart and smoke and do whatever in the wee hours without me around. As I packed my comfy clothes and smart pantsuits, I couldn't get over all our setbacks, and I mentally tried to prepare for a shitshow next week.

OCTOBER 2013, TWO DAYS BEFORE TRIAL

Saturday morning, I drove north to the Poconos. The route was a vivid exhibition of October leaves at their peak color, set against an overcast sky. Philly's NPR station WHYY took me half the way there, but when the signal disappeared, I returned to mulling over some of my own headwinds related to the case.

Over the summer, the girlfriend of an inmate in Victorville messaged me through my author website, asking about the book. Where could she buy it? "Everyone's talking about it," she said. I didn't overthink it and told her I'd put her on an email notification list. But then, a couple of weeks ago, the wife of a Big Sandy inmate found me through my Facebook author page. She said her husband was "an associate" and that I should be careful about what I write. But also, could she be notified when the book comes out?

That one was a little unnerving. But what did I expect? I'd put myself out there and announced to the world I was writing a book. The outside world didn't care, but some tangential players on the inside did, and now the gossipmongers could easily reach me. I'd kept these things to myself, not wanting to burden Scott and Jack in the run-up to trial. And I didn't want to worry Jim unnecessarily. But on that drive, for the first time, I wondered if writing a book about the federal prison underbelly was a good idea.

—

I pulled my SUV into a circular drive behind Jack's Yukon XL with tailgate stickers of the fish and duck variety. One bumper sticker read, "Hooked on Quack," and another said, "If It flies, It Dies." A third sticker said, "DARE to think for yourself!" Scott's Passat was parked off to the side of a sprawling log cabin with a covered a-frame porch, where both guys were rocking in chairs. Jack, with a pipe in his teeth, greeted me first and took a bag. "Welcome to Camp Walleye!" he said.

As he led me inside, he explained the cabin was built in 1900 by Betsy's grandfather. It had been modernized and added onto over the years, and Jack and his wife had recently finished a kitchen renovation. This was their getaway-from-work retreat (this weekend notwithstanding), and Betsy remained at home with their three Irish Setters.

A fire in the cavernous stone hearth warmed the main room, and the cedar walls were covered with the heads of stuffed deer, elk, other local animals, and ones acquired by Jack and Betsy on African safaris. The couple, posing with smiles and rifles, appeared in framed photos throughout the cabin. I had never seen so much taxidermy, which creeped me out more than a little bit. On the way to a bedroom, Jack pointed out the heads of a Cape buffalo and warthog hanging near a full-size Chinook salmon and steelhead trout.

When I saw the room he took me to, with its king-size four-poster bed and ensuite bathroom, I almost gasped. Other than the fully stuffed gray duiker (small antelope) atop my own fireplace, it was charming, and I happily canceled my hotel room. A tour of the rest of the cabin confirmed Jack had given me his and Betsy's bedroom.

We spread our laptops and files on a long rustic table beneath two tall chandeliers. As he unpacked his things, Scott told Jack he'd like to split his defense counsel fee with him now that he wouldn't be paying the expert.

"Scott, your generous offer is appreciated but declined. The court appointed you, not me, and you've done way more work on the case." He pushed his glasses back up on his nose and added, "Besides, I told the judge I was doing this pro bono—what would happen to the Legend of Jackson Bear if I went back on my word? No, my friend," he shook his head. "Unthinkable."

There was plenty to do for the next two days, but the work fell almost entirely to the guys. Jack was handling *voir dire*, or jury selection, so he had to prepare questions for them plus proposed jury instructions for the judge. Scott would give the opening statement, which he hadn't started writing yet. There were questions to draft for Galloway's witnesses and our own, who, at this point, were Kevin, Little Eagle, and a few correctional officers. They would have liked to subpoena Kevin's cellmate, Mark Keys, to corroborate that he would have turned his shank on Kevin if Kevin hadn't helped fight. But Keys hadn't been sentenced yet in his plea deal, and his attorney would have advised invoking his Fifth Amendment right against self-incrimination and to not answer questions.

Scott had received Steven Tremblay's medical and disciplinary records in discovery, and the lawyers needed to process those, plus wade through the horde of pre-trial briefs to re-familiarize themselves with Galloway's arguments. I was there as tech and moral support, but mostly, I observed.

Until yesterday, their strategy had been to use Captain MacDonald to explain to the jury how prison gangs operated. "What's the plan now, guys?" I said.

"Our boy's going to have to do it," Jack said. Scott threw his pen on the table, and I groaned. "The truth of the matter is, he's white, and as racist as that sounds ..." Jack turned his head in my direction.

"Why are you looking at me?" I said.

"... that'll help him with the jury," he continued. "But those facial tattoos aren't doing him any favors." I volunteered to bring some makeup, which they thought was hysterical and quickly panned the idea.

I changed the subject and asked how we could prevent Kevin from having to name gang leaders on the stand, and Scott said that was up to Galloway again. "That's fucking bullshit," I said. "All of this," I waived my arms dramatically over the table, "It's all fucking bullshit," and their eyes widened. "Our case has been eviscerated! No complete videotape. No expert. No *free* expert. Disappeared Lewisburg officers on our witness list. And the COs who do take the stand *lie*! Little Eagle might not even make it here …"

"Little Eagle will make it to DCP," Scott said calmly.

"And a deposition no one will give you—there's a reason for that," I continued. "I don't know how you guys do it. I don't know how you can take on case after case in federal court when it's so lopsided."

Jack chuckled. "Isn't she adorable?" he asked Scott. "She must have been raised by doting parents who told her life was fair." When he saw I wasn't amused, he touched my arm. "Carla, we do this for the joy of the battle precisely because it is unfair. And we pick the fights. That's the fun part."

"And you're forgetting," Scott said, "we did score a victory by getting to use the justification defense."

I wanted to roll my eyes but nodded with a half-smile. I took my laptop to an overstuffed chair near the fireplace, and Jack told me to help myself to anything at the wet bar. It was after 4 p.m., so I opened a bottle of Pinot Noir I'd brought. The guys had already been into Jack's pilsner selections. Until I was needed, I opened my *Under Duress* manuscript and returned to a chapter I was outlining.

Hours later, as my stomach started to growl, the most mouth-watering smells began drifting in from the kitchen. Jack was pan-frying thawed rainbow trout he'd caught in the stream running through his property. Scott and I joined him, and he ordered us around like sous chefs, telling us what to do with the gnocchi and where to find the salad fixings.

Not a morsel remained. Our bellies were full, and we'd finished a second bottle of wine. After we did the dishes, Jack wanted to watch the video again. "Ah, yes, dinner and a show," I said, reaching for my laptop. We replayed it twice, and Jack asked me to go frame by frame over the part where Kevin made a motion inside his rear shorts. "It's possible he lied to you," Jack looked at Scott.

"Jackson, there's no way he carried a knife in his ass. Think about it."

"Do we have to?" I shook my head and laughed. The guys piled on, and we guffawed over to the fireside chairs. Jack added more wood, and Scott found our host's brandy. We were done working for the day.

Maybe it was the wine talking, but I decided to tell them about the prison wife and girlfriend who asked about the book. "I don't think the Aryan Brotherhood approves, not to mention this could hurt Kevin's status with them even more," I said.

"Since your book will probably not portray these people as latter-day saints, their feelings *will* be hurt, and they'll probably take umbrage," Jack said. "They're in jail, so you can be sure they've taken umbrage before." This was not making me feel better.

"Carla, the book's important," Scott said and likened it to an exposé on drug cartels or human trafficking, which I thought was a stretch. "And besides, T-Rex would never sanction a hit on a woman. The AB fucking revere women and children. You're fine … but you should probably get a gun." I looked at him with my mouth open, and Jack immediately concurred.

"Get yourself a concealed carry permit," he said. "Even liberals are allowed to apply for one … ask Santa for a Glock 27 for Christmas. There are lovely shoulder bags on the market with concealed holsters—you should get one of those, too."

"Lucy has one of those cross-body purses with a side zipper that holds her Smith and Wesson. The SW .40 is perfect for girls," Scott said.

"You know what they say," cracked Jack, "a liberal's a conservative who's never been robbed!" They thought that was hilarious and poured themselves another round.

I couldn't believe what I was hearing. I had fired a Glock once as a reporter for a story about a police department's new firearms, but I never considered having a gun in my house. I blinked back tears at the thought, but mostly because they so casually acknowledged I'd dipped my toe into a dangerous current.

"Pass," I said, standing abruptly. I told them I was going to bed and took my brandy with me.

CHAPTER 21
FLY, EAGLES, FLY

OCTOBER 2013, THE DAY BEFORE TRIAL

I was the first one up Sunday morning and made a pot of extra strong coffee. I bundled up in a wool blanket and took a mug to the porch. A light rain fell, and I rocked back and forth to the pitter-patter of drops hitting the roof and wet leaves on the ground. Jack found me and complimented the coffee. Then he said neither he nor Scott meant to be so flippant about my concerns last night. I waved my hand away, pretending not to care, but he knew better.

"For what it's worth, the AB and their minions don't understand your world and are afraid of it, for all their bluster and swagger. They're unlikely to come looking for you. Contact is unlikely if you don't leave your world and enter theirs."

I stared straight ahead and kept rocking while he continued. "*Unlikely*, sadly, does not mean *impossible*. It's up to you if you want to be armed for self-defense."

Oh my God, again, with the gun. "I'm not just going to go out and buy a gun, Jack."

"And I would never suggest you do that—certainly not without the proper training and many hours spent at target practice." Then he droned on about a new Ruger

LCR revolver, a .357 Magnum, that might just be right for me. "Revolvers are simple and don't jam. This one has a Crimson Trace laser sight. The bullets go where the red dot sits ... the response time is .02 seconds from when the trigger is pressed."

I wasn't really listening until he got to the topic of children and how that hadn't been in the cards for him and Betsy. "My daughter would've grown up with firearms and would've likely been a competitive shooter. She would have also had martial arts training from early on, and I would have taught her fencing." He reminded me he'd lettered in varsity fencing at Yale and said that fencing, tai chi, or karate "teach discipline, respect, poise, self-control, situational awareness, and confidence."

He added, "I'm sure she would have taken after Betsy, who shoots anything with a barrel and trigger."

We heard mugs clanging in the kitchen, and I said, "Speaking of situational awareness, I think Scott's up. Shall we?" I rose and smiled.

"Indeed," he smiled back. "But we're going to need more coffee."

We ate scrambled eggs, downed two pots of coffee, worked on our computers, snacked, and worked some more, and by mid-afternoon, Scott was practicing his opening statement on us. Then we gave Jack input on his *voir dire* questions.

Things seemed well in hand. I wanted to check into my Scranton hotel before dark, so I packed up my things and hugged the guys goodbye. We made plans to meet at the courthouse at 8:30 in the morning.

I was five miles from my destination when Scott's call came in through my SUV speakers. "I just got a call from DCP. There's a problem. Can you meet me there?"

Goddammit, what now? I was so looking forward to a shower and room service. "Okay," I said, "what time?"

I beat Scott to the Douglas County Prison and changed from yoga pants to jeans in the car. But I was going in without makeup and my hair in a messy bun. Whatever.

I assumed we were there to talk to Kevin, but Scott said the reason was Little Eagle. He arrived yesterday on an expedited Con Air flight from USP Florence and was now refusing to testify.

"What?" I said incredulously. He raised his eyebrows and sighed. "I know." We were escorted to a visitation room where Little Eagle was waiting at a table in an orange jumpsuit, his long hair in a braid. He and Scott greeted each other cordially, and he called me "ma'am."

"So what's going on, Westin?"

"Yeah, well, Mr. Powell, I'm sorry to disappoint you, but I can't do it. I can't freaking do it this time … sorry, ma'am," he apologized for almost swearing.

Scott pressed for more information, but we both knew who was also housed at the Florence complex at the ADX supermax and probably played a role in this. "Listen, I like T-Rex. I got nothing against him. So I can't go up there and say those things."

Nothing Scott said changed his mind, and my being there didn't matter. Then he asked, "Are you the lady who's writing a book about this?"

Oh my God. I fake-smiled at them both and shrugged. "Listen, can you do me a favor, ma'am? Can you call my mother?"

Little Eagle wrote down his mother's phone number and asked me to tell her where he'd been transferred, how she could write him, and to say that he loved her and his sister. He wasn't sure any letters he'd written her from Florence were getting out because he'd had none in return, and his mother and sister were faithful writers. I said that I would.

Then he asked if Scott or I would write a letter and send it to him at Florence, acknowledging that he refused to testify. We said that we would. And that concluded our business at DCP. We couldn't see Kevin because it was past visiting hours, and the warden had made an exception for this. It was late anyway. I just wanted to get to my hotel, crawl under a luxury down duvet, and pretend we had a winning case.

CHAPTER 22
TRIAL DAY 1

OCTOBER 2013, MONDAY

Jury selection started promptly at 9 a.m. Jack employed his basic rules about picking a jury: "No cops, no security guards, no firefighters, definitely no one who works in the prison industry, and no one who's related to any of the above." His first juror for a peremptory strike was a retired police officer. Galloway's first strike was against an affirmative action coordinator at a local Penn State campus. Jack struck a food service worker at a regional jail. Galloway struck two blacks and a juror who indicated he lived with a male partner. Back and forth it went for two and a half hours, with both lawyers questioning the jury pool and striking or approving ones they could get away with; they didn't have to show cause for the jurors they didn't like. The result was a panel of 12 and two alternates that neither side was pleased with. The mix included a few retired folks and office workers, a shop foreman, a homemaker, a biologist, an accountant, a fry cook, and a customer service rep. All were white. Some had driven 50 miles or more to fulfill their summons and would need accommodations for the week. All 12 would have to agree on the verdict.

After a break, the jury was sworn in. Judge Anderson then gave them preliminary instructions about listening to testimony, considering different types of evidence, and not talking about the case with each other or anyone outside the courthouse until it was over—no email, social media, or texting about it either. No Googling the case when they went home. They could take notes to help them deliberate, which would be destroyed afterward. He explained the government had to prove our defendant's guilt beyond a reasonable doubt. He then explained the unusual situation of our affirmative defense to two of the charges, saying we were claiming Mr. Sanders was "legally justified" and that the burden of proof was lower for this—by a preponderance of the evidence. The judge said he would elaborate on those two standards before they deliberated.

—

We broke for lunch, and Galloway began his short opening statement at 1:45 p.m. He presented an overview of his case, mentioning the rec cage video and recovered shanks. He also preemptively attacked our justification defense, saying he expected our attorneys to present evidence of prison gangs and different rules in prison. "But we submit to you there is one set of laws in this country that everybody lives by. And it has to be that way … Just because you're a gang member doesn't mean you get to make up your own rules."

Scott's opening followed. He said, "We're not here to waste your time, but there's a lot more to this case than the government wants you to believe." He gave some background on Lewisburg's SMU and an overview of our case. He said Mr. Sanders would take the stand to say he participated in the fight but didn't have a weapon and that "my client was put in a cage against his will." He told the jurors the video would be disturbing to watch but also that it was selectively edited because Mr. Sanders "was trying to tell the corrections officer don't put that third inmate in our cage."

Scott touched on the subjects of prison gangs, separate laws behind bars, and what would have happened if his client hadn't participated in the fight. "If he didn't help his cellmate attack this poor victim, then he was going to get knifed himself."

—

Galloway's first witness was Lt. Lippit. He walked her through a long history of the SMU and what the SIS intelligence department did regarding investigating gang-related incidents and inmate separations. He played the video for the jury and had her point out the participants. Two jurors winced, and several leaned forward for a better view.

Lt. Lippit narrated the end of the video, where CO Shemp picked up a plexiglass shank off the rec cage floor. Then, she testified that she picked up an identical shank in the grassy area outside the cage.

On cross-exam, Scott tried to get her to admit that the beginning video portion with his client trying to wave off a CO hadn't been properly preserved. But she stuck to her story that they burned a CD of the video beginning just moments before the fight took place like they typically do. He had her list the five biggest race-based gangs operating at Lewisburg and say that the Aryan Brotherhood was the most prominent white supremacist gang there. They then got into the details of prison gangs and how they operated, and he questioned her on what a kite was. He also had her acknowledge there was no designated "hole" or safe space an inmate could request to go to at the time.

His questioning then returned to the shank that she testified to finding. "I believe your report said you found a second shank out in the grass and you took a photo of it, correct?"

"Yes."

"Where is the photograph?"

"I don't know. I cannot find it anywhere."

"So, how do we know where it was found?"

She didn't have a specific explanation, and he got her to admit that the prison yard was often littered with similar-looking shanks made of the same material—especially after a rec cage assault because all the inmates disposed of their weapons knowing they would be strip-searched after.

Scott then asked for the video to be played again and for Lt. Lippit to point out where his client came into the possession of a shank. "And I also want you to tell me where ..."

But the judge interrupted. "Wait. Stop. Hold it. Stop the tape. Stop the tape right now. Now, Mr. Powell, you ask one question at a time, and then she answers the question, and then you ask another question, please. Because you can't keep asking questions without an answer. I'm not going to keep replaying the tape.

"So you can play the tape, if you want to, or you can have the tape stopped. But ask a question and allow her to answer. Now, ask a question."

This was the first time the judge admonished Scott in front of the jury. Before this, he'd called a couple of sidebars where he asked for clarification on some of Scott's objections, which he overruled, but nothing was within earshot of the jury until now.

"Okay. Can you tell me where in the video Kevin Sanders obtains his shank?"

"Right there, you can see him reaching to his back, and that's where we believe he pulled out his weapon. I've been told by numerous inmates that he ..."

"Okay. I object to hearsay," Scott said.

"He's not letting her answer the question, Your Honor," Galloway complained.

"You opened the door to this," said the judge.

"But, Your Honor, it's hearsay."

"The answer stands," the judge said. "Move on. Ask a question."

"Okay," Scott resumed, "keep playing the video. Can you see the knife in his hand?"

Lippit answered, "Number one, it's in the far corner. Number two, the knife is Plexiglass. You can pretty much see through it, especially at this angle."

"Okay. Are you done answering that question?" She nodded that she was.

"Show me where Kevin Sanders gets rid of the knife," Scott asked, but the lieutenant was, in fact, not done answering the previous question and extrapolated.

"You can also see Kevin Sanders' arm movements," she said. "That's not hitting. That's a stabbing motion, and I have seen lots of stabbing incidents. That's how you stab. That's not how you punch."

"My question is, where did he get rid of the knife?"

"I did not see on the video where he got rid of the knife. I can't see him physically move his hand. It's down in the far corner of the video."

"Will you agree with me that you cannot physically see him take a knife from his butt; you're making an assumption that he did?"

"I'm making a very educated guess based on inmates saying that's the best place to hide a weapon. That's what you do. Plus, the motion of his arm is a stabbing motion on the victim, not a hitting motion."

"Looks like he's punching and kneeing him to me."

"He also kneed him, yes."

Scott questioned her about where on the video she could see Mark Keys pulling out a weapon, and she conceded she could not but that maybe "he may have gotten it out before we started the video on this." Scott circled back to the missing part of the video, asking why officials wouldn't have wanted to see where Keys obtained his weapon. "Does the SIS care whether or not Mr. Sanders was trying to say don't put him in here?"

But she stood her ground through more probing, and the judge had had enough. "All right. I've given you some latitude, Mr. Powell. Let's wrap it up. Let's conclude your examination, please."

—

After a 20-minute recess, Galloway presented his next witness, Lewisburg SIS tech Ehrlich, who copied the video onto CD and testified at the hearing. He told the jury he copied the CD like he'd done dozens of times before, always beginning the video just before the incident occurred.

Jack questioned him on cross, but nothing helpful came of it.

Galloway called a second SIS tech to the stand, who took photos of all three inmates from the rec cage incident. They spent a long time going over photographs of Steven Tremblay's injuries and the rec cage with blood spots in the corner where he was assaulted. Jack, on cross-exam, didn't elicit any helpful testimony from him either.

We were approaching the end of the day, and the last witness the prosecutor called was Officer Shemp, the CO in charge of recreation on the day of the assault.

Shemp's career went back 22 years at Lewisburg, he told Galloway, who then asked, "Okay, now is it fair to say you did not put Mr. Sanders in the rec cage on that day?"

"It is."

"Did you put Steven Tremblay in the rec cage?"

"No."

"Did you put Mark Keys in the rec cage?"

"No, sir."

"Would that have been done by somebody else?"

"Yes," was Shemp's answer, but Galloway was incurious about who that might have been.

After the assistance call came in, Galloway said, "Did you, in fact, recover a shank inside the rec pen?"

"I did, sir," and Galloway cued the video to the place at the end, showing Shemp bending down and picking something up off the cage floor.

Galloway asked him about the order that inmates are placed into a rec pen, and Shemp stated COs typically fill up one cage before moving on to the next. "And you are not involved in deciding who goes in what rec pen, correct?"

"No, sir."

"No further questions."

—

Jack began his cross-exam by asking Shemp about his duties as recreation officer, and Shemp said that meant that he only supervised the inmates in the rec pens, not giving orders to the other COs. A lieutenant or higher-ranked official would do that, but no one of a higher rank was present when the rec cage incident occurred. And no, Shemp repeated, he did not escort any of the three inmates into the rec cage that day, nor did he recall if he had radioed for assistance or if someone else had.

Jack turned to the topic of separation orders and asked, "If a prisoner says to you put me in with somebody or don't put me in with somebody, does that make any difference?"

"On occasion, if an inmate is put into a new rec group and hasn't rec'ed with those people before, they will ask the inmate if that's okay, if he feels comfortable there. Now, whether or not that occurred, I have no idea. What I can tell you is, if an inmate would say to me, I can't go in there,

I would take that inmate back inside and try to find them another rec group. I've seen a lot of brutality in my career, and I hope to God I never see it again."

As the jury lapped up his every word, I wanted to take out the world's tiniest invisible violin and play it over my shoulder. I'm sure I couldn't hide the disgust on my face, but the jurors weren't looking at me. Kevin just shook his head and stared down at his notepad.

—

Court adjourned just before five p.m., and the jurors were instructed to return by 9 o'clock the next morning. Jack, Scott, and I headed to my hotel bar, where they thought the chance of running into anyone from the prosecution side or jurors who had to spend the night was slim. We all ordered martinis.

"They believed every fucking thing Shemp said," I reported. "Did you see their faces?"

"Juries are always predisposed to believe cops," Jack said. "That's just the way it is."

I sighed and took a big gulp of my cocktail. "Little Eagle could have refuted Shemp's testimony," I complained. "He *saw* Kevin wave off Shemp ..."

I paused because Scott and Jack shared a devious smile. "What?"

"Well, Westin Chase may refuse to testify, but that doesn't mean his story can't be told," Scott said. "His hearing testimony can be read to the jury."

"No kidding?" I said.

We clinked our glasses and toasted to a better day in court tomorrow. After a quick and greasy dinner of fried appetizers, we adjourned, and I headed for the elevators, a little less glum. Maybe things weren't as dire as I thought.

CHAPTER 23
TRIAL DAY 2

OCTOBER 2013, TUESDAY

At 9:05 a.m. the next day, Judge Anderson welcomed back the jurors, and Prosecutor Neil Galloway continued with the government's case. He presented three medical witnesses who treated Steven Tremblay after the assault. The first was a Lewisburg paramedic who gave Tremblay an IV and oxygen and then read his X-ray. The X-ray indicated he had a punctured lung, so he called an ambulance to take him to the local hospital.

The second witness was the doctor who treated Tremblay in the hospital. She testified to his treatment, which included the insertion of a chest tube and antibiotics over his four-day stay. The third witness was a physician assistant who assessed Kevin and Mark Keys after the assault and said neither had injuries.

Jack performed the expected cross-exam on all three, but it was perfunctory in each case.

CO Johnson returned to the stand as a prosecution witness. As he testified at the hearing, he said he was the officer who brought Tremblay out to the rec cage—after taking him to a medical appointment—but was not the one who placed him inside. Kevin had written "LIAR" about him on his legal pad then. Johnson repeated the same story for the jury. He said Tremblay never indicated he couldn't be placed in the rec cage, nor did any inmate indicate not to put him in the cage.

Jack began his cross-exam by asking CO Johnson how he knew which cage to take him to, and the officer responded that he got his assigned cage number from the official working Z Block. Johnson said he didn't have the keys to let Tremblay into the sallyport but conceded it could have been Officer Shemp, the rec supervisor for the day.

"I remember him being there. I don't remember if he actually put him inside the cage or not."

—

Galloway also brought back Officer Crone as a witness. He was the CO who set up the rec roster the morning of the assault, and Kevin had also written "LIAR" on his notepad about him during the hearing. He repeated his story for the jury.

"I said to Inmate Sanders, I'm going to set you up in a rec cage with Inmate Tremblay, are you good with that? Inmate Sanders said yeah, I'm good with anybody. I then went across to Inmate Tremblay and asked him the same question. Hey, are you okay to rec with Sanders and Keys? He nodded in the affirmative. So I went back to the office. I put them in the rec group together."

Crone also told the same story about how, after the assault, he spoke to Inmate Sanders in his cell, proclaiming, "Hey, all you got to do is let me know, and I won't put you in the same cage if there's going to be a problem."

"What did he say?"

"He ... it was something to the effect of we have to police our own. I said what do you mean by that. He said, 'I bet he doesn't kick that door tonight.' Apparently, the previous night, Inmate Tremblay had kicked the cell door. And to police their own, they had to take that corrective action to keep peace among the other different races of inmates that we have."

"No further questions."

After some background questions on the SMU's history, Jack's cross ventured into the victim Tremblay and his disciplinary issues.

"Okay. Isn't it true," asked Jack, "that Mr. Tremblay was a discipline problem for you?"

"No, sir. I mean, I can't think of anything that inmate Tremblay ever did to cause me problems."

"Did he ever flood his cell?"

"He did flood a little on his—he'd sit in the shower and just let the water run, and it would come out on the floor. I don't recall it ever coming out on my range."

"Okay. Would it have dripped down into the cell below?"

"I don't know. I never really went to the basement."

"Okay. To your memory, did Mr. Tremblay ever smear fecal material on the walls of his cell or anything like that?"

"After this incident, when I went in to pack up his property, I did observe fecal material on the walls of the cell. Yes, sir. It was on the door side."

"Okay. And when you made this observation, how many days after this particular incident was it?"

"This was the day of the incident."

Jack concluded his cross, and Galloway called his last witness, FBI Special Agent Slater. Slater had taken over the case from Agent Brenner, and Slater testified about the chain of custody of the two shanks that prison officials said came from the scene. Scott handled the cross-exam on Agent Slater but only confirmed the agent had not investigated the incident on his own but relied upon Agent Brenner's overview of the case and notes. Galloway admitted the FBI 302 report into evidence, joining his other exhibits of the assault video, CO memorandums, the incident report, the three inmate health records, and photocopies of two shanks. Then, the prosecutor rested his case.

—

It was our turn to begin Kevin's defense. But before we could start, the judge called a brief recess, and the jury was led out. Once they were gone, the judge said, "The marshal has advised the Court that we have Mr. Chase available. And for the record, I'll say the marshals indicated that Mr. Chase may refuse to testify. I think counsel may be aware of that."

A U.S. marshal escorted Little Eagle into the courtroom. He was uncuffed in his orange jumpsuit and wore a long braid down his back. He refused to step any closer to the bench than the entry door.

The judge asked the courtroom deputy to swear him in, but Little Eagle said, "No. I'm a Navajo sovereign. I don't believe in your laws. I don't want to testify. I don't have anything to say."

"I understand, Mr. Chase. I'll ask you about that," the judge said.

"I have nothing to say."

"If you'll just indulge us for one moment, sir ..."

Scott stood and told the judge that last night he met with Mr. Chase, who "explained to me, in no uncertain terms, that he would refuse to testify."

"He is correct," Little Eagle confirmed.

"If I order you to testify, and I am ordering you to testify, will you testify in this proceeding?"

"No, I will not."

"All right," the judge sighed. "Mr. Galloway, do you have anything for the government?"

"I do, Your Honor. And to make the record clear, Mr. Chase had previously testified ..."

"That's exactly why I don't want this! I don't want ..."

"Mr. Chase, hang on a second," the judge said.

"I don't want to have nothing to do with this ..."

"Hold it, Mr. Chase."

"... absolutely whatsoever, Your Honor."

Galloway said, "I want to make it clear on the record that on page 42 of the transcript, he was asked, 'Did you watch the fight?' And his response was ..."

"Your Honor, this is exactly why I don't want anything like this on the record. I don't want to have nothing like this."

The judge exhaled. "We'll do this outside the presence of Mr. Chase."

"That's fine," agreed Galloway.

"I don't want any more of this guy's mumbo-jumbo," he said, looking at Galloway. "I don't want anything to do with this—no longer, at all, whatsoever, do I have anything to say."

"Mr. Chase is excused then. You make take him back."

"Thank you, sir," Little Eagle gave a little bow. "Thank you, Mr. Persecutor," he said to Galloway as he was led away. The spectacle drew some laughter.

The judge gathered his thoughts and said, "All right. I'll indicate to the jury that Mr. Chase is unavailable, without going into any details, and that, as a result, we will read in portions of his testimony from the prior proceeding.

"Somebody can serve as Mr. Chase on the stand. I would assume one of the defense counsel can do that—maybe Mr. Bear can take on that role."

This was a practical assumption, that Jack or Scott would portray Westin Chase on the witness stand and read his testimony for the jurors. But Scott and Jack had a different idea, one that I had protested mightily, but Scott was insistent.

"This is Carla Conti, Your Honor," Jack told the court. "She is serving as our paralegal. She's a researcher and a writer."

"Very well," the judge said. I took a seat in the witness box, and the judge said to me, "I'm going to advise you, ma'am, when you read it, don't read it with any inflection. Just simply read it if you would, please. Just as it appears."

Without inflection! I panicked a little because I didn't know if I could comply. I've never spoken without inflection in my life. How could I summon a monotone voice under this *pressure*? And how would that do the testimony justice?

The jury filed back into the courtroom. Judge Anderson explained the situation and instructed them to consider this read-in testimony like any other. Jack handed me pages of the hearing transcript marked for my role-play. He had his own copy and would be acting out the part of Scott. It was a bit of a head-scratcher.

"You may proceed," said the judge.

"Did you see what happened with Kevin Sanders and Inmate Tremblay?" Jack asked me.

"Yes," I read from the page.

"Tell His Honor what you saw."

"That morning, I went to rec, and I was in the west side of the rec cages, and I saw a new inmate coming. It was Mr. Sanders, and I said where are you coming from? And he said I'm coming from G Block. I said any new Native American inmates come too? But he went into the sallyport, and I waited for him to go around to where I could talk to him. Then I started to talk to the second guy."

"Would that be Mark Keys?"

"Yes."

"So Mr. Sanders said, no, that no new natives came. Our conversation kind of got cut off because they started coming. Some officer started bringing this guy. So it started getting quiet. Sort of like, we know this guy is trouble, he's a big troublemaker, a problem maker."

"Did you know who that guy was?"

"Yeah, everybody did. The guy's name is Tremblay. Kind of a psychotic type of dude. He does a lot of things:

spit at people, throw feces, kick staff or kick anybody, randomly attack anybody, you know."

"Okay."

"So it kind of got quiet when they were coming with Mr. Tremblay because people didn't know where they were going to put him. And at that time, Mr. Sanders, the guy I met that morning, he was trying to say like, don't put the guy in here, you know, trying to give the officer a stern eye contact and body language."

"Let me stop you. Are you making a motion with your hand that is kind of like somebody cutting their head off?" Jack said to me.

I decided to go for *Best Supporting Actress* and waived one flat hand back and forth under my chin as I gripped the transcript pages and read, "Um-hum. No, no, no, like no, no, no, don't put him in here."

"Describing it for the record, your hand is flat, and you're waving it under your chin?"

I repeated my waving performance while reading. "Like no, no. This guy, don't—hey, don't put him in here."

"All right. Did you see what happened after my client did that?"

"Rec Officer Shemp was determined to put Mr. Tremblay in the sallyport. Mr. Sanders was trying to motion to him— no, don't, no—then he went over and started talking to Mr. Shemp. But at that time, Mr. Shemp put him in the sallyport anyway. So …"

"What happened? Did you hear anything?"

"At that time, I walked away a little bit, but I could still see, you know, that Mr. Sanders was going to have a conversation. I could hear him saying, hey, no, this guy shouldn't be in here."

"What about the rest of the inmates around you? Did you hear anything from them?"

"Well, there's a lot of noise out there at rec. But when the rec officer, Shemp, put Mr. Tremblay in there, he stood there for a minute and put his hand on his thing like he was expecting something to happen. I think he was expecting something to happen from the beginning."

"You are putting your hand on your hip?"

"Okay. He has like a radio. On that radio, there is a little button that they push. So he was standing there for, I would say, a minute. So I knew that, already, something was happening. So I just stood there along the fence line. I walked around a little bit, and I came back."

"What happened then?"

"I heard people yelling—excuse my language—but get that punk. You know, do it. Get him now. Everybody yelling, different people, from Z block."

"Did you watch the fight?"

"Well, at first, they said stay over there, to Mr. Tremblay. They didn't want no problems with this guy. But their people were yelling, and they had to do what they had to do, or else maybe they would be in jeopardy. And that Tremblay guy, they tried to say something to him, like, hey, keep it cool. But he didn't want to greet them. He started walking around, acting aggressive and crazy. So they said, stay over there, stay over there.

"Then Mr. Sanders and Mr. Keys went over to the other side of the cage by the camera. And then more yelling was getting louder and louder. So then it just—all of the fighting started. It went over into the south part of the cage and stayed in that corner."

"All right," the judge said. "Mr. Galloway?"

The prosecutor read from his transcript. "From what you can see, were both inside stabbing Tremblay?"

"I never saw a weapon," I read.

"You never saw a weapon?"

"I never saw a weapon."

"Did you have a weapon on you that day?"

"No, I did not."

"You never saw a weapon in that cage?"

"I never saw a weapon at all. Absolutely not."

"Thank you," Galloway said to me.

"All right. You may step down," the judge told me.

—

Mercifully, court adjourned for an extended lunch break. Kevin was taken by a marshal for another sack lunch, and we gathered our things.

"Wow, that was not fun, gentlemen," I whispered. "Possibly the longest seven minutes of my life." The guys just grinned all the way out of the wood-paneled courtroom like we'd scored some sort of victory. In the hallway, a petite blond in a navy business skirt and jacket was waiting for Scott. I had seen her from the witness stand observing from one of the back benches.

Scott kissed her cheek and introduced Jack and me to Lucy Sandburg. We shook hands, and she said she'd heard a lot about us. Jack, predictably, told her not to believe a word.

"Lovely to meet you, Carla," she smiled. "That was some performance. Well done."

"And the Oscar goes to …" Jack said, making us laugh all the way to the elevator.

Lucy joined us for lunch at my hotel—Jack ordered chicken wings all around—and was upbeat about the case's prospects. But at the same time, she said, it was always hard to get a jury to *want* to know what goes on behind prison walls. I liked her and could see why Scott did, too. He had long since overshared with me some of their relationship details, and I wasn't quite convinced they were through. The way they slid in next to each other in the dining booth, how she picked lint off his collar, and the looks they shared—it was a little suspect.

Lucy was due in Williamsport and wished us luck with Kevin's testimony, coming up next. She said she would try and make it back tomorrow for closing arguments.

CHAPTER 24
TRIAL DAY 2 CONTINUED

OCTOBER 2013, TUESDAY

Court resumed shortly before 2:00 p.m., and Scott presented his star witness. Kevin was sworn in and took the stand, and Scott began by asking him about his conversation with Officer Crone right before recreation that day.

"You heard CO Crone tell the jury that he specifically asked you if you could rec with Steven Tremblay. Do you recall that testimony?"

"I do."

"Was that testimony true?"

"No, it's not."

"What happened?"

"He came up to the cell and asked me if we could rec with *whites*. I told him, yes, we can. There was no indication of Steven Tremblay whatsoever."

"Is there any particular reason why you would not agree to rec with the victim, Steven Tremblay, in this case?"

"Because he was flooding his cell, creating issues and problems. And he was a known target for the gang, which was housed in the lower level of Z block."

Scott then went backward in time to try and paint for the jury the ugly picture of prison gangs, hit orders, and running afoul of gang rules, with a dose of CO incompetence thrown in for good measure.

He had Kevin testify about his trouble with the Montañistas in Allenwood. Kevin recounted how he refused an order from the gang leader Lorenzo Cruz to assault his best friend, which resulted in Cruz putting out a hit order on Kevin, necessitating his transfer to Lewisburg. Then, soon after he arrived in Lewisburg, he found himself in a rec cage with Cruz and had to fight for his life, he said.

Scott had to fight at the sidebar to present this backdrop to Kevin's defense. He told the judge the jury needed to know that, from Kevin's perspective, Lewisburg officers could not, or would not, keep him safe in a rec cage.

After being admonished for getting too far into the weeds about Lewisburg's various prison gangs, Scott focused on the continuing threat from the rec cage fight with Montañista leader Cruz.

"Are you afraid of the Montañistas?"

"Yes, I am."

"Why?"

"Because they are dangerous and have been known to kill and maim."

"You said they are a very organized group. What do you mean by that?"

"They are very militant. You could kind of compare them to Arab-type suicide bombers. They are individuals who die for their gang. They work out. It's mandatory. They are not allowed to use drugs. They are not allowed to drink. They are very up to par with weapons, education, and knowing who their enemies are."

Kevin testified that his cage fight with Rey opened the door for him to associate with the Aryan Brotherhood, or AB, for protection.

Scott had the video cued up and paused as Kevin testified about what occurred before the part of the video that was captured: his conversation with Westin Chase; his trying to wave off Officer Johnson, who walked Tremblay to the rec cage; his telling Officer Shemp not to put Tremblay inside; Shemp standing by with his hand on his radio alarm.

"Now you heard Officer Shemp say he didn't put Tremblay in the cage. Do you agree with him on that?"

"No, I don't."

"On a scale of one to ten, how sure are you that it was Shemp?"

"I'm very positive. I could say a ten."

Scott resumed the video and paused it to where Kevin made a motion in the back of his shorts. "Okay. So, let's get this out in the open. Did you have a weapon in that rec cage?"

"No, I didn't."

"When you're reaching into your butt on the video, are you pulling out a knife?"

"No, I'm not. I'm securing information."

"What do you mean by that?"

"If they had preserved the video and shown more than what there is, they would have seen me reach into my shoe and take out what is called a kite." Kevin described the tiny rolled papers that contained valuable gang intelligence and how they got passed along to "higher-ups" through a "fishing line" underneath cell doors. Kevin explained that the AB tasked him with securing a kite, and his cellmate, Mark Keys, was authorized to carry one of the many plastic shanks prevalent inside the prison. There was no need for both of them to have weapons, and in fact, Kevin said his cellmate didn't want Kevin to have a weapon for fear he might use it on him. Inmates, he explained, concealed the plastic shanks inside a pocket in the front of their boxer shorts. The weapons were attached with a string for easy retrieval.

Scott returned to the topic of the kite and produced a facsimile of one for the jury. Kevin testified he prepared it for the trial to show jurors how small and detailed everything was. Scott asked permission to show it to the jury, and Galloway had no objections but asked the court, "Your Honor, could we at least ask maybe where this one came from, considering previous testimony?" prompting many jurors to laugh.

Knowing he walked right into that one, Scott asked Kevin, "Was that ever in your rectum?"

"No, it wasn't."

"Is it in relatively sanitary form?"

"Yes, it is." Kevin's testimony continued as some jurors examined the kite and others passed on touching it.

"Is securing a kite hard to do?"

"Not really, if you're prepared, and you've been doing this for a while and know what you're doing."

"I guess I have to ask you how you do it."

"Normally, if it's real high sensitive information, it's wrapped in plastic and sealed. You usually keep yourself greased up. You spit on the kite, and you insert it. It's real fast. It's just real easy."

Scott resumed playing the video and asked Kevin what he was hitting the victim with in the corner of the rec cage. "My hand," Kevin said. Scott let the video play to its conclusion.

"All right. Now, Kevin, why were you involved in this?"

"Because I was told, you're going to get in this, or it's on. You already know what the business is. I was directly ordered by Mark Keys to engage in combat and aid and assist him in this assault."

"And what would have happened if you didn't?"

"He would have took it as a direct threat and stabbed me instead of the victim."

"Why do you say that?"

"Because I know him. It's based on fact. He has a knife. I've seen him do this before. I know who he is. I live with this character. He's in a county jail now stabbing inmates and facing prosecution for it."

"Okay. Is it also against the rules to try and avoid a fight?"

"If I blatantly told Keys no, I'm hit. I'm targeted. I'm targeted anyway just for being up here talking about it."

"Just for testifying today, you are targeted?"

"Just for testifying today and letting it be known, I'm a marked man. I have to go into protective custody. I no longer can live on the yard. I'm done. There is no getting around it. Just for letting it all be known of how it unfolded, who ordered it, who did it."

"So just by telling this jury about kites, for example, marks you?"

"Yes, it does."

"One more question related to that. Why didn't you just raise your hand and say take me out of this cage?"

"Because there was no protective custody at Lewisburg."

Scott then tried to produce two letters written by Mark Keys: the first to his sister, where he stated, "I stabbed some lame 45 times," and the second to Kevin, where he said he would sign an affidavit stating he would have attacked Kevin if Kevin hadn't participated in the fight.

Galloway immediately objected, and Judge Anderson called a sidebar. "They look like straight hearsay to me." The judge said.

"Well, they're not being offered for the truth," Scott said, out of earshot of the jury.

"Oh, they certainly are," said the judge

"It's going to *state of mind*," Scott countered.

"It's being offered for the truth because it goes right to the heart of your defense. I'm not going to allow these in. Now, let's finish up here. I've given you a lot of latitude. You've had this guy on the stand for hours, for the entire afternoon. I want to allow you to put on a full and complete defense, but the fact of the matter is that you're asking repetitive questions. I'm not going to admonish you in front of the jury, but you've got to finish up with this guy. You cannot get these letters in. They are hearsay, and they are excluded already. All right. Let's go."

The judge turned off a white noise maker, and the lawyers returned to their tables.

"Okay Kevin, you are in Douglas County Prison right now and have been in for some months, correct?"

"Yes, I am."

"What are you doing in Douglas County Prison?"

"Painting."

"Painting?"

"Painting."

"Are you an artist?"

"Yes, I am."

"That's all I have, thanks."

"We'll take cross from Mr. Galloway," the judge said.

—

Galloway started by asking Kevin about his affiliation with Lewisburg's white supremacists. Kevin repeated that he fell under the AB umbrella for protection, but said he wasn't considered a full member because of the short time he knew them. Furthermore, he wasn't authorized to have any official tattoo markings, like the AB's shamrock or Nazi Low Riders NLR initials. This opened the door for Galloway to point out all of Kevin's visible tattoos, and he went over them one by one for the jury.

The prosecutor touched on CO Crone's testimony that he told Kevin he'd be rec'cing with Tremblay, "and that's completely incorrect, right?"

"That is incorrect."

"So he lied under oath here, according to you. Is that right?"

"Yes, he did. He asked me if I could rec with whites."

Galloway showed Kevin an internal BOP disciplinary report from his time at Allenwood. "Now it says there, 'While housed at USP Allenwood, Sanders participated in a multiple assailant stabbing of another inmate. This took place on July 1st, 2008. Sanders was observed by staff chasing another inmate in his housing unit. The inmate being chased was later found with multiple stab wounds. Sanders has been discovered in the possession of homemade sharpened knives on two occasions. On January 8th, 2008 he was found with a sharpened metal rod, while on February 27th, 2007 Sanders possessed two sharpened metal rods.'"

"Do you see that?"

"Yes, I do."

"Is that information all accurate?"

"It's correct."

Galloway turned to the rec cage fight with Montañista leader Lorenzo Cruz and pointed to a report that said he and his cellmate Mark Keys attacked Cruz first. "Cruz didn't start any fight with you at all, did he?"

"No. But I know who Cruz is. And I know what he's about. And I'm not going to take the chance of letting him pursue me or engage me in any altercation."

"Okay. Your counsel said in his opening that you're serving time, a ten-year offense. Is that right?"

"Yes, I am."

"And that was for felon in possession of a firearm. Is that correct?"

"Yes, it is."

"Okay. Well, to be a felon in possession of a firearm, you had to have committed another felony before that. Is that correct?"

"Yes, I did."

"How long have you been in prison?"

"Most of my adult life."

Galloway switched gears and asked some bullet-point questions covering parts of Kevin's long testimony. "You talked about bylaws of the gang. Are these rules that are set up for the gang to follow, but they aren't necessarily rules of civilized society?"

"Yes, they are."

"Okay. And you said Shemp was the one who put Tremblay in the sallyport?"

"Yes."

"Oh. So, his testimony was wrong and incorrect under oath?"

"Yes, it was."

The prosecutor went over photos of the victim and asked, "So, every one of those puncture wounds that was on Tremblay was put there by Keys?"

"Yes, they were," said Kevin. "Let's count the strikes on the video. What I find real funny, Galloway, is the most important photo in the entire line-up is missing, the one where they supposedly found my shank. Why isn't that photo there, but every other photo is? The one where it shows the placement outside the cage, that's the only photo that's missing."

"But we had testimony, didn't we, about where that shank was?"

"It's lost. The most important photo in the entire investigation is lost."

"The most important photo would have been you waving somebody off, wouldn't it?"

"That's in the video. We're talking about the photographs where they found the weapon outside the cage. The most important photograph in the entire case just disappears. Why?"

"Must have been Lieutenant Lippit, I guess, has a vendetta against you, huh? Along with Shemp, Crone …

"I don't know about a vendetta. But I do believe that they are trying to cover themselves for their wrongdoings."

"Okay. And your testimony is that it wasn't you taking a shank out of the back of your pants with your left hand, transferring it to your right hand. But it was actually you putting a kite there for security reasons. Is that right?"

"Yes. In the institution, there is no air conditioning. It's very sweaty. It's during the summer. Our bodies are sweaty. I'm not going to carry a knife in my ass walking up and down the stairs from the institution, all the way down into the rec cages, in case it might fall. We don't carry them like that. We secure a weapon a lot more easy in the front of boxers where I know it's not going to fall. If I was going to get a weapon, I would have gotten it out of the front of my boxers just like Mark Keys did. I reached into my shoe, pulled out a hot piece of information, and secured it."

"Wasn't it secure in your shoe? Wasn't it safer there?"

"No. Because as soon as they cuff you up, they are going to take you directly out of the cage into another cage, strip you down, and find the information."

"You said they did a full body search on you, didn't they?"

"Yeah, they did."

"Doesn't that involve having you spread your butt cheeks, so to speak?"

"If it's in your ass, where's it going to be? How are they going to see it?" Kevin asked sarcastically.

"If they had you do that, spread them, so to speak, wouldn't they see the kite?"

"Galloway, if you strip and you spread your ass, are they going to see the shit in your asshole? No. C'mon, let's be realistic. Let's keep it real." A little laughter came from some jurors and a few spectators.

"I'll finish up here, Your Honor," he said. "You're telling this jury that just before you are going to begin combat, you take something from your sock and put it up your anus, and it's a securer place there?"

"It's very secure. It's where we keep our contraband. It's the same place everybody keeps their drugs. This is prison. This is how we live. It's an institution."

"And you live by the rules of gangs?"

"In the institution, you have no choice."

"I see. No further questions, Your Honor."

—

The attorneys gathered at sidebar to argue over the admission of exhibits, and Scott opted not to pursue redirect in favor of having one last witness testify before the day ended. The judge warned him to be brief. "Not so ponderous. Okay. This is not a deposition. This is a criminal trial. Let's step it up a little bit. We'll take his testimony so he doesn't have to come back."

An imposing man with a shaved head in a dark uniform was sworn in and took the stand. He said he was a Douglas County Prison officer who had known Kevin for three of the five months he'd been placed at DCP.

"What kind of trouble do you have with Kevin?"

"We haven't had any problems with him there. He's in general population. He's out with anywheres from 35 to 40 inmates all day. I haven't heard any reports. I haven't seen any write-ups."

"He said that he's been painting there."

"Yes."

"What kind?"

The CO explained how Kevin touched up the lettering on an overhead beam that said, "Respect is earned on both sides of these doors," which led to the large mural of the covered bridge in a hallway.

"In your opinion, is he a gifted artist?"

"Oh, definitely."

"Do you feel any personal insecurity around Mr. Sanders?"

"I haven't had a problem."

"Okay, that's all I have, thanks."

"Any cross, Mr. Galloway?"

"Yes, Your Honor. Did I get this right—he's been on your block for three months?"

"Roughly three months, yes, sir."

"During that period of time, there hasn't been a problem, for three months?"

"Not that I'm aware of, no, sir."

"And he was pending trial during that entire lengthy three-month period of time. Is that right?"

"Sir, I couldn't tell you that."

"No further questions."

And with no recross, the judge said, "All right. Folks, that concludes the testimony in the case. Please be here ready to go at 11:00 a.m. tomorrow for closing arguments." And he warned them once again not to look up the case or talk about it to anyone.

CHAPTER 25
TRIAL DAY 3 CONCLUSION

OCTOBER 2013, WEDNESDAY

T he lawyers were due in court at 9:30 a.m. for a charging conference with the judge. While they discussed the proposed jury instructions and charges to be presented, Kevin and I chit-chatted. I snapped a picture of him in Scott's bulky, dark gray suit, navy polka dot tie, and a borrowed watch, and the federal marshal standing at the door sprang into action. "Ma'am, you can't do that. I don't want to have to take away your phone." I offered a charming apology but couldn't get him to smile.

The jury filed in at 11:00 a.m., and Assistant United States Attorney Neil Galloway began his closing argument.

"May it please the Court. Counsel, ladies and gentlemen of the jury, good morning. The government, as I'm sure the defense and the court, is very thankful for your service in this particular case, your patience with us, and for paying close attention to the evidence presented. The case is very important not only to the government and the defendant but also the victim in this case, Steven Tremblay."

He said jurors would have access to a binder with exhibits, mostly photos of the victim's injuries, shanks recovered by officers (except no photo of Kevin's purported shank in the grass), and the CD so they could watch the video as many times as they wanted.

Galloway went over the charges—assault with a dangerous weapon, assault resulting in bodily harm, possession of a dangerous weapon—and said, "The Judge will instruct you on a defense of justification or an alleged justification defense that the defense has to prove by a preponderance of the evidence. We anticipate the Court will instruct you on four specific elements of that affirmative defense. We would submit that the defense can't establish any of the four."

The AUSA characterized the rec cage assault as a "vicious, cowardly attack from behind by two inmates, including this defendant, armed with shanks on an unsuspecting, unarmed victim, who suffered 41 stab or puncture wounds." He said the defense wanted the jury to believe the defendant inflicted none of the wounds, and that instead of arming himself for combat, Mr. Sanders put a kite in his rectum for safekeeping.

"But does it make sense that, gee, before I engage in combat or attack somebody, for safekeeping, I'm going to put a kite up my rectum before I begin the attack? Does that make any sense whatsoever? We submit no. As a result, his testimony is not credible."

Galloway cued up the video again and paused it seven seconds in. "Ladies and gentlemen of the jury, it appears the left hand goes into the back of his pants, and it appears his left hand then goes to his right hand. Now run it a little bit further until—boom, boom. Okay. Stop it there. What does he do? Is that a stabbing motion, as SIA Lippit has testified to? We submit it sure is."

I thought Galloway could have saved his breath, that less was more, but he continued recapping the government's case. He went over all the witnesses he called and what they said. When he came to Lt. Lippit, he couldn't deny the photo of the shank in the grass she said she took was missing. "If you had the photo, would it help? Perhaps," he said.

The AUSA talked about prison gang "bylaws" and reminded the jury that Officer Crone testified that he told the defendant, "'If there's a problem, tell me,' and, 'Why did you do that?' And what was his response? 'I bet he doesn't bang on that door tonight.' What does that indicate to you? They were taking care of Tremblay, and they did it together."

Eventually, Galloway focused on the justification defense by asking, "Was there a chance to avoid the harm?" The prosecutor repeated the testimony of CO Crone, who claimed Kevin said he could rec with Tremblay, and at that point, he could have said, "I don't want to rec today, I don't feel good today ..." Likewise, Kevin could have refused to go into the rec cage later, knowing Tremblay would be placed there.

Our defense team believed none of that was true, and it was hard for me, at least, to hear the story twisted to fit the prosecutor's narrative. Galloway then touched on the immediacy of the threat posed to Kevin in the rec cage.

"Where is the evidence that Keys threatened Sanders in any way that morning? Other than the defendant saying, hey, Keys threatened me. Keys told me if you don't join in this assault, you're in trouble, I'm going to get you. None whatsoever. All we have is the defendant saying well, gee, I felt he might get me."

And that's because the prosecutor and judge blocked our expert witness, I wanted to scream.

But in case the jurors thought the testimony I read of Westin Chase was corroboration of a "wave-off," Galloway suggested Kevin and Chase had coordinated their testimony, right down to insisting CO Shemp had put Tremblay in the cage. "It certainly wasn't Shemp who put him in," he said, based on Shemp's testimony. "And Johnson didn't see any wave-off."

Yes, my dry inner monologue continued, *because all the COs told the truth on the stand.* Galloway finished his closing in just over 30 minutes.

———

Jack didn't know he was delivering our closing until yesterday at lunch. Over a plate of chicken wings, Scott asked him to do it. "Oh, fuck me," Jack looked up at the ceiling, BBQ sauce stuck to his beard.

Today, dressed in a crisp dark suit, white shirt, and red striped tie, he told the court his co-counsel asked for a quick restroom break before beginning his closing argument.

"Well, he can take a bathroom break while you commence," the judge said. "We're going to keep moving here. So, go ahead." I saw Lucy in one of the benches, and I sneaked back to join her for the show, hoping Jack would find some brevity that generally eluded him.

"Thank you, Your Honor," Jack said. "This case brings me full circle in this courthouse. It was 23 years ago, in this very building, that was my first federal defense—a stabbing at Lewisburg. At the time, Lewisburg was the toughest institution in the federal system." He then discussed Alcatraz prison, which closed around 1966, and the supermax at Marion, which opened in 1990. Returning to Lewisburg, he said, back in the day, inmates could learn metal-working in the prison shop, "and they made metal desks and metal rockers."

"Your Honor, I'm sorry. I really hate to object at this point," Galloway said. "That's really none of the evidence in this case. It's irrelevant."

"I understand you are trying to give an example, Mr. Bear," the judge said. "Why don't you make sure you contour it to evidence in this case? I'm going to give you some latitude. But why don't you move into the case if you would, please?"

"Well, the point I'm making," Jack said, "is that sometimes the government does stupid things." This perked up some jurors' ears. Jack linked his thesis to Area 51, the Nevada Air Force base synonymous with tales of UFOs and government coverups, and the NSA claiming they didn't collect information on Americans when it turned out they did. "The point is people get up on the witness stand, and even if they work for the government, and even if they shouldn't, they sometimes tell things that are not the truth under oath."

Jack cited the many references to the Aryan Brotherhood and said the prosecutor would like them to believe there is only one rule of law that everyone should follow. "But that's not the case. Within the prison system, there's a very elaborate gang structure."

And this gang structure, he said, impeded Kevin Sanders' freedom of movement the same as prison walls did. He told the jurors his client couldn't make the choices to avoid the incident as Galloway claimed. A man in prison "goes where he's told to go. He gets up when he's told to get up. He goes to bed when he's told to go to bed. And in the Special Management Unit at Lewisburg, he doesn't go anywhere without an escort and without handcuffs. He's got to be cuffed up. He doesn't have these choices. He can try to wave off a rec or something like that. And if the guard deigns to listen to him, he might not be taken out to rec, or he might be taken out of that cell. But if the guard doesn't listen to him, he's there. And that's where my client found himself."

Jack moved on to "burdens of proof," "standards of evidence," and "preponderance of evidence." He said, "If this case were a law school exam, some students would be in the bathroom throwing up right now. This is a complicated case." He discussed the instruction they would get from the judge about reasonable doubt—about 25 pages worth of material that he called "almost a half-year course in law school."

Then he got into the weeds of those definitions and used buying a second-hand car as an analogy that went on way too long. "We liken it to a set of scales," he said. "If the scales stayed dead-leveled or tipped to the prosecution, then we haven't carried our burden of proof and have not succeeded in convincing you by a preponderance of the evidence. If the scales stay level, that's a tie. The tie goes to the prosecution. As soon as those scales tip, as soon as you say to yourself, you know, it's more likely than not, it doesn't have to be a certainty, it's just more likely than not … as soon as the scales tip, then the affirmative defense is made, and then you must find the defendant not guilty, even despite all of the other evidence that has been presented. As long as you find the elements of the affirmative defense of justification by a preponderance of the evidence, you must set aside the proof beyond a reasonable doubt that you had previously, and you must find the defendant not guilty on count one and count two."

My eyes glazed over, and I tried to determine how focused the jurors were on these technicalities. My conclusion was, for about half of them, not very.

Jack returned to simpler concepts, such as whether his client had a knife and all the evidence that supported he did not. But that took many minutes. Jack meandered into tattoos and swastikas, Kevin's background growing up speaking Spanish, and his Montañista history, all of which supported a repeat telling of the prison gang culture based on racial separations. Lucy and I looked at each other. He was losing the jurors, and nothing could be done about it.

He turned to the four elements of the *Taylor* case that, if met, would satisfy the justification defense, including Kevin's fear at the hands of Mark Keys in the rec cage and that Kevin hadn't recklessly placed himself in the situation.

He all but called CO Crone a liar for saying he asked Kevin if Kevin could rec with Tremblay, when Kevin said Crone asked him if he could rec with whites. "I believe that my client is telling the truth. And that's why he was surprised when they came to the cage with Tremblay. He thought he would have a nice quiet recreation hour with his cellmate and that there wouldn't be a problem."

Jack discussed the video and said if the beginning part had been captured, it would have shown his client waving off CO Johnson and then talking to Officer Shemp to try and avoid the conflict.

In the end, after 45 minutes, Jack left the jury with a truism. "My client participated. Absolutely. You see that. But he was not participating willingly. He was putting on a show. He was doing what he had to do to avoid being knifed himself.

"I ask you to find in his favor by a preponderance of the evidence on the defense of justification. We have met all of the elements. They are there. And I ask you to find him not guilty. Thank you."

And, because this was federal court, Galloway got the last word with a short rebuttal, refuting all of Jack's highlights. The AUSA told jurors that the theory of justification applied to only one person in the rec cage that day—if Steven Tremblay had been able to turn his assailants' weapons against them, he would have been justified in doing so.

—

At 12:35 p.m., court recessed for a one-hour lunch. Scott, Jack, Lucy, and I grabbed deli sandwiches a few blocks away. We complimented Jack on his closing with no mention of its length. Jack had a lot of challenging concepts to impart to the jurors, we all agreed, and his calling the case complicated was a vast understatement. I didn't think Scott could have done much better.

When court resumed, the judge talked directly to the jurors for an hour. He covered general and then case-specific instructions on how they needed to reach a unanimous verdict, repeating many things he said at the trial's outset and some of what the attorneys said in their closings. He read all 25 pages of instruction even though the jurors would take the paper version to deliberate.

As Judge Anderson discussed selecting a foreperson, weighing the different types of evidence, and the elements of our affirmative defense, the courtroom grew warmer. Sun streamed in through the tall windows, whose curtains were open, and that combination plus having full stomachs from lunch was sleep-inducing. Some jurors seemed to drift—I know I wanted to—and at one point, I had to kick Jack under the defense table to wake him up.

For some reason, the judge made the two alternate jurors endure his hour-long soliloquy in the hot courtroom before he dismissed them. He sent the remaining 12 to the deliberation room with their instruction pages, any notes they had taken, a copy of the CD, and a verdict slip. It was 2:25 p.m.

Kevin was taken to his holding cell. The federal marshal, who wouldn't smile, let Kevin keep Scott's watch on to track the time since there was no wall clock nearby. Kevin paced and checked it frequently.

Lucy joined us, and we sat in the near-empty courtroom for a while and then paced the hallway outside. Then, she and I went on a coffee run and exchanged some post-game analysis. We both agreed that our case had been severely hobbled by the lack of an expert witness, COs covering their asses on the stand, and the general imbalance that favors the prosecution in federal court. But she wouldn't say anything disparaging about the judge.

"At least Neil didn't ask your client to 'name names,'" as he did at the hearing," she added. I nodded and said by extension that had kept the prison riot memo out of evidence—two good things for Kevin's safety.

At 4 p.m., Scott texted us that the jury had two questions, so we raced back to the courtroom. The judge read the questions to the counsel without the jury present. The first was: Did the jurors have to be unanimous on each of the four points of the justification defense? The judge and lawyers agreed that the answer was yes.

The second question was: What was the definition of "immediate" as in the "immediate, unlawful threat of death or serious bodily injury to himself?" The foreperson wrote, "Is immediate the next ten minutes or the next 24 hours or some other time period?"

The judge asked for input from the lawyers, and the best they could all come up with was to give the panel a Webster's dictionary definition: "Near to or related to the present, of or relating to the here and now."

The judge called the jury back and answered their questions, but the foreperson wanted clarification on the first. "I believe point four in the defense is, you know, did the defendant recklessly put himself in a situation which could have been avoided? Does that mean all 12 of us have to sit there and say yes, he did, or no, he didn't, in order for that one to be counted? Like, we can't take a seven-to-five vote and say that's yes?"

The judge repeated that all 12 had to be unanimous on each of the four elements. He essentially told them that if even one of the four elements failed because there was no unanimity, they didn't have to debate the other three because that meant the justification defense failed overall. Full stop.

The relief on the jurors' faces was undeniable. It was nearing the end of the day, and they returned to the deliberation room, knowing exactly what to do now. No de-coding was necessary to understand that seven jurors thought Kevin either went into that rec cage knowing he would have to fight Tremblay or could have left the cage before the fight ensued.

At that moment, the grim scale of our uphill battle washed over us, and I expected them to return quickly with unhappy news. But to their credit, they deliberated 45 minutes longer. At 5:15 p.m., they rendered their verdict.

Count One, assault with a dangerous weapon with intent to do bodily harm—*guilty*. Count Two, assault resulting in serious bodily injury—*guilty*. Count Three, possession of a weapon by an inmate—*not guilty*.

Though the verdict had been telegraphed an hour earlier, it still stung. We were somber even while pleasantly surprised they'd found Kevin had no weapon. I cynically thought that was probably a peace offering made by jurors who wanted to go home to the holdouts. We would never know.

The judge asked the panel to stay for a few minutes so he could personally thank them for their service. Scott, Jack, and I hugged Kevin goodbye before the marshal led him away, and Jack told him quietly that we'd all be working on the appeal, adding, "Our work's not done here, Kevin, not by a long shot."

CHAPTER 26
KING CON

OCTOBER 2013, WEDNESDAY EVENING, DOUGLAS COUNTY PRISON

A few hours after the verdict, the DCP warden let Scott and me visit with Kevin. We had changed into jeans but weren't feeling comfortable or casual, just sad about the outcome. Scott shook hands with the prison officer who testified for us, and the CO said he was happy to help and sorry for the verdict.

In the visitation room, Scott reiterated that we'd all be focusing on the appeal but added, "Buddy, you do have another option, too. You can file a 2255. I'll even help you write it. No hard feelings at all."

"Are you crazy? That's *Ineffective Assistance of Counsel*. After all you've done for me? No way, man, no way." Kevin shook his head, and I thought he might break down. Then he looked in his lap and said, "I was just supposed to take my five years and shut up. Like Arson did."

"Well, we don't know what the sentence will be—maybe less than that since we got a not-guilty on Count Three," Scott said. The sentencing date was yet to be determined, but Scott guessed it could be before the end of the year.

We filled the rest of our time with small talk. Kevin explained how fishing lines were made out of the tiny, thin elastic bands inside the tops of inmates' boxer shorts. With careful removal, the bands could form a long enough string to carry a kite or book of stamps pinned to the end. The line would be flung underneath a cell door, down a hall to another door, and so on until the recipient received it. Or, sometimes, it was cast out a window and made its way across the prison's exterior wall.

The absurdity of what he described made us laugh out loud, and I said something about "necessity being the mother of invention." Still chuckling, Scott said, "Or maybe it's, *idle hands are the devil's playthings*." I roared almost to the point of tears and was struck by the notion that Scott and I had come there to make Kevin feel better, but here he was doing that for us.

When it was time for goodbyes, Kevin asked. "Do you think they'll let me stay here until the sentencing?"

"Maybe," Scott smiled.

After Kevin was led away, I said, "Really? Do you think he can stay here?"

"Not a chance."

"Why'd you say it, then?"

"I didn't want to take his hope away."

—

The following week, Scott filed a motion with Judge Anderson asking that Kevin be allowed to remain at DCP until his sentencing. A sentencing conference had been set for the end of the year, and Scott and Jack planned to present evidence of mitigation to obtain the lightest sentence possible. Scott said they'd need to confer with their client as part of this mitigation prep. In the motion, Scott also referenced Steven Tremblay's deposition that the prosecutor wouldn't give him.

Scott stated Kevin was securely housed at DCP, where the warden was aware he was now a target for gang reprisals and was keeping him safe, and that "if returned to USP-Florence, Mr. Sanders will be in mortal danger."

The judge responded by expediting Kevin's sentencing. He did not order the U.S. Marshal Service to keep Kevin at DCP but *suggested* Kevin be kept locally, and wrote it was his "fondest hope" that would happen.

However, digital arguments over the deposition—who told what to whom, and how and why Scott hadn't been able to see it—stretched into the next month, and the sentencing was delayed. So, by early November—for bureaucratic or some other reason—Kevin was sent back to USP Florence in Colorado.

—

NOVEMBER 2013—THE STORY OF KEVIN SANDERS' LAST DAY AT DCP IN HIS OWN WORDS (EDITED FOR BREVITY AND CLARITY)

"KING CON"

It's 9 a.m., and I'm on a bottom bunk in the softest jail I've ever sat in. Never in my criminal life have I tasted the freedoms of any facility like I have here. It's con heaven, and I'm King Con.

"Sanders, get your ass up!"

"Damn, Gronk, everyone knows I get up at lunch. Why you stressing my downtime, hoss?"

"The marshals are here to get you, boy, so roll your shit up and see me at the Bubble."

As CO Gronk walks off, I spin out of bed and look at my cellie "Farmer." I tell him, "What the fuck, homie? I'm not ready to leave yet. I'm not even sentenced." Farmer looks at me with his stoner's glaze, lost for words, 'cause I know he's only thinking of the tattoos I started that won't get finished.

Farmer is one of the most trusted inmates in my circle. I call him Farmer because he got busted growing a large crop of marijuana in his house. He looks like one of those *Duck Dynasty* guys with a full, long beard but with a shaved head and lots of tattoos I've been doing for the last few months. I pull on his beard to help him snap out of his daze and get him to roll out of his rack.

"Come on, Dawg, get down here and roll us some smokes. You know I can't think straight without a smoke." Because of his hobby, Farmer can roll a smoke better than most.

"I don't know if that's a good idea, bro, with Gronk working the block. You know how he is over smoke."

I just stare at my cellie for a second before spitting out a rant in Spanish, then finishing it with, "Fuck the Gronk. What's he gonna do, put me in the hole? The marshals are here, homeboy, and we need to smoke. I don't have this pleasure in the feds, and I'm not stepping out this cell 'till I've blown smoke." I smile and tell him, "Let's just call this my goodbye to the Gronkster."

Farmer laughs and starts rolling the loose tobacco, fatter than usual, inside bits of magazine paper. I light up using a battery, a thin strip of foil, and toilet paper rolled into a wick. As we smoke our contraband, Farmer says things won't be the same around here without me. "You have this place relaxed, and they don't mess with you," he says.

"It's all about respect," I say as a cloud of smoke blows out my mouth. "It's their world, and sometimes they let us rule it—always let 'em know you know that.

"You take care, Farmer, and keep these boys in line. Don't let 'em slack on their workouts. Keep 'em strong," I say as I hug my cellie.

"Damn, bro, I'm gonna miss you," he says.

I can't explain the bonds that grow between men who have to do time together and have their limits tested. Maybe it's like soldiers who have to stand together through thick and thin.

"Goddammit, Sanders!" yells Gronk as he rips the cell door open. "You're smoking on my shift, boy? Where's the respect?" I flip my stub into the john and say, "I know, hoss, I know." I smile and give the Farmer a wink as I grab my stuff and head out.

"What if the warden comes down here and smells smoke? He'll think I can't do my job."

"I know, hoss," I say, as Old Gronk lets out a rant that is just putting on a show for the other inmates 'cause he don't want them to test the air with smoke of their own now. I follow Gronk down the tier and look at the lettering I painted, "Respect is earned on both sides of these doors." On the other side, I painted, "Nothing is impossible." The word "impossible" says *I'm possible.*

That I am, I think.

I set my stuff down at the end of the range, and Old Gronk turns to me and thrusts his hand out. I grab it and shake it. "You know, Sanders, I've seen a lot of inmates come and go through this jail, but you're one of the few I hate to see go, especially back into the feds."

I've known this old hoss for the last five months and will miss him and all the COs I have built an understanding with—our mutual respect about our ways of life, theirs and mine.

"So long, hoss. Pop this door and let me go before all these boys start to cry 'cause I'm leaving 'em." I popped out the sallyport into the hall and walk down to the Control Bubble. I stop and look at the wall that holds a large painting I did of a covered bridge, and the warden steps out of his office and walks over to me.

"You smell like smoke, Sanders!"

I smile and say, "You know I got to blow my last smoke, boss. The road ahead is smoke-free from here."

"So is this jail!" he screams at me. "Get your ass out of here before I lock you up."

"I wish you would, boss. I've had a real nice run here with your staff and all my painting. I wish you would."

Two officers dress me out in cuffs set into a belly chain. I am walked out a door, through a garage, and into the back of a van. In the front seat are two jail officers wearing flak jackets and strapped up with a pair of AR 15s. I sit back and watch my former jail hacks turn into part-time chauffeurs, driving me to the airport to hand me off to the U.S. marshals.

There's not much to talk about on the ride, and the thick plate of bulletproof glass between us makes us almost have to yell. Within a few minutes, both officers start playing with their phones. No wonder I hear so many news reports about crashing cars with all these new phones around. The officers can't keep their hands off them.

I give the safety glass a few swift knocks, making both of them jump. "What the fuck?" says Officer Todd in the passenger seat.

"How about more driving and less phone time?" I say. "How 'bout you pass that back here and let me check it out for a minute?"

I get a laugh from both officers. "There's nothing to see on my phone," Officer Todd says, "but Mike—he's got porn on his."

I quickly shoot back, "I don't like farm animals. I know Mike chases them sheep out in the sticks."

So now I have both officers holding their phones up to the glass, showing me pictures of everything they can think of—cars, bikes, women, hunting kills they made, and more women. Then, Officer Todd cracks his window and lights up a smoke.

"Hey! Hey! Todd! Give me a smoke, hoss!"

"No way, Sanders. You already smoked today, and I'm not getting no shit over you burning holes into the seat."

"Well, I have to try, Todd. You know I have to try," I say.

A few minutes later, Mike slides a Chew Skoal Bandit pouch of chewing tobacco through the crack of the divider. I snatch it like a bird grabbing a fat worm. "Don't be spitting back there," I hear as I sit back and enjoy the ride.

In a little while, I test my luck and ask, "How 'bout lunch, boys? Some fast food or something for going away?" They look at each other and think about it, then go with the better idea of the paper bag lunch from the jail kitchen.

Once we reach the airport, we sit and eat cold sack lunches while waiting for the U.S. marshals to show up. Soon, the big white federal Con Air plane appears in the sky and touches down. She looks like a prisoner herself, with no detail and only a black registration number to identify her.

"Let's go, Sanders, you're up," Officer Mike says. As I step out, I spit my chew Bandit onto the tarmac. "We don't want the marshals to flip out over that, now, do we?" I smile.

"So long, boys. You watch them sheep, Mike. I don't want to come back and hear you're in jail for that shit. I might have to whoop ya for it. You know, convict rules and all."

We laugh, and I get the old joke about dropping the soap and some other slick lines to send me on my way. I start my slow shuffle to the marshals, 20 yards out, shackles and chain jangling along. I look back and give them a nod, and they give me one in return. Not bad for a couple of soft-ass jail hacks.

But as I make my way to the marshal line, my heart is heavy, because I know the good times have come to an end.

PART II

CHAPTER 27
A TINY HIT

MID-NOVEMBER 2013, USP-FLORENCE-HIGH

On his third night at USP Florence, Colorado, Kevin didn't sleep at all because someone was going to try to kill him the next day.

Kevin's new cellie, Diablo, had heard the gossip at recreation, and so Kevin got to work immediately on a "stab vest" to wear for his debut release on unit E-A. Kevin was at the end of his precautionary 72-hour lockdown when Diablo told him an Aryan Brotherhood of Texas (ABT) associate named "Tiny" was concerned about Kevin's arrival and was asking around for a shank. Kevin stayed up late sewing magazines into strips of cloth and then sewing that layer inside a T-shirt. Three of his tattoo magazines in front and three in the back covered his vital organs, and he hoped the stab vest would help keep him alive until COs intervened.

Diablo, a Mexican Paisa member, offered Kevin a knife for tomorrow's fight for protection and entertainment. He pulled a 9-inch flat blade from under his sleeve, handed it to Kevin, and said, "Here, *carnal*, we think you need this filo, homie. Just in case."

"No, Diablo, I don't need that. I'm not a gangster no more, and I need to do this right. If I move with that, homie,

I'll be hit with more hard time, and I'd rather die than do more time in these trick bags."

Because Kevin wasn't a Paisa, Diablo couldn't help him fend off Tiny, but Diablo agreed to bring the shank with him for Kevin to use as a last resort. "I'll do what I can, but it's not the Paisa's problem," Diablo told him. "Tu no eres Paisa, *carnal*," meaning, "you're not under us, brother." As much as the two cellies got along, Kevin understood the rules and why his cellie's help would be limited.

Kevin tossed and turned and tried to doze, but all he could think about were various combat strategies and how, once again, due to the negligence of prison cops, his life was in danger. At intake three days ago, he told two counselors and two SIS officers that he needed to be kept away from any active white gang members because of his trial testimony. Kevin even asked who might be a potential problem on his new range, and they singled out Tiny. But don't worry, they said, Tiny and his cellie were ABT dropouts, completing phases three and four of the SMU program like Kevin was sent there to do. The Florence officials assured him there would be no problems.

And it wasn't like Kevin could now call a CO to his cell door to say a fight was brewing. There would be a cell search, and if Diablo's knife weren't found, Diablo would turn that 9-inch shank on Kevin in retaliation—because Kevin's cellie lived by the same set of convict laws in play at every prison. Kevin considered taking Diablo's knife as a preventative measure, but that could have ended badly for his cellie, and Kevin figured he was in deep enough shit already.

His only option was to show his enemies he was ready and defend himself as well as possible with his bare hands.

—

After lunch the next day, the range officer popped open the doors one by one for indoor recreation. Kevin's and Diablo's cell was one of the first unlocked, and Kevin, wearing a baggy gray sweatshirt to hide the stab vest, immediately walked over to Tiny's cell. As Tiny and his cellie exited, Kevin said, "What's up *woods*?"

Tiny emerged and was anything but his moniker. He was large, with a shaved head, and wore the Aryan Brotherhood of Texas signature twin lightning bolts tattoo on his forearm. His cellie was of similar size and had the same tats. "Let me speak to you before we get off on the wrong understanding up here," Kevin said as the two white gangsters stopped and registered the tension in the air. Everyone was watching, including some officers, ready to hit their body alarms if needed.

"I'm not here to start problems," Kevin told them. "And I don't need the drama in my life over this shit. I'm through with the gang-banging, and I'm stepping back."

He continued, "We can either get the fuck out of this program, or we can smash head-on into it right now. I know you and homeboy here have been looking for bangers, and I'm ready to get it popping." Kevin tapped his chest so they'd hear his magazine shield and know their task wouldn't be as easy as they imagined.

"No, no, wood," said Tiny. "We just thought you was on some power trip, and we don't want to take no chances. If you're stepping back, we have no issue with that. But we can't back you if you get into any racial drama."

"I'm good on that," said Kevin. "From here on out, I'm doing this bid alone. I don't need the gang drama to hold me down anymore."

The exchange might have seemed like a truce to any officers paying attention, but Kevin knew he was just holding them at bay for now. They rec'ced without incident that day, and over the next few days, for the two to three hours outside his cell, Kevin wore his stab vest. He also approached his unit manager and told the officer the SIS was not protecting him against active white gang members and that he should be in safety housing because his life was in danger. The unit manager told Kevin he was aware of his situation and that officers were developing a plan for him. But also, Tiny and his cellie hadn't moved on Kevin yet, so "they probably won't," the unit manager told him. "Don't worry about it."

If you stupid fuckheads would just do your job right the first time, I wouldn't have to wear a vest of magazines and bluff my enemies into thinking I'm armed, he thought.

More days passed with no protective action from the SIS or other officers. More days with Kevin wearing his stab vest on the open range and inmates walking by, poking his chest, just to make sure.

Five days after Kevin's confrontation with Tiny, he left the stab vest behind to run a few miles in the outside rec yard with his MP3 player to blast heavy metal music into his ears. But as Kevin descended the stairs, the other inmates stared at him, and those not rec'cing had their faces glued to their cell windows. Kevin knew it was on.

He was only wearing a light T-shirt, shorts, and running shoes, but for some reason, he was calm. Tiny walked over to him with his hands in his pockets, then pulled out dual shanks, one in each fist, and said to Kevin, "Let's do this."

Kevin delivered the first blow into Tiny's stomach, followed by another, that set the big gangster back on his heels. Kevin kept at it, punching so hard and fast that Tiny lost his focus and swung his shanks wildly in the air. Kevin blocked more thrusts than he took, but he still got sliced, and the worst shot landed under his left armpit mere inches from his heart. Kevin felt a knife break his skin and slide off a rib bone. Fifteen seconds into the fight, officers arrived and screamed for both inmates to stop and lay on the ground. Kevin wasn't about to give Tiny that split-second advantage, and officers broke it up by pepper-spraying both inmates' faces and subduing them on the range floor.

"This one's bleeding all over the place!" said one of the three COs who tackled Kevin. With his eyes, nose, and throat searing, he was pushed inside a shower to rinse off the spray. He couldn't see or breathe while an officer yelled, "Get him the fuck out of here now! Look at all that blood. Assess! Assess! Medical assess! This one has stab wounds!"

Kevin was rushed to a medical room, where they cut off his bloody T-shirt because he was handcuffed behind his back. A nurse who put three staples into his armpit slice and another one into a gash on his hand told Kevin he was lucky, that his worst wound could have been fatal if it had been an inch or two to the right.

Through watery, burning eyes, Kevin saw his unit manager arrive and look worried. "I fucking told you what would happen," Kevin said. "Are you happy now?"

Right after getting his staples, he was interviewed by the SIS, and one had the audacity to ask him what had just happened. Kevin went on a rant about their stupidity and how he couldn't trust them and said he would not take a cellie and allow another inmate a chance to stab him up. So, for protective custody, he was taken to the hole, a bare cell with nothing but a bed, a john, a shower, a sink, a desk, and a window with a view of a brick wall.

The officer who walked him there appeared again in his cell door window. "What do you want?" Kevin snapped, tears and snot still running down his face from the pepper spray.

"I thought you might need some of these," he said, holding up some Sugar Twin sweetener packets.

"What the fuck do I need that shit for?"

"Look, asshole, I just thought you might want to rub some of this on your skin to help the burn of the mace," the CO said and tossed the packets under his door.

No shit, Sugar Twin—who knew? Kevin opened some packets and rubbed the grainy substance over his face, but the second it touched his skin, it was like being sprayed all over again. And then washing it off in the sink further re-activated the oleoresin capsicum irritant. Kevin flipped off the CO, grinning at his window, and curled up on his bed on his right side. He ached all over and tried to drift off with thoughts about what he'd like to do to that officer if he ever managed to slip his cuffs in his presence.

CHAPTER 28
SEE NO EVIL, SPEAK NO EVIL

EARLY 2014

K evin spent 83 days in the hole with nothing to do except draw, read from the boring prison collection, and write letters to Scott and me. That's how we learned of the hit, in a 25-page letter that Scott received two weeks after the assault.

Scott arranged a three-way conference call with Kevin in his counselor's office and me in Philadelphia. We were frantic for more details, but Kevin mostly gave us one or two-word answers because he couldn't talk freely.

It was the winter of the Polar Vortex, and for the first three months of 2014, Scott, Jack, and I froze off our behinds while plotting Kevin's best legal strategy—namely, how to reduce his sentence. Work on the appeal couldn't begin until we knew how much additional prison time Judge Anderson would give him.

Right after the trial, Kevin's former cellmate, Mark Keys, a.k.a. Arson, was formally sentenced to five years. We learned through the grapevine that part of his plea deal involved him *not* testifying for Kevin and that AUSA Galloway dropped two of his charges. This wasn't surprising; it was just further evidence of the government's power imbalance.

Jack was optimistic, though. "Wow! Mark Keys gets 60 months! Our guy had no knife—he should get 30! I can't wait to see how this develops!"

One possible silver lining from the AB's attempt to murder Kevin in Florence was that we'd have compelling new evidence to try to sway the judge. Florence officials would have to investigate, and Scott and Jack planned to subpoena the report when it was complete. Based on this, Scott filed a motion to extend Kevin's sentencing date.

—

While we waited for the Florence report, Scott finally got his hands on a copy of Steven Tremblay's deposition—but not his own copy. Nearly two months after asking for it, AUSA Galloway's boss acquired the deposition, and Scott was told he could sift through the 200 pages in Galloway's office and take notes. If he wanted a copy, he'd have to pay the California court reporter for it. As a party to that civil suit, the government finally agreed to Scott obtaining it.

He sat there for four hours with his yellow legal pad and ballpoint pen, diligently taking notes from a transcript of Tremblay being asked questions via video link by an AUSA from a Harrisburg office.

The first 65 pages included a discussion of Tremblay's background, his mental health struggles, and his troubled history in various prisons, including Big Sandy, where he was incarcerated with Dennis MacDonald, who was a lieutenant then. Tremblay gave the AUSA a bizarre and disturbing account of being four-pointed by MacDonald, who instructed a female CO to electrocute his toe, pelvis, and genitals.

Finally, on page 80, the AUSA questioned Tremblay about the rec cage fight with Kevin and Arson that sparked his civil suit against the BOP. Tremblay said Kevin and Arson "had to hit me because they put me in there" and that COs had set it up while the cellies told the officers not to put him in the cage.

Tremblay even said Kevin and Arson gave him more of a beat-down than a real hit, and "That's probably why I'm still alive. So it's almost, like, thank you for not killing me …"

And then Tremblay expanded on the role of CO Crone, who refused to tell him who he was going to rec with that day, and said, "If you don't go out to rec, I'm going to have you four-pointed."

Tremblay also said that Captain MacDonald, whom Crone reported to, orchestrated the cage fight for an altercation that took place between him and MacDonald months earlier, which I took to mean the snowball incident. He recounted the threat MacDonald made in front of other inmates about putting him in a cage to get hit. "All the corrupt people involved … were in communication with each other and plotting. It's from top to bottom." Tremblay also mentioned, twice, an unknown officer who told him that COs are "trying to kill you."

Halfway through the deposition, Scott took photos of a few pages and emailed them to Jack and me with the subject header "Brady Goldmine."

But as the depo continued, Scott was dismayed to read that Tremblay lumped both Kevin and Arson together as assailants, saying both had stabbed him. He appeared confused about whether Kevin and Arson were told they would be rec'cing with him ahead of time. Tremblay tried to recall Crone's conversation with Kevin at his cell window about rec'cing with "whites," but his memory was fuzzy.

The AUSA was very interested in whether Tremblay had told anyone about MacDonald's threat, and the answer was yes—his parents, in a letter, and the Lewisburg Prison Project staffer who had helped him file his initial civil suit. The AUSA also asked him which other inmates witnessed the assault and would back his story, and Tremblay gave him two names, both different from Little Eagle.

Finally, Tremblay said he would never testify for the government, which is why Galloway hadn't called him as a witness, but he indicated he was open to testifying *for* Kevin. The depo was taken three months before Kevin's trial, and I assumed that's why he had written to Scott. But I could also see why Jack's instincts not to have him testify for us had been spot-on. Tremblay's memory was hazy, and Galloway would have used his mental illness to discredit him. Plus, just like in his civil suit, he said Kevin stabbed him along with Arson.

Merde. What a mixed bag, I thought. Nonetheless, Scott and Jack felt the depo contained enough Brady material to file a motion for a new trial. However, they decided the motion should be written solely by Jack because Judge Anderson had not taken kindly to Scott's earlier motions to extend Kevin's sentencing and to force Galloway to give him a deposition copy. Our case was the proverbial fly encircling His Honor's head; it wouldn't go away no matter how much he swatted.

In his argument for a new trial, Jack included the depo and regurgitated two things the judge denied us: the expert witness and the use of Mark Keys' letter, where he admitted to stabbing someone. And, as a warning of documentation to come, Jack added that the AB had tried to kill Kevin in Florence and that Kevin's request for protective custody had fallen on deaf ears.

It was a succinct and impactful filing that was all about record-building for the appeal. Best of all, he'd attached the 200-page Tremblay deposition that was now part of Kevin's growing case file.

"I have a crystal ball," Jack said. "Neil will file a brief in opposition. It will contain a lot of shouting and hand-waiving. Anderson will deny the motion. He will schedule Kevin for sentencing. The sentence will be vindictive. We will appeal."

—

In February, Kevin turned 39 in the hole. He was bored and lonely but safe. Some of his prison reading included a passage about how blind people's other senses were more acute, their hearing in particular. And, since he had nothing better to do, he tested that theory by bandaging some leftover adhesive pads to his eyes. On the first day of his week-long experiment, the officer who banged on the food/handcuff slot with his dinner tray asked him what was wrong with his eyes.

"Nothing's wrong with my eyes," he said, feeling his way to the door to find the tray. "I'm blind for a while." He heard the cuff slot slam, and the officer walk away.

Halfway into figuring out how to eat his first meal as a blind man, he heard a lot of boots stomp down the range and stop at his cell door. "Sanders! Cuff up!"

"Why?"

"What the hell did you do to your eyes?"

"Nothing. I'm doing a self-awareness experiment on how it is to be blind, so scoot off and let me be."

"We still need to check your eyes to make sure, so get over here and cuff up."

Damn, these bastards, he thought, as he reached the door and felt around for the slot. "You know, none of you worried about me getting stabbed up, but as soon as I patch up my eyes, you're all concerned."

After cuffing him, the officers opened his door, and a medical staffer stepped in and lifted the eye patches. "Where did you get these," he asked. Kevin explained they were left over from his injuries.

"What the hell?" said one CO.

"What's wrong with you?" asked another.

"Nothing's wrong with me. I told you I was doing a self-awareness experiment. Now give me the patches and run along."

The COs said he absolutely could not keep the patches and took the two he was wearing. But Kevin had more in his laundry bag. "Make sure you put a note up there that I'm blind for a week and to leave me be. I'm not hurt," he called after them. He applied two more patches and kept them in place with a bandanna.

The few things that used to occupy his time—drawing, writing letters, reading—were now impossible. He couldn't listen to music because Tiny's Aryan cellmate stole his MP3 player in the heat of their battle. He kept himself clean easily enough but didn't want to try shaving. And he ate his meals without difficulty. But mostly, he was alone with his thoughts more than he'd ever been. Surviving Tiny's dual knife attack weighed heavily, and he wondered what the future might hold.

On the fourth day, Kevin really wanted to rip off the eye patches because it was so itchy underneath. But he stayed disciplined and focused on listening. He could hear the COs sneak up on his cell and watch through the door. *They think I lost my marbles*, he guessed.

He persevered for seven whole days. When he finally removed his eye patches, he was surprised to see what a mess he'd made of his cell. As he cleaned and reorganized things, he started the second phase of his self-awareness experiment—wondering what it would be like if he couldn't talk. He figured that would be an easy test because he had no cellie and wasn't allowed out anyway.

As soon as the officers saw his eye patches were gone, they had many questions for him. "So, how was the blind experiment, Sanders?"

Kevin just shrugged.

"That bad, huh?" one CO said.

Kevin shook his head.

"Don't want to talk about it?" a second officer asked.

He shook his head no once more.

"Are you pissed off?"

He shook his head no again but also smiled.

The two officers looked at each other, and one said, "Hey, Sanders, listen, we didn't have anything to do with you getting stabbed. So don't take it out on us, okay?"

Kevin shrugged his shoulders with a head tilt that indicated okay.

The officers left, but a lieutenant soon appeared at his door. "Sanders, you alright?"

He shook his head yes.

"You planning to do something stupid?"

He shook his head no.

"Well, what the fuck you got going on, then?"

He shook his head no one more time and tried to keep from laughing.

"You're playing games, and I don't like this shit," the lieutenant said before leaving.

Kevin could have written on paper that he was conducting another experiment to ease their minds, but he thought, *fuck these assholes. A little stress in their lives should do them good.*

The next morning, "the head doctor" showed up at Kevin's cell door. "Mr. Sanders? Can I talk with you?" he said through the cell window.

Kevin was washing his face in the sink. He grabbed a towel, dried off, and just stared at him.

After a good spell of silence, the doctor said, "I know what you're going through. Here are some handouts on how to deal with stress." He slid some papers through the door's side crevice. Kevin did not move to retrieve them while staring at the doctor.

"Well, Mr. Sanders, I can see you don't want to be bothered, so I'll let you do your thing. I'm going to see if I can help you, though."

Really? thought Kevin as he snatched the papers from the door. *I could have used some help before I was stabbed up.*

Mid-way through his mute week, the COs started to ignore him. Then, after the 7th day, when Kevin started talking again, they gave *him* the silent treatment. *Sensitive assholes*, Kevin said to himself.

In a letter to Scott, he talked about not wanting to come out of the hole for fear of another hit. "That was a death shot, not a warning, Scott. The next time could be the last time," he said.

"It's a long way from paint on the jail wall. Now it's blood on the prison floor," he wrote. "But I'm still alive." And he noted one upside to the attempted murder that gave me chills. "I can say it's good for the book."

CHAPTER 29
NO GEM IN JUDGMENT

SUMMER 2014

USP Florence-High officials spent two months investigating Tiny's assault against Kevin, and their report had been filed at the end of January. But it took over half a year of legal wrangling before we could see those results.

The first Florence hit documents, as we called them, trickled in over the summer and were a bland compilation of the expected: Kevin's incident report about the stabbing, his DHO hearing report exonerating him for fighting because he was defending himself, and many memos by officers who witnessed the fight. But the assault video that Scott requested by subpoena was missing, and there was no mention of Tiny's motive.

The circumstantial case that the AB ordered Kevin's hit was overwhelming. But the guys were looking for something in writing to confirm this so Jack could add it to Kevin's sentencing memorandum. The Florence Prison legal center finally agreed to send the video plus another batch of documents they said they found related to the assault. They noted that batch would contain redactions to protect confidential informants.

However, weeks went by, and nothing was sent. At this point, Jack was bumping up against the deadline to submit the memo, as Kevin's sentencing was firmly on the judge's docket for late August.

Ultimately, under threat of Scott filing a motion to compel with the court, all the additional Florence hit docs and video arrived in Neil Galloway's office for Scott to pick up—ten days before sentencing.

Jim and I were in California on one of his business trips, and in anticipation of the doc reveal, I set my Blackberry to vibrate, ping, and flash purple when either of the guys texted or emailed. Right on cue, my pocket chimed and buzzed just after martinis were delivered to our table at a surfside gastro pub south of L.A. I excused myself from Jim and a trio of executives and walked out onto Sunset Beach with my phone and lemon drop cocktail in a paper cup. The moment did not disappoint.

Scrolling and pausing through the PDFs felt like reading that anonymous prison riot memo only tenfold. I could not believe what was on my phone. I was incredulous, not just over the content but also because the BOP actually turned this stuff over. The documents included the official investigative report and all of its backup material. As promised, much of it was heavily redacted.

Sitting in the sand and sipping from my to-go cup, I lingered over two intercepted inmate letters and a transcript of a recorded prison phone call—all threatening Kevin, either blatantly or in barely disguised code, for speaking out in his trial.

I couldn't wait to process it all before texting Scott and Jack. "Holy shit, guys! I was skeptical the BOP would ever deliver these golden nuggets … I can't imagine that video will be nearly as valuable as these docs."

"Chock full of diamonds bigger than cherries in a fruitcake. Lovely, lovely," Jack replied, saying he would add the whole lot as another appendix to the sentencing memo.

One key letter was written by an inmate at USP Canaan. It was included inside a letter to his girlfriend, with instructions for the girlfriend to pass it along to a [REDACTED] individual at another prison because inmates weren't allowed to write to each other.

"You asked about Kevin," the letter said. "In case you run into anyone who is confused about it, Kevin does not eat with us. I have no desire to make his life any more miserable than it is now, but there is no seat for him at the table. Period."

Another letter from an unnamed prison written by a Nazi Low Rider/AB associate to an NLR member (delivery method unclear) said, "I want to shoot you a brother's name. He is out of the Golden State and living in Colorado right now. [REDACTED] should get to work on Kevin real soon, but I don't have a way to get at him, so if you can, you might want to say hello."

The SIS in Canaan monitored a recorded phone call between one of their NLR inmates and an NLR at a halfway house. The transcription indicated that multiple inmates had seen Kevin's court filings that the caller described as "completely out of line" and said Kevin signed off on the "crazy shit" motions his attorneys filed. "We all read it. We don't care what anybody says, *it's* dead. That's all that needs to be said."

The letters were intercepted after Kevin's hearing when Prosecutor Galloway made him and Little Eagle name T-Rex on the stand. The phone call was placed after the trial concluded. Based on that letter and the phone call out of USP Canaan, Canaan's SIS unit informed USP Florence in writing that Kevin could face a possible threat if he were returned there due to his testimony—and that was the smoking gun Scott and Jack were looking for. Even the official Florence report couldn't deny Kevin's attempted murder was an AB retribution hit.

Later that night, at our Huntington Beach hotel, I re-read the docs on my computer—especially the pages I'd glossed over on the beach—and started taking notes. One that I missed gave me instant heartburn. It was a memo from Kevin's Florence counselor recapping the conference call with Scott, Kevin, and me in his office. The counselor wrote that we discussed Kevin's safety concerns and that Scott said he felt the judge had been vindictive in sending him back to Florence, where he knew he would be in harm's way. But this was the part that gave me acid reflux:

"There was another attorney on the phone with Mr. Powell ... I do not recall her name. She asked if I thought that the BOP let inmate Sanders get assaulted in the unit. I told her absolutely NOT! In defense of the BOP, I explained that we do extensive background checks to ensure the inmates' safety before placing them in any housing unit. She seemed to be fishing for something that would say we were negligent in placing inmate Sanders at USP Florence. I notified the SIS department of the conversation."

For fuck's sake. Yes, I was creeped out to read about myself in those pages (and for the record, I hadn't represented myself as anything, much less an attorney, to the counselor). But I was equally outraged to see the Florence SIS incompetence laid so bare—especially compared to their counterparts at USP Canaan, who gathered the intelligence and warned them in writing of the dangers Kevin faced. Not to mention, Florence officials heard this in great detail from Kevin himself at intake.

At that point, the only good thing I could say about USP Florence-High was that Kevin had finally earned his way out of there. After his time in the hole, he'd been moved to a secure tier where he completed the last two phases of the SMU program. All spring and summer, he sent me letters, drawings, and copies of psychology class certificates as he earned them: Understanding Yourself, Basic Cognitive

Skills, Feelings, Chemical Dependency, Quiet Moments, and Making Choices That Work, among others.

To celebrate the achievement, I sent Kevin the five-book series *A Song of Ice and Fire* by George R.R. Martin, adapted into HBO's *Game of Thrones*, which Jim and I started binging to see what all the fuss was about (fuss warranted). Kevin wrote me that they were the best books he'd ever read.

Soon, he'd take that boxed book set to his new home, an open-compound prison in Central Florida. The high-security USP was geared toward gang dropouts, high-profile inmates, and prisoners who were targets of violence. That last group included "kid touchers" or "CHOMOS" (child molesters), the brand of inmate most despised by fellow convicts. But first, Kevin had to return to Pennsylvania for his sentencing.

—

Jack completed the 3553 sentencing memo at Camp Walleye and attached all the mitigating documents in our arsenal. His appendices included copies of Kevin's excellent work performance review in Allenwood, a transcript of the Douglas County Prison CO who testified on his behalf, Kevin's SMU certificates, samples of his artwork, and copies of the Florence hit docs proving the AB tried to kill him—all to hopefully sway the judge toward leniency. Jack asked that Kevin be given a sentence in the 30–37-month range because of the duress he faced and because he was not the man with the shank in the cage that day.

The government's Presentence Report, on the other hand, contained two and a half pages of Kevin's voluminous institutional history, including many assaults and incidents of weapons possession, and suggested a sentence of between 8.3 to 10 years.

Jack was of the opinion that Kevin should not speak at his sentencing because any apology he might make would be a tacit admission of guilt, and we were seeking a retrial.

"And anything Kevin says *other than* an apology will be tantamount to pouring gas on a campfire. Spectacular, but it will make the room unpleasantly warm," he added.

This left Scott and me to try to convince Kevin not to *allocute* before the judge, which we attempted to do the night before on a visit to the Douglas County Prison. But we were unsuccessful.

The next day, after Jack pleaded his case for leniency, Kevin stood in his prison-issued khakis and addressed the court.

"I've done everything I can to try to move forward. I struggled. I tried," he told the judge. "Everything I did when I was with the gang, I was backed up, pushed against the wall. But I moved forward. I've completed the SMU program. I'm now able to be on an open yard where there are no gangs."

Kevin was close to breaking down, and I could feel my own throat swell, but he managed to finish with, "This is the only opportunity I have left. I come to you wholeheartedly. It's all I can say."

After Neil Galloway had his turn arguing for a harsher sentence, Judge Anderson began a long monologue leading up to the *fait accompli*. He mentioned Kevin's lengthy criminal history and called him a "career offender." And while he accepted the jury's verdict that Kevin had had no shank, he was convicted of aiding and abetting the crime nonetheless—a brutal and legally unprovoked assault upon an unarmed fellow inmate.

"I understand that from Mr. Sanders' perception he felt that it was necessary to take certain steps. The world inside prisons is not a world that I fully understand. However, I understand the law. The law is that you cannot, without legal justification, participate in an assault that results in an individual being stabbed 40 times. And that is the finding of the jury in this case after a full and fair trial."

The judge turned to *acceptance of responsibility* and said Mark Keys properly received credit from the government for admitting his guilt. "That's why we have acceptance of responsibility, to incentivize the defendants who are, in fact, guilty to face up to what they did," he said.

He reminded everyone that "we have had this case in our docket literally for years now." Still, he added, " I want to be clear on the record that even though ultimately the defense that Mr. Sanders proffered was unavailing, I do not in any way hold that against Mr. Sanders in sentencing him today."

I don't think any of us believed that statement for a millisecond.

"It is not the law of the jungle that prevails, although a jungle it may be in federal prison. We have to work with the law as we find it," he added before passing judgment.

"Pursuant to the Sentencing Reform Act of 1984 then, it's the judgment of this court that the defendant, Kevin Sanders, is hereby committed to the custody of the Bureau of Prisons to be imprisoned for a term of 84 months, to be served consecutively to any sentence which the defendant is currently serving."

I did some quick math while the judge talked about fines and restitution. He gave Kevin seven years—less than Prosecutor Galloway asked for but much more than Jack argued for.

Jack, in all his wisdom, had told us how this would play out, yet the rest of us still hoped against hope for more compassion from Anderson's bench.

Hours later, the three of us met with Kevin at DCP.

"I shouldn't have said anything," Kevin berated himself. "I should have listened to you guys."

"Kevin, Anderson already had his mind made up," Scott said. "Nothing you said or didn't say would have changed that."

Jack agreed and tried to make us all feel better. "This is federal court, where they hand out decades like parking tickets. Remember, sentencing is just a speed bump on the appeal highway."

CHAPTER 30
NOTORIOUS

I n early September, Kevin made his way in chains and cuffs down the retractable stairs of a prison transfer flight that landed in Orlando. The airplane was part of the Justice Prisoner and Alien Transportation System (JPATS) that flew about 375 inmates daily. However, JPATS, established in 1995, never caught on with the inmate crowd, but "Con Air," from the 1997 film *Con Air*, starring Nicholas Cage, did. Cage played an inmate on his way home after eight years in prison who got caught up in a prison flight hijacking—a scenario wholly removed from any drama that ever occurred on a JPATS flight but it made for a searing thriller and box office hit.

At the bottom of the stairs, Kevin, in his brown transfer uniform, got another pat-down by a U.S. marshal, including a search of his navy slip-on shoes. He joined other shackled inmates in different-colored jumpsuits from other prisons and jails, with facility names spelled out in bold black letters on their fronts and backs. Any inmate still in street clothes was coming to the feds for the first time.

After the rubdown, the marshal pointed him toward his bus, and Kevin shuffled off on the boiling tarmac to a row of buses, vans, and unmarked cars that encircled the plane. By the time he reached his designated bus, the Florida humidity had quickly drenched the top of his jumpsuit. A correctional officer, to whom he'd given his name and inmate number, told him, "Don't be looking around here. There's nothing for you to see." That was a true statement because the buses were blocking the view—the only things for Kevin to see were smug guards and chained-up inmates.

An old convict in an orange jumpsuit and white beard standing next to him grumbled in a New England accent, "Muthufucka, I'd like to give you something to see, ya fucking hack." Kevin turned to him and said, "Wouldn't we all, old timer." Before the CO could tell them to shut up, they faced the bus wall and kept busy with their thoughts.

Before boarding, each had to state their name and inmate number and keep the line moving. The old-timer was one step ahead of Kevin, and he told the CO that he was James Bulger. Kevin registered the name as Whitey Bulger, the infamous Boston mobster, and he kept his composure while taking a seat right next to him. *Ain't that something!* Kevin thought and couldn't believe his luck.

But an inmate in street clothes sitting behind them across the aisle caught Kevin's attention. He was Ricky Richardson, a guy Kevin had entered the feds with ten years ago and had just served with him at Lewisburg. Richardson ratted Kevin out to Lewisburg COs, telling them about his handcuff keys and stainless-steel knives—tools Kevin kept handy to prevent getting stabbed up in his cuffs. Richardson had squealed in exchange for some coffee and because he thought he could get away with it due to an upcoming release.

The first thing Kevin did after the bus pulled away was slip off his waist chain and call out the snitch, who hadn't noticed Kevin until then.

"Hey, Rat Richardson, looks like your punk ass can't stay out of the feds," he said, prompting a terrified look in return. While the guards weren't looking, Kevin held up his removed belly chain, tight between his hands, demonstrating how easy it would be to strangle him with it.

"No, Chico, you don't understand ..."

"I understand two things, fuckhead. Either you're going to stay away from me at Coleman, or I'm going to wrap this chain around your neck and turn my bid into life 'cause you're a no-good turd just taking up good air."

Everyone on the bus was watching to see how the conflict would play out. Richardson shook his head as if he understood, but to make sure, Kevin added, "Respect this, and you can walk. Cross me, and you know who I am."

Whitey took it all in and asked Kevin about *the rat*. After getting the backstory, he said, "If I were you, I'd kill the muthufucka. Just no place for a snitch like that."

Then he asked, "Hey kid, that move you got, ya know, the chain slip—how'd you pull that trick?"

"You got to be ready for anything in this fucking zoo, Old School," Kevin told him. "How is it I'm schooling you on this shit, and you're the infamous one here?" and they both laughed.

Kevin explained how he "slipped the rig" by pushing out his belly and leaning back with his "dick all in the way" when the chain was applied, making the CO unable to "sinch the bitch down good."

"Nice trick, kid. You sure you don't want to grease the rat?"

"Fuck no, you kidding?" Kevin said quietly. "I'm not doing no life for that lame. I just did the thirteen-and-a-half, Old School, no way."

"Thirteen and a half? What's that?"

"Really?" Kevin said, surprised the old convict wasn't up on the lingo. "The thirteen and a half is 12 jurors, one judge, and half a fucking chance."

Whitey roared with laughter, and they talked about how the mobster had gotten busted and ended up on that bus to Coleman II.

—

Whitey, who had just turned 85, was a notorious Irish-American mobster who got his nickname as a child because of his whitish blond hair. He started as a teenage gangster on the streets of Boston, graduating from forgery and assault and battery to loansharking, hijacking, and extortion. He eventually robbed banks, which landed him in some famous federal prisons, including Lewisburg, Atlanta, Alcatraz, and Leavenworth. In the 1970s, he joined Boston's Winter Hill gang and rose to become its leader, and for 15 years, he controlled most of South Boston's organized crime. Folklore suggested he was a Robin Hood of sorts, who gave generously to and protected his neighborhood, particularly in his early criminal career. But he was also known for his ruthless tactics and ability to evade law enforcement—a skill directly related to his controversial role as an FBI informant.

In 1975 Whitey agreed to work with the FBI to help take down a rival gang, but the relationship with his handler, Agent John Connolly, became corrupted. It was an unprecedented scandal for the FBI when decades of dirty deals were revealed. Before that, though, in 1995, Connolly tipped off Whitey about an upcoming indictment, prompting Whitey to flee to California with his girlfriend. The pair lived under assumed names for 16 years until an anonymous tip led to their dramatic capture in 2011. Around the same time as Kevin's trial, Whitey was tried in Boston and found guilty of 31 criminal charges, including participation in 11 murders. He was given two consecutive life sentences and sent to federal prison in Arizona.

Whitey, who always denied being a "rat" and instead considered the FBI to be his personal paid lackeys, spent eight months at USP Tucson. But he was abruptly moved to Coleman II after it was learned that he'd gotten favorable treatment there from a female psychologist. According to press reports, the psychologist arranged for him to have his own cell and lobbied for him to be allowed to write to his incarcerated girlfriend, Catherine Greig, in a Minnesota women's prison.

This famous gangster, now sitting next to Kevin and headed for Coleman II, had been the subject of countless books and some movies. Whitey was the inspiration for the character of Frank Costello, played by Jack Nicholson, in the 2006 Martin Scorsese film *The Departed*. And filming for a new biopic about him had just wrapped in Boston called *Black Mass*, starring Johnny Depp in the feature role. That film was set to premiere next fall. Whitey Bulger was about as high-profile of an inmate who existed in the feds on an open range, and whether his status would lean toward celebrity or pariah remained to be seen.

As he'd done periodically while listening to Whitey's recap of what landed him on that prison bus, Kevin looked behind him again at Richardson in his street clothes.

"Don't worry, I'll tell ya if Rat Boy gets up," Whitey said. "How are you gonna play it when the chains come off?"

"Any way he wants to swing it, Old Man. He knows how this can go." Then Kevin added, "I know you've been around the block a few, but there's a lot of young fuck heads in the feds now. So if you need some muscle, just ask for me, I'll help you out."

Whitey smiled and said he would be just fine. "Don't let the old man role fool you. I still got it ... But if it's my time, I'm ready to go."

Kevin thought that was a curious attitude, but then again, the old convict would dance with the Grim Reaper sooner versus later. Whitey was just being realistic about it, he guessed.

As with all the maximum-security federal prisons, inmates at Coleman II were double-bunked—each man had a cellmate, no exceptions. Twice, when prison officials tried to give Whitey a cellie, he told each of them, "I *will* kill you in your sleep. So go tell the cops you don't want to cell here because you'll end up dead."

And that's how, according to Kevin, Whitey got to cell alone.

CHAPTER 31
SECRETS

EARLY 2015

T he deadline for the appeal to the Third Circuit Court
was January 9th. So, like freshmen with a term paper
due, we started putting it together the week before. Kevin's
giant case file, with its myriad motions and briefs, already
contained the material, so it was a matter of repackaging
and laying out a persuading argument that Judge Anderson
erred at the trial court level. Chances of winning an appeal
from the three-member circuit court were as slim as winning
the case in district court, but the guys felt we had a pretty
good shot. We had to convince two of three appeals judges
of any of these four things: 1) that Tremblay's deposition
was *Brady* material the government failed to turn over, 2)
that Judge Anderson shouldn't have denied us our expert
witness, 3) that the judge shouldn't have denied us the two
letters written by Mark Keys, 4) and that the judge gave
Kevin an excessively long sentence.

We worked remotely by email, sending drafts with edits
and attachments back and forth. It was our great fortune that
Jack had done this before—and, in fact, had appealed once
to the U.S. Supreme Court—and Scott was eternally grateful
to have him take the lead. I organized and kept track of the

drafts while checking for grammar and typos, which I did on my laptop from my mother's condo in The Villages near Orlando.

With Jim on a week-long business trip, our oldest son in the workforce, and our college student son skiing, I happily escaped Philadelphia in January for a working vacation to see my mother. And I would also see Kevin at USP Coleman II, only 12 miles from her home in central Florida.

My mother, Marilyn Parello, was delighted to have me all to herself for most of a week. She fussed over the linens in her spare bedroom and served us sun tea on the lanai. Her two Shih Tzus, Ozzie and Harriet, were excited about having company, too, but remained dutifully by her side. She and my father had moved to the retirement mecca more than 30 years ago to be close to her parents. My grandparents started out there as Pennsylvania snowbirds in the late 1970s and then permanently joined the conglomerate of planned over-55 communities that later became known as The Villages.

Marilyn knew Scott and my Diners Club besties well because she'd been our freshman English teacher. Scott always gave her credit for whipping his ass into shape at the end of high school to raise his GPA just enough that he could get into the local community college, and eventually accepted to Michigan and the University of Alabama law school.

In his version of the story, midway through our junior year, my mom asked him to stay after one of her study halls, where he usually either read *Time* magazine or played cards with some of the others. In a private conversation, she asked him how many study halls he had. She already knew his GPA was hovering just below 2.0.

"Scotty, do you want to be a goddamn coal truck driver the rest of your life? Or do you want to use the brain God gave you and make something of yourself?"

She wouldn't take no for an answer and immediately moved him into an AP English class. They revised his schedule together, and for a little while, she became his de facto academic advisor, helping him raise his GPA to a decent 3.0 at graduation.

Our parents socialized regularly at card clubs, dinners out, and the like, and my mother and Scott's mom, Joanne, were very dear friends. Sipping iced tea on her back patio, I asked my mother if she would have taken as much interest in Scott's academics if she hadn't loved Joanne so much.

"Possibly not? Probably not? That's sad to say, isn't it?" She reached for her pack of Newports and a lighter. Marilyn lit up and took a deep drag, carefully blowing the smoke she knew I hated away from me. "But Bill and Joanne were at their wit's end with him."

"You mean over his grades?"

"Well, of course, that was part of it. His sweet sister Pam was an angel in comparison. Straight As, basketball star, never worried them a day in her life."

"Say more," I prodded, adding sugar to another glass of tea.

"Well, he just got into trouble a lot, you know that. He was always cutting class. There was the drinking ..."

"Everyone drank in high school, Mom."

"And the epilepsy. They were beside themselves ..."

"What?" I interrupted.

"Yes. Bill and Joanne drove him everywhere to see specialists for a couple of years. They went to Scranton, down to Philadelphia..."

"Wait, what?" I said incredulously.

"Oh, that's right. This would have been in middle school while he and Pam were at the Catholic school. You didn't know him then, honey."

"Still, I can't believe I didn't know that about him *later*, Mom."

"Well, why would anyone advertise that, Carla?" she countered. "His condition resolved in high school. But his parents were deathly afraid of him getting his driver's license, I remember that."

I searched my memory for images of Scott behind the wheel of that funky red Renault Le Car he and Pam used to tool around in. They both drove it, I decided.

"And then there was the pot. Joanne once found a baggie of it in his room and called me crying."

"No!"

"Yes. I told her to flush it down the toilet."

"Oh my God. How did I not know *this* story?"

My mother shrugged and smiled through a smoky haze.

"Okay, I see your pot story and raise you this—did you know Scott gave me my first joint ever?"

Her mouth almost dropped to the ground.

"We were in 10th grade, and it was on one of your pinochle nights. Somehow, I ended up down at the river with him, and he introduced me to *mar-i-juana*," I annunciated for effect. "I coughed and gagged all over the place. But he was so sweet. He pretended not to notice that I didn't know what I was doing."

"Carla Jean!" my mother found her voice. "I thought I raised you better than that!" But then she burst into hysterics, and we laughed until tears formed. She dabbed her eyes and got up abruptly, saying she wanted to show me something, and disappeared inside. She returned with a color photograph of her with Joanne. It was taken in the early 2000s in front of a restaurant when Scott's folks came to see my parents and check out The Villages. Their heads touched with their arms around each other, and their smiling, more youthful faces squinted in the sun. They wore short haircuts, matching lipstick, and different flower-embroidered tops.

My mom said the photo was taken about a year after Joanne's bladder cancer surgery. I snapped a picture of it and texted it to Scott.

"You know that white afghan on your pull-out sofa? Joanne crocheted that for me when we left Douglasville. I want to be buried in it."

"Really?" I said, looking up from typing on my phone.

"Really."

"Well, there goes Tony's and my plan to cremate you, then," I said, finishing my text to Scott where I reported that my mother said "hi" plus her burial wishes.

"Pause, change of thought," my mother said. "When we go to Tony's, please don't bring up Obama or politics of any kind."

"Mom! What on Earth ..."

"He's very angry these days. Fox News is on every time I go over there. I can't stand it."

"Well, no wonder ..."

"Just promise me, Carla."

"Mom. I think I know my own brother. But I'm not going to pick a fight. I just want to enjoy an afternoon at the pool with my niece and nephew."

—

The next day, I drove the short distance to the Coleman penitentiary complex over my mother's misgivings ("What has Scotty dragged you into?" she demanded). I briefly panicked in the parking lot until I felt the front of my bra, having wholly forgotten Jack's warning not to wear an underwire one unless I wanted a very handsy pat-down after tripping a metal detector. I was good; no underwire today.

Kevin had been at Coleman II for four months and had settled into life on an open *gen pop* (general population) range without organized gangs. He had access to sports like basketball, softball, football, and soccer, but mostly, he liked running around the track or hitting the exercise bikes and equipment. But he really enjoyed this new thing called *email,* which gave him immediate access to his legal team via me. We knew the Bureau monitored all emails—as they did with letters and phone calls—so Kevin and I often corresponded in code. I chose to write under the name "Angela Lansbury" as a tribute to the actress who portrayed a mystery writer and amateur detective in the 1980s-90s TV series *Murder She Wrote.* Kevin, who was too young to get the reference, went along and called me "Gela" for short.

We met in a private conference room for the legal visit that Jack arranged and hugged hello. I explained how we'd all worked on the appeal that week from different locations on our computers, and he repeated an endearing refrain about how honored he was that we believed in him that much.

"But you do need to know that the chances of the Third Circuit overturning Judge Anderson are exceedingly low," I reminded him. "I think the statistics are even worse than winning in district court." Kevin said he understood, but I knew he was pinning his hopes on us.

We talked about his cellmate, Ricky Richardson, someone he'd known in Lewisburg, and he told me about how he had ratted him out in Lewisburg.

"Why would you want to cell with him?" I asked.

"You know what they say, 'Keep your friends close but your enemies closer,'" and he gave me a devilish grin.

I asked about Whitey Bulger, and Kevin said, "He don't like that name, he wants to be called *Jimmy,*" and that they often spent time together jawboning. He said Jimmy got pushed around in a wheelchair by a couple of white gang dropouts, although it was just for show, he didn't need the chair, but he napped in it sometimes. Jimmy told him about getting experimented on with LSD in the Atlanta Federal Penitentiary in the 1960s in exchange for having his bank robbery sentence reduced. It was some kind of secret CIA program that left him with night terrors for the rest of his life. He could only fall asleep with the light on and didn't sleep for more than a few hours at a time.

Jimmy was running a side business of signing old black-and-white photos of himself to put money on his books, and Kevin offered to get me an autographed mugshot.

We said our goodbyes, and I told him I would visit again when I came down to see my mother and brother. In the meantime, we'd email and wait for the decision from the Third Circuit Court.

—

Back at my mother's condo, I Googled "Whitey Bulger and LSD experiments" and learned that he had indeed been part of a Cold War mind-control program called MK-Ultra that ran from the early 1950s to the early 1970s. It seemed the CIA, fearing they were losing ground to the Soviets in thought-control interrogation methods, were at first trying to come up with a truth serum to be used against Soviet spies and prisoners of war.

MK-Ultra expanded its goal to manipulate and control human behavior using various techniques, including administering massive doses of LSD and other psychedelic drugs, hypnosis, isolation, sensory deprivation, electrocution, and other forms of physical and psychological torture.

It operated throughout various college campuses, hospitals, research centers, and prisons on unwitting subjects with no agency, including Canadians and others throughout the world. Test subjects included mental health patients, terminal cancer patients, sex workers, drug addicts, and prisoners like Whitey, who thought they were volunteering to help find a cure for schizophrenia. Over 18 months in the Atlanta prison, Whitey and other inmates were injected with massive doses of LSD on a weekly basis, reportedly more than 50 times. This left Whitey with life-long anxiety, nightmares, and violent hallucinations that he'd been very vocal about.

The military intelligence goal of MK-Ultra was to instill amnesia, shock, and confusion in an individual who could then withstand torture and coercion and even kill another person.

Due to the paranoia of the early 1970s Watergate scandal, the CIA ordered the destruction of all MK-Ultra files. But a 1974 *New York Times* article on the secret brainwashing program launched a congressional investigation. Enough documents survived the purge, and a report the following year revealed the appalling human experiment to the public for the first time. Program overseers eventually admitted it had failed to produce the military mind control weapon they sought.

Untold numbers of test subjects—Hundreds? Thousands? It wasn't clear—were left with psychological and emotional distress, and cognitive and functional impairment. Many survivors were still seeking compensation.

It was unbelievable, and yet not. This was no conspiracy theory. A shadowy sect of the American government really had spent tax dollars illegally and unethically in search of a *Manchurian Candidate*, with no thought of consequences or concern about the well-being of their unsuspecting guinea pigs.

CHAPTER 32
SLINGSHOTS

MID-2015

S hortly after Scott filed the appeal—all 1,800 pages that absurdly had to arrive at the court building bound and printed—Scott called to say he was fed up with trying to make a living in private practice. He'd been looking to join a law firm and working on the appeal had been his last official task as Kevin's attorney. He already talked to Jack, who agreed to stay on as Kevin's attorney if *I agreed* to help him with a new trial—*if* the Third Circuit granted our appeal. "Of course, I will," I said.

Scott's father's health was slipping, and he wanted to stay within driving distance of Douglasville, so he was primarily looking at firms in Philadelphia, Harrisburg, and Pittsburgh.

"I need a change," he said. "There's nothing left for me here." And that included Lucy—their on-again, off-again relationship was off for good. Also, his sullen teenage daughter Ashley preferred the company of her newly remarried mother. I got it. I heard the weariness in his voice. And I also knew that Kevin's case, the way it dragged on for years as Scott pushed through and fought the system, played a large role in his decision.

Scott sent Kevin a thoughtful letter of explanation, promising to stay in touch and saying he'd always be his friend. He also said he'd been holding his breath on the Third Circuit, "knowing full well that they could write one of the greatest decisions on *Brady* in the history of federal jurisprudence, or they could say that inmates don't have a right to a justification defense. If it is the latter, remember that *fair* is a weather report and do what you need to do to survive."

—

That spring, Kevin wrote me that his younger brother Martin died of a drug overdose. He'd had a stroke on his front lawn, worn out from years of alcohol and drug abuse. Only 18 months younger than Kevin, the two were best friends and had grown up together until Kevin was hauled to juvenile detention for street crimes and petty thefts. It was a devastating loss, and Kevin told me that he'd be "checking out" in solitude for a while.

I sent him Malcolm Gladwell's book *David and Goliath: Underdogs, Misfits, and the Art of Battling Giants*, which discussed adversity's role in shaping our lives. When he resumed our correspondence, he said it helped him cope with his brother's death.

In one letter, he told me that while Coleman II didn't have active gangs, it was still a violent place, much of which was drug-related. He guessed that 80 percent of the inmates were either strung out on prison wine, a synthetic marijuana called Spice, or a new drug, Suboxone. Suboxone was a Schedule III drug that physicians prescribed to help fight opioid withdrawal symptoms, and it was smuggled in invisibly on corner pages of legal documents. The dealers who controlled the supply could get $10 for a tiny piece of paper the size of half a pinky fingernail (paid in books of stamps) that the inmates licked to get high.

I looked forward to Kevin's long letters filled with stories for the book and the artwork he sometimes enclosed. One drawing he sent me on cardboard was religious in nature. It depicted a crucified Christ and the weeping Virgin Mary with prayerful hands and a delicate rose. The words *Conti Family—in his love, they are blessed* rounded out the sketch.

Another drawing couldn't have been more opposite in tone, yet it was the same gesture of appreciation. It was an untitled black and white drawing on a handkerchief that I dubbed *Sexpot with Slingshot*. It featured a buxom and scantily clad fairy with wings in platform boots (one of which partly concealed a knife) pulling back a slingshot. A tiny gremlin was the ammunition, and other gremlins and cute toadstools surrounded the pointed-eared, plump-lipped fairy. I winced when I first saw it until I decided it represented me figuratively as an advocate and not literally.

He told me he was thinking about getting his high school equivalency certificate, and naturally, I encouraged him. Each time he passed a class, I'd send him a book. He particularly liked the recent bestseller *Just Mercy: A Story of Justice and Redemption* by Bryan Stevenson, a lawyer's memoir of fighting the wrongfully convicted on death row.

—

Scott and I were still on Jack's stupid email list, and once in a while, one would slip through my auto-filer and remind me why I'd set it up in the first place, such as this one from May 1st: "Hoo-ray, hoo-ray for the first of May, outdoor fucking starts today!"

Scott emailed us both progress reports on his job interviews. By summer, he had a second one scheduled in

Pittsburgh. One week, Scott said that he'd gotten a letter from Steven Tremblay, the rec cage victim, who was trying to reach me about the book I was supposed to be writing but was really just building a database for. My excuse was that the Third Circuit was taking too long—were we, or were we not, getting a retrial? How could I possibly write a book if I was going to help Jack with a new trial?

"No news is good news," Jack said about the circuit court's silence. "Turning down an appeal is easy. We may yet get turned down, but we've made 'em think, and that, in and of itself, is a victory."

Before I reached out to him, Steven Tremblay found me through my Facebook author page, so he and I exchanged a few messages that summer. He emailed from his mother's computer in Canada, where he'd been deported after his release from Victorville six months ago. He wanted to contribute to the "wonderful true story" I was writing and believed that Kevin's self-defense case was the truth. "I can't believe we have the chance to expose everything that's being documented by yourself," he wrote. "All of us who are willing to fight are being given the chance to win."

Oh my God, did I feel guilty for the minimal progress I'd made on that book so far.

Steven and I set up a phone call, which I kicked myself later for not recording, but I'd taken careful notes. He was in his early 30s and living on government disability in Ontario near his parents.

He was open about his physical and mental health struggles. He said he'd been going through a psych episode preceding the rec cage fight due to the prison withholding his antidepressant medication. He'd been taking Trazodone (along with migraine medicine and an allergy nasal spray), but the Trazodone had been stopped abruptly with no explanation, causing him to hallucinate, he said. His behavior spiraled, and he lashed out at officers and cellmates, earning him a temporary solo cell. He asked to be put back on Trazodone but was denied.

The weekend before the Monday rec cage assault, Steven stopped up his toilet so that his wastewater filtered down into T-Rex's cell. COs discovered Steven in his cell amid filth and rotten food, covered in feces, and not making any sense.

That was his condition a day before he was placed in the rec cage with Kevin and Arson.

Steven's story correlated to his Lewisburg medical records that we'd been given at trial, including a suicide attempt a month after the rec cage fight. One report, dated two weeks after the cage fight, stated, "Inmate states he is very hot living on the third floor. He feels like he is going to fall out and his feet are numb. He states he feels dizzy. Started a new medication today as well. Requests to be put on suicide watch because it will be so hot."

Three weeks after that, medical staff responded to Steven's cell because he'd tied part of a bed sheet through the vent over the cell door and wrapped the other end around his neck. But the final assessment of that report stated, "No Significant Findings/No Apparent Distress ... follow up at sick call as needed." Two days later, he was four-pointed.

I asked Steven about the suicide attempt, and he said, "I honestly don't remember doing it. I was in such a psychotic state."

Steven said he still suffered from a lot of back and nerve pain from the rec cage assault and had turned to street drugs/painkillers to cope. But he didn't hold his injuries or the assault against either Kevin or Mark Keys, reiterating what he said in his deposition. "They had to do it. T-Rex was yelling out the window with everyone else," he said.

Without being specific, I asked if Kevin indicated Steven shouldn't have been put in the cage that day. Steven described Kevin waving his flat hand back and forth under his chin. Steven also said he heard Kevin tell CO Shemp not to put him in the cage.

And then he surprised me by backing up Kevin's story that Kevin didn't have a knife, saying all his injuries were on the side Mark Keys was stabbing him from.

"But in your civil suit, and even your deposition, you said both Kevin and Mark had knives and stabbed you," I said.

"Well, I maybe wasn't as clear about things then. But I never saw Kevin with a knife and didn't get any stab wounds on that side … plus I told this to the FBI. Twice," he added.

"You told this to the FBI?"

"Yeah, two different times they came to see me to ask me to testify for the government's case …"

"In Kevin's trial? Do you remember their names? Was it one or two agents?" I interrupted.

"No, I can't think who it was, but it was the same man both times … so I told him that there was no way I was going to testify for them and that they should be investigating MacDonald, who set up the rec cage fight to begin with."

A knot in my stomach twisted with this new information, and I asked him to pause so I could catch up on my notes.

I asked him why MacDonald set up the cage fight, and he gave me the same version of the snowball story I'd heard from Kevin, right down to Steven kicking the Captain in the groin to the cheers of on-lookers and MacDonald's line, "Who around here can I put you in a cage with?"

"Why did you throw the snowball at him that day?" I asked.

"Because he's just a evil person, likes hurting people."

"You mean at Big Sandy?" I said, referencing an incident he recounted in court documents.

He said that MacDonald, a lieutenant at Big Sandy, was on a power trip and four-pointed him for complaining about sexual harassment coming from a female prison counselor. Steven said he'd been taken to a basement, put into paper clothes, and four-pointed on a gurney. Then, a female officer, under MacDonald's orders, used some device to send electric shocks through his big toe and testicles. He remembered vividly MacDonald laughing and saying, "I'm turning you into a girl."

My head was spinning, and I asked for another pause to capture his quotes. Before we hung up, he asked if I knew anyone who would take over his civil suit against Lewisburg Prison. Steven had been trying to represent himself in the case but was missing filing deadlines. He'd petitioned the district court twice to be appointed a lawyer but was denied. Steven wondered if either of Kevin's lawyers could be persuaded to take on his case, and I told him frankly that Kevin was down to one attorney now who didn't have the resources as a one-man operation.

"Okay. Well, if Kevin gets another trial, I would testify for him. Tell the lawyer," he said. "But, also, I'm not allowed back into your country, so you guys would have to figure that out."

I thanked him for his time and willingness to help and promised to let him know when the book came out.

—

"It never fails to astonish me how much useful information and exonerating testimony one uncovers AFTER the damned trial is over and AFTER the client is convicted and sentenced," Jack said after I emailed a recap of my conversation to him and Scott.

In a retrial, Jack was very interested in having Steven testify for us by video now that he knew how it would go. We would also subpoena both FBI 302 reports that the mystery government agent would have had to file after meeting with Steven twice to try and get him to testify against Kevin. And, of course, we would have time to track down and subpoena Captain MacDonald, ambush him, so to speak, with the snowball incident, and lay out a case for vengeance. "It would be finer than frog's hair if one of these reports mentions the snowball," he said.

Jack, who described himself as a "cautious optimist," felt extra hopeful about our chances that summer. He thought if we were granted a retrial, AUSA Galloway might favor a quick and easy plea of Kevin's "time served" versus enduring another week-long trial with our expert witness, new evidence, Steven Tremblay testifying for us, etc., especially since Galloway was close to retirement.

Jack typed out these sunny thoughts in his first letter to Kevin as his official counsel of record. While stating that the appeals court "hates granting new trials," Jack opined that our brief was "making them sweat" and "they couldn't just dismiss us." Then he talked about which judge he thought might get the retrial (it wouldn't be Anderson), said he'd ask Galloway for "time served," and then wondered where Kevin would go to live after his release.

Goddamnit, Jackson. Really? I was livid that he filled Kevin with such hope. I toned down my complaint in Scott's, Jack's, and my email thread, where Jack replied, "Well, the guy could use some cheering up."

He said the odds were better than 9 in 10 that the appeal would be denied, but then again, the briefs were submitted six months ago and they usually issued denials quickly. "It IS a good case. It IS a good brief. I did the best I could to warn him about their prejudice against Appellants. If he's happy for a few days, well, okay."

CHAPTER 33
REVELATIONS

LATE 2015

In August, Scott joined a small firm of criminal defense attorneys just outside of Pittsburgh. He was hoping to try murder cases but soon realized he'd have to prove himself first with mundane drug, fraud, and DUI files like a first-year associate. But at least he wasn't chasing ambulances, fracking cases, or handling invoices and begging to be paid.

He bought a cute bungalow with a covered porch just minutes from his office and reconnected with Gordo and Leroy, our two Pittsburgh Diners Club members. The three started meeting for drinks in the Strip District on Fridays after work, and Scott settled into a new life with familiar faces. But by September, he had an unexpected roommate.

With little warning, Brad—my high school boyfriend and alcoholic member of our Diners Club—arrived on a bus from New Jersey. He couldn't drive because he'd lost his car and his license; he'd just been released from another 90-day jail term for driving drunk despite the license suspension. Countless stints in rehab and religious-based counseling hadn't saved his marriage or his job as a government intelligence contractor. He'd lost his security clearance and been out of work for over a year. After his divorce, he moved in with his parents, who retired down South. But his mother was on his case all the time about his drinking, he said, and he asked Scott if he could come to Pittsburgh for a little while so he could get back on his feet.

It was immediately clear that Brad had no intention of drying out. While Scott was at work, Brad wasn't job searching; he was just day drinking. Gordo and Leroy were supportive, but their get-togethers were now awkward. Even if it was a Pirates game where drinking wasn't the main focus, Brad always over-indulged. The two of them finally stepped back from the gatherings because it was too painful to watch Brad's self-destruction, too sad to remember the once bright, promising young man who'd been such a good friend in high school back when he seemed to have it all.

—

Brad was the baby of four brothers, born into a moderately religious Catholic family. Athletic and good-looking like his siblings, he was an honor student and track and football star. (All of us who later formed The Diners Club were academic athletes, except for Scott, whose high school career included playing the drums for one year and starring in two musicals). Brad and I started going together in our junior year. We made for a pretty couple walking hand-in-hand down the hallways, he in a football jersey, I in my cheerleading skirt and sweater, with his class ring on a chain around my neck.

As I'd told my mother, everyone I hung out with in high school did a fair amount of drinking. I learned my lesson in 10th grade by consuming way too much cherry vodka one night and throwing it up in a snowbank next to my front door before stumbling in by curfew. In my impaired state, I hadn't covered up the red, splotchy evidence, which my father discovered the following day. To my surprise, my parents didn't ground me because they figured my massive hangover was punishment enough. And they were right.

Never wishing to repeat the experience, I drank very little from that point on and was often the designated driver among our friends before anyone gave that a label. I recall at least one time wresting the keys away to Brad's Trans Am and the drunken idiots I drove home praising my father for teaching me to drive a stick shift.

Few high school romances last—our Pam and Russ were an exception. Whatever path Brad and I were on took a sharp turn at the end of our junior year when my parents moved my younger brother Tony and me to Florida. It was a tearful and melodramatic transition for me, leaving my small town and the bosom of my friends and boyfriend for my senior year at a sprawling, humid high school ten times the size of Douglasville High. That next year, Brad and I flew to see each other several times, wrote gushy teenage love letters back and forth, and rang up expensive long-distance phone charges.

We kept it going—sort of. We both dated other people but stayed in touch, and Brad even got accepted into a Central Florida college. But by then, I didn't feel the same way about him anymore.

Before Brad's divorce, he called me in response to an email I'd sent him urging him to get treatment for his alcoholism. It was part of a Diners Club campaign, an e-mail/phone call intervention of sorts. I told him he owed it to his kids to get help, but he denied there was any problem to fix. And, sadly, he chose to tell me this on the phone.

"I loved you with my whole heart," he told me, obviously drunk.

"We were kids, Brad," I said and tried to circle back to him getting help for his drinking.

"Carla, I loved you with my whole heart," he repeated, and I replied only, "I know." Then, I ended the call as graciously as I could.

Florida grew on me. I managed to enjoy my senior year of high school, and I graduated from a well-known state university with a journalism degree. A few weeks before getting that diploma, I met Jim on a bar stool at a Bennigan's. He had graduated as an engineer from Penn State two years previously and was on a new assignment for Westinghouse. He only walked into that eatery and sat next to me because a friend who was supposed to visit him had missed his flight. No airline mishap, no Carla and Jim, we would later say when asked the proverbial question of how we had met.

Not long into our relationship, Jim and I discovered we had someone in common. My Douglasville High classmate Eric, our fearless class president and a founding member of The Diners Club, had also been one of Jim's fraternity brothers at Penn State. And that's when I realized the world was small and that my universe was a mystifying mashup of luck and fate that only a fairy godmother could explain.

I never went to a single reunion from my Florida high school. Instead, I stayed connected to the Douglasville High crowd, especially after a handful of corporate relocations when Jim and I landed in Philadelphia. Over the years, I think we all forgot that I hadn't actually graduated with them.

—

As October approached, Scott said he was planning to visit his dad during Apple Fest and that he'd be driving to Douglasville with Brad. Leroy and Gordo were coming too, and so were his sister Pam and her husband Russ. I hadn't seen anyone other than Scott in three years, so I booked the only room I could find at a Hilton amid the big box stores near the highway exit. The four guys from Pittsburgh booked their rooms there, too. Eric, in Wisconsin, couldn't make it, and we promised to eat a platter of apple fritters in his honor.

Six of us—Scott, Leroy, Gordo, Pam, Russ, and I—walked the length of Main Street, stopping for funnel cakes or ice cream as the din of laughter and carnival rides swirled around us. Brad chose to sit alone on a bar stool at the edge of town.

We talked about how unwell he looked, what a saint Scott was for taking him in, and what his future might hold. Scott said he'd been in touch with one of Brad's brothers about coming to get him because Brad wasn't capable of establishing an independent professional life in Pittsburgh, or anywhere, for that matter. Brad had worn out his welcome and even began picking fights with Scott.

"Carla, he accused me of bringing you into my criminal case so I could sleep with you."

"Oh my God," I said, shaking my head because I had no other words.

"Yeah, he thinks I'm the reason you two broke up in high school," he added, to which I repeated, "Oh my God!" even louder. "Such revisionist history."

"He never got over you," Gordo chimed in. Pam seemed to want to agree, but I snapped, "That's not true!

"I know for a fact he and Susan were *very* happy—until they weren't, of course. But ..."

"Let's face it, Susan is no Carla," Scott said.

"Nope, nope, nope, none of this is true," I protested. There was no delicate way of escaping the belief that I had broken a heart while dodging a bullet.

At the end of the weekend, after Leroy, Gordo, Pam, and Russ had left, Brad crawled off his bar stool and joined Scott and me for a last Sunday night hurrah before heading home Monday. We shared a booth at a brewery, and Scott disappeared to get drinks for us and a soda for Brad. I hadn't been alone with Brad all weekend, and sitting there was dismal, waiting for Scott to return.

Brad sensed my discomfort and slurred, "Don't worry, he'll be back." I pretended not to understand.

"The knight in shining armor, the *protector*, the *lawyer*, he will return to claim his prize," he continued dramatically.

"His prize?" I said sarcastically.

Brad raised his glass and nodded at me like I was the prize.

"You're shitfaced and don't know what you're talking about," I said and thought about getting up and leaving.

"But you don't know ..." his slurring continued. "You don't know."

I kept looking at the packed bar of festival-goers, hoping to see Scott carrying beverages.

"Don't you want to know what you don't know that you know?"

"No, I don't. This was a bad idea, and I'm going back to the hotel." I started to gather my coat and purse, but Brad reached for my arm and wouldn't let go.

"He is our wounded *hero*," Brad said, letting out a belch.

"Get off me," I demanded and jerked my arm free.

"Carla, Carla, Carla, Carla, Carla," he slurred. "Listen. For real. Scotty was hurt at the Catholic school."

"Wait, what?"

"In sixth and seventh grade," he said, looking toward the bar to see if he had time to reveal more. Then he whispered, "The science teacher used to take him into the supply closet and make him *do things.* "

I sat there paralyzed, unblinking, with my mouth open, and he added, "Terrible things. Sexual things." He downed the rest of his beer, wiped his mouth, and put a finger to his smug lips. "Shhhhhhhh. No one else knows ... except his sister."

Then he put his head down on his arms on the table and closed his eyes as if the mission to violate Scott's privacy had worn him out.

I had no time to process what had come out of Brad's mouth because Scott finally returned with the drinks. But when he saw his passed-out roommate, he said he should call it a night and get Brad to bed. I volunteered to help.

Back at the hotel, we unloaded Brad onto one of their beds, and I tried to catch my breath. Tears trickled down my cheeks, and I didn't even try to stop them.

"Oh, Carla, it's okay," Scott assured me. "He goes to bed like this almost every night."

I hugged Scott and let him think Brad was the cause of my heartache when, really, I was sobbing for an innocent, curly-haired boy who suffered unspeakable harm inside a closet in the town's Catholic school.

CHAPTER 34
DISTRACTIONS

2016

After almost one year of waiting, we finally had our answer from the Third Circuit Court of Appeals—no relief. There would be no retrial. The three-member panel affirmed every decision Judge Anderson made. In other words, they found the judge hadn't abused his discretion in denying us our expert witness, the Mark Keys letters we wanted to use, or in sentencing Kevin to seven years. And they said the Tremblay deposition wasn't *Brady* material, that Prosecutor Galloway didn't know about it to turn it over.

Statistically speaking, we shouldn't have been surprised, but we had all started to buy into Jack's optimism as 2015 dragged on without word. The decision came down two days before Christmas, and I copied and pasted the entire six-page judgment in an email to Kevin with the team's heartfelt condolences.

I had ordered two book sets for him that arrived between Christmas and New Year's (Stieg Larsson's *Girl with the Dragon Tattoo* series and the *Hunger Games* trilogy by Suzanne Collins). However, the first week in January ended with no email reply to either the court decision or the books, which was unlike him. After another week of radio silence, I asked Jack to call Coleman II for an explanation.

Jack learned that Kevin failed a drug urinalysis test the day before the appeals decision occurred and had been sent to the SHU with no email privileges. When he was released three weeks later, he told me a story about his cellie Ricky Richardson having "set him up" by placing Suboxone in his shoes. But also, he said, COs must have known the appeals court decision was coming and were worried about his reaction to it, and so concocted a "dirty urinalysis" to place him in the SHU as a preventative measure. Neither story made sense to me, but I didn't question it, knowing the court order had been a gut punch for him.

Plus, I had to deliver more bad news by relaying Jack's opinion that the case didn't contain the kind of overarching legal principle—a broad public policy or conflict between circuit courts—that would make the U.S. Supreme Court take it up and, therefore, another appeal would be a waste of effort and hope.

Kevin emailed back that his cellie Richardson had sold all of his property while he'd been in the SHU—his art supplies, books, tennis shoes, etc.—to repay a drug debt and that Richardson asked to be put into the SHU for protection when Kevin was released. "This prison is the worst I've ever been in," he told me. "There is no structure or shot-callers to keep assholes from doing crazy things. It's all a test. Tell Jack and Scott that I don't want to do no more court, just ride it out and get this over. I got to go eat."

—

Now that his criminal case was fully adjudicated, I supposed it was time to revise the book proposal—with the short name *Under Duress*—and reach out to the West Coast literary agent who expressed interest at that NYC writer's conference. But that had been three and a half years ago. Would she even remember me? Could she sell a book about an inmate battling prison gangs and corruption who'd lost his trial and still had five years left to serve?

Regardless, I decided that if I were going to write that book, I needed to keep my lines of communication flowing with Kevin. Despite earning meager wages for sweeping up the prison compound, he often didn't have enough money on his books to pay for email and expensive phone calls to me, which brightened his days. So I started wiring him a modest monthly stipend by Western Union so we could communicate and he could shop at the commissary. He was almost embarrassingly appreciative, mainly because he stopped having to resort to side hustles, like tattooing other inmates, for needed funds. If he'd been caught with a tat gun, that could have set him back from his now-2021 release.

Also, for my book purposes, I wanted to record our phone calls. I switched from an iPhone to an Android for an automatic recording app that dumped the calls into cloud storage. Jack lectured me on one- and two-party state rules, telling me that Pennsylvania was a two-party consent state, meaning I had to have explicit permission to record someone during a private conversation. Of course, Kevin was agreeable, and I told Jack, "If the BOP is recording all my calls with Kevin, I can sure as hell do the same."

—

I'd been a news junkie ever since my college journalism classes. Later, as a newspaper reporter, the disorder magnified, leading to a lifetime of choosing National Public Radio over music in the car and working at home with cable news on in the background.

Jim tolerated my habit when he was home, and the third weekend of January was no exception. The Mid-Atlantic and East Coast were hit with a historic blizzard dubbed *Snowmageddon,* and we stayed indoors all weekend watching the 2016 presidential election coverage. Hillary Clinton and Bernie Sanders were the last two remaining Democrats vying for that nomination, while 17 Republican hopefuls had winnowed down to four. However, at that point, most of the GOP's primary endorsements were going to TV reality star Donald Trump. The 69-year-old New York businessman, always wearing heavy orange pancake makeup and a sprayed-in-place blond combover, yammered comically about policies he had no intellect for.

From the moment he descended a golden escalator at New York's Trump Tower to announce his candidacy, he blathered, bullied, and bragged his way into free media advertising and my family room. One of his stunning quotes included deriding Arizona Senator and Vietnam prison of war hero John McCain because "I like people who weren't captured." Another doozy was him saying Mexicans were rapists who brought their drugs and crime into our country but that "some, I assume, are good people." He also wanted to ban Muslims from coming into the U.S. In six months, Trump had become a fantastical gift to late-night comedians and news organizations, which used his imbecilic soundbites to drive up their subscriptions and ratings.

Buried under two feet of snow, Jim and I were eating junk food on the couch when we heard Trump say at a rally in Iowa, "I could stand in the middle of Fifth Avenue and shoot somebody, and I wouldn't lose any voters, Okay? It's, like, incredible."

"Jesus," Jim said. "The *shit* that Trump says. Somebody should start recording all this idiot's best lines." That was a cartoon lightbulb moment for me. I bolted from the couch and grabbed my laptop, navigating to a domain name service. And with just a few clicks, I was the proud owner of *ShitThatTrumpSays.com*.

I spent the rest of the winter designing my new blog and writing snarky op-eds about The Orange Man's exploits. I paired articles about his word salad nonsense with political cartoons from a subscription service and started getting more web traffic than I ever did with Kevin's blog.

—

Only one other member of The Diners Club would appreciate my new blog, so for fun, I shared it just with Gordo, Leroy, and Scott, knowing it would piss off two of them. I texted them my blog story links with hilarious cartoons, like one of a baby Trump in diapers or Trump as Humpty Dumpty sitting on a wall between the U.S. and Mexico that he said he'd force the Mexicans to pay for. Gordo was the only one who replied with either a thumbs-up or a laughing face emoji.

One night, Scott texted me a selfie of him, Leroy, and Gordo at an outdoor eatery, and I gasped to see Scott in the middle wearing a red Make America Great Again ball cap. Gordo, possibly expecting some blowback, made a face with his eyes crossed as he pointed to Scott's MAGA hat. Leroy, however, was all smiles. I replied with an animated gif of a Trump-faced pile of poo with a blond combover and circling flies.

—

Toward the end of summer, I had a proper catch-up phone call with Scott that steered clear of politics. He'd been in his new job for about a year and had been roommate-free since the fall. He was still taking on property crime and drug cases but had recently assisted in a manslaughter case and the defense of an accused rapist, so he was climbing the ranks, he said. In addition to his Happy Hours with Gordo and Leroy, he often went out after work with some of his firm's younger associates, who considered Scott a mentor. And he was even seeing someone he'd met through a dating app.

Brad had returned to live with his parents right after Apple Fest the previous year. Scott stayed in touch with one of Brad's brothers, who told him that Brad's life was filled with simple pleasures like listening to Christian music, taking hours to prepare a special meal, and pitching in with dishes, laundry, and cleaning. He often talked about his love for his wife and children, even though he didn't see them, and appreciated the company of his brothers and parents, whom he was careful not to drink in front of. But everyone understood his condition.

At times, when Brad spoke, he didn't make any sense, and his brother asked a doctor about it. The doctor said Brad's liver had stopped functioning—his brain was getting too much ammonia as a result—and that he probably only had six months or so to live. Brad's mother said she thought her youngest son had come home to die.

I had no intention of piling on to that heavy topic by bringing up what Brad told me about Scott's Catholic school abuse. I accepted the story as true because it was too sinister and inconceivable for Brad to make up, but also because it explained so much.

Most assuredly, Scott's temporary middle school "epilepsy" had been a physiological reaction to the trauma. And it made sense now why the young man who enrolled in our high school, on the heels of that abuse, would flounder academically, act out, and turn to pot and alcohol. Perhaps he still would have grown into the subversive adult who mistrusted the establishment, yet Pam, his twin, carried none of those personality traits—they were polar opposites. All his adult life, Scott had been prone to depression, for which he never sought help, and there was his divorce and tendency to self-medicate, mainly with vodka. It all added up to a convincing circumstantial case of this alleged abuse which I couldn't ever imagine confronting him with.

We ended our long phone call with an update on Kevin, which reminded Scott of a letter he'd seen a few months ago that was mailed to him from an inmate at Florence ADX. The letter was in a pile of forwarded mail from his old home office, and he'd sent it off, unopened, to Jack.

I was miffed because now I had to track down this letter for my book database. I hadn't worked on the proposal since launching the Dumpster blog, but I did carve out time to update the database with emails, phone calls, transcripts, and new information, which this letter might fall under.

"Scott!" I complained. "You didn't even open it? Weren't you curious? And why didn't you send it to me?"

"Sorry, Luv. I don't have your reporter's thirst for knowledge," he laughed. "And I'm not Kevin's lawyer anymore, remember? Get it from Jack. He'll give it to you."

I groaned before we hung up at the unnecessary work I'd just been given.

CHAPTER 35
OCTOBER SURPRISES

FALL 2016

J ack did not recall the mystery letter from the federal inmate that Scott forwarded to him. But he invited me to his home office in Northumberland County, where he thought we could find it. He said I could also meet Betsy, and they'd take me to lunch.

My two-and-a-half-hour drive northwest was lovely once I left the main thruways for less traveled roads. It was still warm in late September and green as summer, but some of the red maples I passed already wore fringes of scarlet.

At the edge of a quaint little town, I pulled into the gravel driveway of a stately red brick Victorian with a wrap-around porch. Jack greeted me outside with his familiar tobacco-spiced bear hug. I'd parked next to a lamp post hung with a sign that advertised his services—Jackson B. Bear, Attorney at Law—and I took a couple of selfies of us in front of it for Scott. Jack looked dapper in a coral shirt and suspenders and posed for a portrait, pointing at the sign with his pipe between his teeth. He still wore his ponytail, and his white beard was trim, but his belly was not and may have grown since I'd seen him two years ago at Kevin's sentencing.

He and the Irish Setters took me on a tour of his 2 ½ acres, which included a spectacular red barn with a workshop where he restored Revolutionary War-era muskets. Beyond the barn, his property gave way to the rolling hills of a neighboring farm and a pasture with a windbreak of trees. What a tranquil place to work from, I thought.

The house, built in 1890, was in great shape and bore all the hallmarks of the period, like warm woodwork, trim, pocket doors, and wallpaper. I looked around for Betsy, but Jack said we'd meet her in town for lunch. She, too, was a solo practitioner and the only veterinarian on duty for miles. Like Jack, she made her own schedule, and if he weren't traveling for court appearances, they'd usually have lunch together.

Jack's office took up half the first floor in what looked like a combined parlor and dining room, and those walls, just like at Camp Walleye, were covered in stuffed animal heads. There were too many to count, and I asked Jack for a quick inventory of his mostly mounted African safari trophies. He walked around, pointing to a cluster of waterbucks in one corner, a moose and a warthog over there, a few gazelles over here, and an impala and kudu in another corner. There were *dozens*. It was a dizzying array of African deer and antelope species with either tall, ribbed horns, lyre-shaped horns, or spiral, tightly curved horns. I recognized a native black bear head and stuffed Walleye, both showing teeth, and a gigantic, hideous water buffalo graced the mantel above the potbellied stove. I was sad to see a black and white striped zebra head with its neck mounted over his cluttered desk, but I tried not to show it.

Surrounded by all those dead animals, I'd almost forgotten my mission. When I processed the disarray and jumble of files, boxes, and papers, my worry must have been written on my face because he told me, "Well, Carla, it may look like a mess, but I assure you, this is controlled chaos. I know where everything is."

In a corner near two filing cabinets and another water buffalo, Jack picked up a box labeled *Sanders*. There were three others like it, and I helped drag them over to a sitting area. He said these were the latest files he'd received from Scott, and we started rifling through them. I wasn't just looking for the mystery letter but for anything I thought I should have for my database. I came across a black-and-white drawing of a fishing scene featuring a man with a pole in silhouette surrounded by trees, birds, and cattails that Kevin had made for him at some point. Then I found another drawing, this one of a mystical deer-like creature surrounded by clouds and trees, with strange antlers unlike any on Jack's walls. I asked if I could take them home to scan in, and Jack didn't mind at all.

Two boxes were heavy because they each contained a copy of the thick-bound appeal with transcripts. There weren't many loose, unidentifiable papers or envelopes, and it wasn't long before I found a large manila packet with Scott's Pittsburgh return address. Inside was the unopened letter from the Florence Supermax prison, postmarked a year ago, which Jack could have found on his own. But I did come across other documents I wanted and was looking forward to meeting Betsy, so I told myself to stop complaining.

—

Jack drove us into town in his Yukon, and I opened the letter. There were actually two letters, one written to Scott asking him to pass on a second letter to Kevin. The handwriting was messy and hard to read, and I tried to decipher it on the drive into town. I'd never heard of the letter writer, but he knew Kevin, and his tone was one of a friend writing to a friend.

"Holy shit!" I said as Jack pulled into a downtown parking spot. "This guy says T-Rex called the Florence hit on Kevin—that he was the actual shot-caller who gave the hit order!"

"Surprises you, this does, young Jedi?"

"I guess not. But it's good for Kevin to have confirmation. This guy seems well-connected to the Aryan Brotherhood and names multiple AB sources for the allegation."

We walked to a Korean BBQ place and sat at a table waiting for Betsy. I read a part of the letter aloud, indicating that T-Rex had initially okayed Kevin's duress defense and was prepared to testify for him. But AB leaders at ADX felt he'd overstepped his authority and disapproved. So, to save his standing, T-Rex ordered the hit.

"This guy also says that Kevin's hit didn't get T-Rex out of trouble with the AB, that T-Rex was still *in the hat*, as they say, and so T-Rex dropped out of the gang and went into a debriefing program."

"That, right there, is a whole chapter for your book, Carla," Jack said, standing with a kiss for Betsy when she appeared. We shook hands, and she said, "Did I hear you two mention the book? How's that going?"

"Fine. Slow," I both lied and spoke the truth.

Jack gave her the background on the mystery letter, and I said I worried that the Aryan Brotherhood still posed a threat to Kevin in Florida. And I verbalized something that troubled me ever since Tiny attacked Kevin in Florence with a shank in each hand. "I don't even know if I should still write a book about this case. I mean, isn't that irresponsible? To put something out there, where Kevin has to look over his shoulder the rest of his life?"

"Is it not the case, Carla, that Kevin wants you to tell the story despite the risks?" Jack said.

"So he says," I replied. "But I don't know if he's really thought this through."

"Have you considered using a pseudonym or maybe changing people's names?" Betsy asked.

"I've thought about both of those things," I said, and in fact, I had already deleted my personal author website, author Facebook page, and the few references I'd made about the book on my social media.

"I've also thought about writing a fictionalized version ... maybe that's how I can tell it where no one gets hurt."

"Aliases and nicknames won't fool anyone," Jack said. "And a fictionalized version would rob the story of all its fun and impact. What makes this story compelling and interesting is that it's true—real names, real events, real people. Remove this, and you've gutted the story."

I frowned, and a waitress took our order. "Any shithead can write fiction," he continued, and Betsy punched him in the arm. "Ow!" he looked at her. "It takes a real person, with real experiences, and maybe even some real courage, to write a real story. In the end, truth is always better than fiction.

"Write exactly what you saw and what you felt. Have fun with it," he added. "Give the civilians out there a window into this scary, insanely dangerous, twisted world of guards and gangs and prisons and courts, lawyers, and judges, with all its dirt, misery, hopelessness, and gritty heroism. Do that and be proud of it. ... and buy yourself that Glock."

I gave him the stink eye, and Betsy changed the subject.

"Did you tell Carla about your stories, Jack?"

"Oh, yes, Dear, thank you for reminding me." He said he wanted to give me a collection of short stories he'd written, mostly about their Safari hunting adventures, and that maybe I'd know how he could self-publish them.

We chit-chatted through lunch—Jack with a large platter of ribs, Betsy and I with fried chicken and Japchae glass noodles—until Betsy looked at her watch and said she had to return to work.

She was lovely, spirited, and every bit Jack's equal in intellect and charm. Lunching with her had definitely been worth the trip.

I almost escaped their driveway without the short stories, but Jack remembered to run in and get me a neatly bound copy, about half an inch thick. He handed it to me through my car window, and I promised to look at it and get back to him. "That would be delightful," he said, kissing my cheek.

I tossed the story collection in my back seat and reached out for his firm grip for one last goodbye. "May the Force be with you, Jack," I smiled.

"And also with *you*," he said, eyes twinkling. "Drive Safe."

He tapped my SUV roof twice with an all-clear signal and lit his pipe as I pulled away. I caught his wave in my rear-view mirror and thought Scott had been right; Jack looked exactly like Santa Claus.

—

Late in the afternoon on the first Friday in October, I was making potato salad for the big Penn State/Eagles football weekend. As usual, cable news on my iPad entertained me while I toiled away at the sink. But I had to stop peeling potatoes and increase the volume to process some breaking election news that appeared, on the surface, to be a game-changer for the Democrats.

The Washington Post had just released a shocking video of Donald Trump making vulgar comments about women to television host Billy Bush. In the 2005 video for the *Access Hollywood* TV show, Trump bragged about using his fame and status to make unwanted advances toward women. He was first recorded saying he "did try and fuck" (unsuccessfully) a particular married woman, who later "got the big phony tits" and "totally changed her look."

Then, referring to an actress he and Bush were about to see on the TV set, he told Bush:

"I better use some Tic Tacs just in case I start kissing her. You know I'm automatically attracted to beautiful—I just start kissing them. It's like a magnet. Just kiss. I don't even wait. And when you're a star, they let you do it. You can do anything. Grab 'em by the pussy. You can do anything."

Boom. Mic drop. I called Jim at work, and later, we agreed there was no way that bloated, misogynistic pig could become president now. The fallout would destroy him, and it should be smooth sailing for his opponent and the only adult in the race, Hillary Clinton.

I felt a huge sense of relief because now I could kill my *ShitThatTrumpSays* blog. I'd been keeping it going out of frustration and therapy, but now that The Orange Man's downfall was imminent, I could return to less poisonous, more productive writing, like the book everyone thought I was working on—after the election, of course.

—

In the last week of October, a Google alert I'd set up for "Lewisburg prison" paid off big dividends in my inbox. I opened my email to find links to a joint investigation by National Public Radio (NPR) and The Marshall Project into the horrors of Lewisburg's SMU program.

The exposé's eight-minute radio segment, *Inside Lewisburg Prison: A Choice Between A Violent Cellmate Or Shackles*, appeared on NPR's *All Things Considered* that Wednesday. The print version—*28 Days in Chains* with the subtitle "In this federal prison, inmates have a choice: live with a violent cellmate or end up in shackles."—was posted to the website of The Marshall Project (a nonprofit news outlet focusing on criminal justice) and included shocking photos.

The investigation centered on Lewisburg inmate Sebastian Richardson, whose lawsuit I'd found in PACER nearly four years ago. He'd been four-pointed and chained in hard restraints for a month in the winter of 2011 for refusing a violent cellmate. The news organizations interviewed prison staff, over 40 current and former inmates, some of their lawyers, and the Lewisburg Prison Project (LPP) to present a damning portrait of the deadly environment and its tortuous conditions.

Photos showed the closet-size decaying cells with a discussion of the double-celling, nearly 24-hour lockdown, and unaddressed or ignored mental health issues that had led to extreme inmate-on-inmate violence since the SMU opened.

Another photo featured an inmate being held down by COs and four-pointed, which was somehow smuggled out. It illustrated the punitive, inhumane policy that left inmates stewing in soiled clothes because they couldn't use the bathroom in their excessively tight restraints. Reporters talked to numerous inmates with lasting scars and nerve damage, not to mention PTSD, from the experience.

The report detailed two murders that had occurred in Lewisburg last year. Two inmates were each killed by their cellmates, and a mental health component was attached to each slaying.

One searing quote by an LPP board member really stuck with me. "If you did to your dog what they do to men here, you would be arrested."

Finally, I thought, the world was starting to learn what so many of us knew but didn't have a platform to share—and, in my case, which included resources and access. I emailed the stories to Scott and Jack but was disheartened to see the exposé fade quickly from the news cycle. The election was less than a week away, and The Orange Man was sucking up all the media oxygen.

That weekend, Jim and I celebrated a niece's art show in New York City with local family. Twelve of us booked a dinner cruise on the New York Harbor, and we wined and dined as we floated past Manhattan's brilliantly lit skyline. We took selfies on the deck as the yacht approached the Statue of Liberty and indulged in rich, savory multi-courses and endless bottles of wine.

Our niece, the painter, had brought her long-time boyfriend, and our young adult sons had brought their girlfriends. Both were fantastic, engaging, bright women Jim and I dared not get too attached to, but the glow of young love at the table added to everyone's high spirits. Plus, the election was only three days away, and we were excited to be on the verge of history.

"Here's to the first woman president—Hillary Clinton," my sister-in-law said and raised her glass. We clinked our goblets and decided it was an amazing time to be alive.

—

Even though the polling looked good for Hillary, watching live election night coverage was far too nerve-wracking. So Jim and I hunkered down and distracted ourselves with the *Hell on Wheels* TV series we'd been binging. Once in a while, we'd flick over to CNN for an update but then quickly return to our show.

As the night wore on and our CNN check-ins grew scary, we doubled down with our binging, preferring to lose ourselves in the mid-1800s and episodes about the construction of the first transcontinental railroad. When our sons started calling and texting, saying they were trying to comfort their girlfriends, the Earth's axis snapped in two, and the world fell out of orbit.

He had done it. The Orange Man had eeked out a win, and I couldn't watch any more TV. Jim and I staggered to bed, reminding each other of our blessings. We were grateful for each other, our families, our health. We didn't know what lay ahead but would get through it together.

—

When Hillary finally called Trump to concede around 2:30 a.m., the usual overnight quiet at Coleman II prison was pierced. One inmate, who'd been listening to his radio on headphones, started kicking his door. Another joined him. And then another, and so on, until a thunderous rumble of feet bashing doors spread like kudzu and ushered in a new era of dread and despair.

CHAPTER 36
BAD THINGS HAPPEN IN THREES

2017

I appreciated the apolitical banter that flowed from Scott and Jack after the election. Their restraint in gloating showed a maturity I wasn't sure they possessed. In the year since the Third Circuit Court ended Kevin's criminal case, our three-way emails or texts had mainly been of the silly variety or contained updates from me about Kevin. Around the holidays, I even removed the filter on Jack's stupid emails because I needed the laughs.

On New Year's Day, Jack shared an email with the header "Never Squat With Your Spurs On" that listed some famous sayings of Will Rogers, a cowboy actor from the 1920s and 30s who was also a humorist and social commentator. Some of the quotes included:

> *Always drink upstream from the herd.*
> *Never miss a good chance to shut up.*
> *If you find yourself in a hole, stop digging.*

I emailed back, "I like this one, Jack! Happy New Year to you and Betsy!" and wished Scott a happy New Year, too. Scott replied, "Happy New Year to you both. You are beautiful people."

Jack replied with a follow-up email, "About Growing Older," with sage phrases like:

> *Eventually, you'll reach a point when you stop lying about your age and start bragging about it.*

> *Being young is beautiful, but being old is comfortable and relaxed.*

> *Some people try to turn back their odometers, but not me. I want people to know why I look this way. I've traveled a long way, and some of the roads weren't paved.*

—

On Saturday, January 7, I took an Acela train from Philly to Providence, RI, to meet Jim and look for a corporate apartment. He was in charge of a new business acquisition in New England, and because he'd be spending so much time there merging the manufacturer and plant operations, it made sense. We had done this once before in Milwaukee, so I was fairly skilled at finding and setting up a *pied-à-terre*. And as a bonus, the train ride, at just over four hours each way, would give me some built-in writing time.

I was ready to return to my book *Under Duress,* but it had been so long since I touched it that I wasn't sure where to start. I also didn't know what the ending was supposed to be. Rather than stew on that, and because I was a master procrastinator, I caught up on my email instead. I saw one from Jack from two days ago, sent to his special friends list, called "Questions That Haunt Me."

> *Can you cry underwater?*

> *What disease did cured ham actually have?*

If Jimmy cracks corn, and no one cares, why is there a stupid song about him?

If the Professor on Gilligan's Island can make a radio out of a coconut, why can't he fix the hole in the boat?

Can a hearse carrying a corpse drive in the carpool lane?

Do you ever wonder why you gave me your e-mail address in the first place?

Oh, Jackson, *yes, yes, yes,* and *yes,* I laughed to myself, but I certainly was enjoying the diversion. Before I opened my book file, my phone buzzed with a text message. It was from Scott and made my heart stop. "I'm calling you in two seconds," I texted back and had to leave business class for the luggage area so I could talk. Brad had died last night. He was 52.

He'd just spent his third Christmas without seeing his children and, in recent weeks, started talking about wanting to join Jesus. Yesterday morning, his parents found him in bed, non-responsive, with an empty vodka bottle on his nightstand.

"The last time we talked, I knew he was sad. I knew he had lost hope," Scott told me. "I wasn't surprised to hear. Just disappointed. I loved him, but I couldn't save him … I really don't have any other words."

"No one could save him because he didn't want to be, or couldn't be, saved," I said. "He loved you like a brother. You did all you could, and you'll eventually have to come to peace with that. Some people just can't be helped."

I spent the weekend apartment shopping and having long phone conversations with high school friends about the loss. Brad's Facebook page started filling up with condolences and photos of him as a child and teenager.

Plenty of resurfaced pictures showed our Diners Club crew with Brad, including one of just him and me, arm-in-arm at our junior prom, beaming for the camera.

—

Three days later, I woke up to a text from Scott: "Jack Bear died Sunday. Fuck."

Oh my God, I thought. *No. This can't be*, and I called Scott immediately. He told me he'd heard from one of Jack's attorney friends whom Betsy asked to spread the word. Jack had gone to bed Saturday night—only hours after I'd read his last emails about growing older and questions that haunted him—and died of a massive heart attack in his sleep. He was 64.

For a long time, I couldn't leave my bedroom. Eventually, I made coffee but then couldn't leave the couch. I definitely couldn't get out of my bathrobe that day. What. The. Fuck.

—

Jack's public memorial service was held at his county courthouse on the second Friday of February. It was widely attended by friends and colleagues, some of whom had driven a great distance through a snowstorm to pay their respects. I sat with Scott in a historic courtroom with wonderfully tall, coved ceilings and a center medallion with a hanging chandelier. The wood accents and floor-to-ceiling windows reminded me of the Scranton courtroom where we defended Kevin. I quietly told Scott about my end-of-summer visit with Jack and Betsy, the giant plate of ribs he ate, how I thought his girth had expanded, and my last view of him with his pipe between his teeth. And then I tore into Scott, asking about his cholesterol and blood pressure and whether he was exercising. "Did you get a colonoscopy yet?" I demanded to know.

He rolled his eyes. "My job is stressful, but I'm fine," he said. "And, no, I'm not dating anyone either."

There was so much we didn't know about Jack. One colleague or close friend after another spoke at the lectern, recounting stories of his hobbies, personality, and achievements. Jack had been close with his nieces and nephews, and everyone called him "Uncle Jack," even his mother-in-law. He was of Russian descent and studied Russian and chemistry at his Ivy League school. And he earned a language certificate from the University of Leningrad in the Soviet Union, now the University of St. Petersburg in Russia. In addition to the muskets he built, he refinished bamboo fly fishing rods and made Damascus hunting knives with a friend. Two of his favorite accomplishments were writing the township zoning ordinances that protected his local trout streams and helping an elderly woman regain her independence from a scheming relative.

Scott and I mingled after the service, and by that, I mean I mostly sat with my phone while he shook hands and talked with former colleagues. I didn't know anyone but Betsy and didn't want to intrude into her private time with mourners. When it was time, we hugged her goodbye and walked to a coffee shop.

Scott didn't have to rush off because he would be making the easy drive to Douglasville to spend the weekend with his dad. His father, Bill, was recently hospitalized with pulmonary fibrosis and bacterial pneumonia. We touched on our families and his job, but mainly, we talked about the stunning losses of Brad and Jack. I told him I'd been waiting in terror for his next text message telling me someone we both cared about had died.

"My mother always says, 'Bad things happen in threes,' so I'm just waiting for that next shoe to drop, Scott." He looked at me and shook his head as if he didn't want to find out either.

I pulled the bound copy of Jack's story collection titled *Moyowasi Safari Stories* from my tote bag and explained that I had promised to help him self-publish it but never even read one story. "I threw it in the back of my car and forgot about it," I said. "And when I finally cleaned out my SUV a few weeks ago, I saw it and burst into tears." Just recounting this made my eyes well again, and I declared, "I'm such a terrible person," while dabbing my cheeks with a napkin.

"That's ridiculous, Carla," he said, covering my hand with his. I sniffed and said I'd recently skimmed through the pages and confirmed the tales were mainly about his and Betsy's safari adventures, with one about fly fishing and another about a pheasant shoot. "There's a section on firearms and a suggested reading list for hunters," I added. "Mostly, the stories are about killing animals," I sighed. "I should ask Betsy if she wants me to do anything with them."

—

Kevin was terribly sad to hear the news about Jack. I told him I now possessed the fishing silhouette and mystical deer sketches he'd made for Jack and that I could add them to his other artwork for our loosely defined "book project" that might include a related website. He was writing me so many stories that, between those, our emails and phone calls, I already had enough material for two or three books, so I said we'd have to offload some of it digitally. In one email, he told me, "My whole life is this book and what we have to do to get u the info to grab the world."

Our phone calls were regular (and always recorded, with his happy knowledge), and 99.5% of what we discussed was his prison life. I kept my family life private—I don't think he even knew my boys' names—and sometimes, I struggled to fill in the last bits of our 15-minute call increments. One time, because I couldn't think of anything more to say or ask him, I told him that maybe his friend Jimmy/Whitey Bulger would like to know some celebrity gossip about the actor Johnny Depp, who portrayed him in the recent movie *Black Mass*. Depp, I said, was accused of abusing his young actress wife, who'd divorced him after only a year. Photos of her with a black eye and bruised lip had circulated online, and a judge granted her a temporary restraining order. I said it all seemed to be related to the actor's long history of drug and alcohol abuse. This scandal was old at that point, but I was trying to fill our phone time.

Kevin wrote me later that he'd told Jimmy the Johnny Depp gossip, which made the old convict furious that anyone would treat their wife that way. Jimmy told Kevin about his girlfriend Catherine Greig, who was 20 years younger and whom he loved so deeply he would die for. When they both were captured after 16 years on the run, Jimmy tried to bargain with prosecutors—life in prison or even the death penalty for him if they would forgo a prison term for her. However, no deal was struck, and Catherine was sentenced to eight years for aiding and abetting. She remained in a low-security women's prison in Minnesota.

Kevin had formed a "household" with three trusted inmates, Bomber, Snake, and Big Chop, who shared a goal of wanting structure, respect, and purpose in their lives. Kevin was a natural leader, and this didn't surprise me. And he told me he could possibly move to a medium-security prison if he met certain not-very-clear conditions, so he was making a concerted effort to stay out of trouble (a bold claim, I soon learned) and further his education. He had gotten an outstanding work performance rating on his compound sanitation job, which earned him $36 per month, and he was now down to about four years left to serve on his sentence.

In the spring, Scott typed him a letter on his law firm's letterhead, saying, in part, "My life has been up and down. The only consistent thing is that I love the job. I'm in court every day, and I love criminal defense. I am surrounded with 35 other like-minded people, although I am the only one in the office to vote for Donald Trump."

Scott said he would help Kevin get back on his feet when he got out, and thought Kevin would like Pittsburgh, with its vibrant arts scene and culture. "Hit me back and let me know how you are doing. I think about you often, I'm just a shitty correspondent. That's my biggest problem in this office, keeping in contact with my clients. You became a friend a long time ago."

—

The same week in May that Trump's bootlicker attorney general, Jeff Sessions, wanted to reverse an Obama policy and return to harsher punishments for low-level drug crimes, The Orange Man fired his FBI director, Jim Comey. Comey was leading the investigation into whether Trump's cronies colluded with Russia to influence last fall's election. I texted Scott a link to an article about Sessions' sweeping new criminal charging policy and said, "Of all the shit that's gone down this week, this is actually the most alarming."

"Yeah, I agree with you on that one," he replied. "Time for the RINO Republicans to get with Dems and change the laws. I don't blame a prosecutor for enforcing the law. But I don't like bad laws."

—

The Orange Man really hit his stride that summer after a deadly neo-Nazi rally in Charlottesville, Virginia, threatened to spark a new Civil War. In August, hundreds of neo-

Confederates, neo-fascists, white nationalists, Klansmen, and far-right militias gathered to protest the removal of a statue of Confederate General Robert E. Lee. The mob, marked by Confederate flags and swastikas, carried tiki torches and spewed racist chants, and one participant rammed his car into a crowd of counterprotesters. A 32-year-old paralegal, Heather Heyer, was killed, and dozens were injured.

Hours later, a helicopter conducting aerial surveillance on the rally crashed with two members of the Virginia State Police on board. Killed instantly were Lieutenant H. Jay Cullen, 48, and Trooper Berke M. M. Bates, 40.

When first asked about it by a reporter, Trump said Americans had to learn to set bigotry and hatred aside. But then two days later, when questioned again, he showed his true colors by stating there were "very fine people on both sides." The supposed leader of the free world, who had yet to condemn white supremacy, was equating violent white supremacists to the protestors opposing hate speech, racism, and brutality.

Instead of deterring such behavior, The Orange Man emboldened it. Every angry, hateful, often arms-bearing fascist now had a green light to crawl out from under their rocks and inflict a new cycle of bigotry and bloodshed upon the landscape.

—

I coped with this fresh dystopian world the way anyone would: by ordering a stuffed Trump voodoo doll that I'd stuck with 30 colorful pinheads. That paired nicely with his *Time* magazine feature cover, on which I'd drawn devil horns, googly eyes, and a curly mustache with a black marker. I started collecting a whole shelf of mementos, including a pair of tiny plastic hands and a Trump and Vladimir Putin *Best Comrades* finger puppet set.

Jim and I survived the year by watching and rewatching comedian Melissa McCarthy's outstanding parody of Trump's mean and farcical press secretary, Sean Spicer, on *Saturday Night Live.* And the joy we got from The Orange Man's first chief of staff's name was almost criminal. Jim turned Reince Priebus into *Rice Penis,* and we were distraught when Priebus only lasted six months. "Does this mean we can't say *Rice Penis* anymore?" I asked Jim.

On the contrary, he said. "We shall say *Rice Penis* daily and be thankful for this small gift from the grifter-in-chief."

—

As the year came to a close, I thought about my mother's belief that bad things happened in threes. There were no more deaths in my world, or Scott's, for that matter, so we must have foiled the prophecy. But then, the more I thought about it, the more I realized the third bad thing was really the first bad thing and had preceded Brad's and Jack's deaths. It was The Orange Man's election and infernal rise to power.

CHAPTER 37
GONE FISHING

2017 BONUS STORY FROM COLEMAN II DURING WINTER LOCKDOWN

In the early winter of 2017, Coleman II officials locked down the prison for two weeks due to their misguided belief that a war between white and Mexican gangs was imminent. They came to this conclusion because "all the white boys had their prison-issued boots on," but the real reason for that was that the whites had all sold their regular shoes for drugs, according to Kevin. Nevertheless, the COs thought "this was going to be the big one" in gang wars.

The lockdown meant Coleman's inmates were restricted to their cells except for three weekly showers. On the 11th day of their lockdown, Kevin wrote me this *Lockdown Loot* story (edited for brevity and clarity) about the first three days.

—

"LOCKDOWN LOOT"

JANUARY 9TH, FIRST DAY OF LOCKDOWN, 10:30 A.M.

The Special Investigative Services cop, Lt. Applehead,

walks down my tier and makes it clear that if something happens, then they're going to lock this motherfucker down and tear shit up. *Whatever* is our attitude, along with some real slick sexual comments like, "How 'bout you tear this dick up in your mouth?" or "Lock down your jaw, and we'll tear up your mouth, pig!" Everyone is laughing as his face turns red.

"Who said that?" the lieutenant asks, and no one steps up to own the outburst.

But then another con yells, "Hey, lieutenant, see if you can get that approved with the captain!"

"Get what approved? I don't need to ask the captain anything."

"To suck us all off, you do, fag!" someone yells.

Now Lt. Applehead is so pissed off he turns three shades of red to almost purple. "Motherfuckers think I'm playing?" he says.

"If you're gonna fall for that shit," another con yells out, "come over here and kneel for this, head-humper!"

Lt. Applehead storms out of the unit, shaking his head, knowing he lost the moment, taking more shit than he was selling. He could have locked down the unit and flexed his muscles right there, but that would have stopped the race war they want. They want the whole prison to feel the wrath but will settle for trashing our unit due to the outbursts instead.

11:40 A.M.

Knowing that we are going to get locked down, I shoot out for lunch and go eat. Halfway into a taco salad, a CO's body alarm goes off, and everything is shut down. Everyone has to get up and leave the chow hall. I'm pissed because I can't finish my meal, so I knocked my tray off the table, spilling shit all over the floor, but I act like it's an accident. I give the mess hall cop a look like *my bad* as I walk out.

Then I hear lots of trays hitting the floor "by accident" while the mess hall cop cusses, "Motherfuckers. Knock that shit off!" because he has to clean that shit up all by himself—lockdown means no inmate chow workers to sweep up for him. I smile 'cause I feel the home team just scored a home run.

As soon as I reach the unit, I smell the mace gas and feel it touch my lungs. The cops are yelling, "Go straight to your cell, or you can go to the SHU!" Two inmates had gotten into a fight, and I look at a cop and ask if there was "knife play." He shakes his head no and points me up to my cell.

After everyone is locked in their cells, Lt. Applehead walks through the unit, yelling, "Thought I was playing, boys?"

One con responds, "We know you play with boys, dick-licker!"

And now I know this shit has reached a point where there'll be hell to pay.

"I'm fucking tired of your shit!" the lieutenant says, which only opens the door to another round of insults. Someone says in a high-pitched voice, "Then stay out my ass, boss!" This brings the house down, and everyone starts kicking their doors.

Lt. Applehead stands there with his hands on his hips and smoke coming out of his ears. He finally walks off in disgust at the nature of our rebelliousness, and I know we are in for it.

12:20 P.M.

I lay back on my bunk and kick my shoes off with nowhere to go. My cellie does the same 'cause this is routine when we get locked down. We keep the talk small and laugh about all the shit the officers take. I read one of my study books until I feel a good nap coming on, but just a power nap, so I'm ready for anything that might be coming next.

4:00 P.M.

I wake up for stand-up count and wait for dinner. I study some on the Renaissance of Northern Italy and how great works of art and science came from famous Italian figures like Leonardo DaVinci, Dante, Michelangelo, and Christopher Columbus.

4:20 P.M.

The cuff port opens up, and two brown bags are stuffed through, our dinner for the night—four pieces of bread, one slice of cheese, one slice of baloney, two packs of peanut butter with jelly, and a small pack of four little cookies.

Eat, study, sleep is all I do. I don't really interact with my cellie because his level of smarts is very low and he has no drive to learn anything new. He stays out of my way on the top bunk. Every now and then, he'll burst out laughing from one of the urban hood novels he likes to read.

He's never been nowhere but this prison. A little taste of that gangster shit in the active SMU program would shape his ass up real quick. He loves my war stories, that I only share if I have to teach him a lesson in convict nature and slow his ass down.

JANUARY 10TH, SECOND DAY OF LOCKDOWN, 6:30 A.M.

I wake up to the cuff port slamming down and Styrofoam trays being pushed through the opening. "Let's go! Turn the light on!" the cop yells. In a hurry for nothing, I take my time to grab the two breakfast trays, set them on the desk, and get back to bed. With nothing to get up for on lockdown, I sleep the morning away, and so does my cellie.

9:30 A.M.

I wake up to officers storming the unit like the Gestapo—handcuffing inmates and walking them to the showers to be strip searched and held there as their cells are ransacked. Two sets of officers do this. The male cops do the strip-searching, and the female cops, who work in education and the prison offices, do the cell searches. They trash our cells, take everything they can, and throw it in their big black garbage bags. They even take shit they're not supposed to.

No fucking way, I say to myself as I walk back in and see what they've done. Everything is upside down and everywhere. You can't even tell what's gone until you sort it all out.

12:20 P.M.

After about 21 cells of this hard labor, the cops have to take a break and go to the downstairs office to gossip. But they leave their work behind—lots of black trash bags in the hallway with everyone's contraband inside. I make a fishing line out of strips of sheet and shoot it down the tier to the homies who haven't been hit yet. I pull back hordes of contraband that slide under my door. It's all safe unless I get caught.

Next, I take a staple, hook it to my slider with the pointy side turned up, and shoot it out to the trash bags. After a few tries, I hook a big one and pull it to my cell door, reaching under and ripping it open. But I only have two inches of door space to work with, so I take some magazine covers, roll them tight into two long poles, and use them like chopsticks to pull out anything that'll fit under the door. I get stamps (prison money), headphones, radios, shirts, and magazines with nude girls—the real money in any man's prison.

After getting all I can find, I shoot the line across the way and have a homie pull the bag back to the center. Then I go for another bag of hot loot and snag my next one after three tries. With my chopsticks, I pull out more porn (the female staff take that shit every time), a watch, and more magazines. If it fits, I'm pulling it under. As I do this, the homeboy across the way is watching out for me, ready to whistle if the Gestapo comes. I shoot the fishing line over to my *crimey,* and he pulls the raided bag away from my door to cover my tracks. When he shoots the line back to me, I see a little bag of stamps that came from The Store Man's house.

The Store Man is another convict who buys commissary items and sells them at a 50% markup 'cause not everyone can shop, or maybe they lost their store privileges. Also, somebody might need an item now and can't wait for store day, which only comes once a week. In all those cases, The Store Man gots you.

Now, here is where one man's ideas and all his hard work turn into monkey see, monkey do. Three other inmates are now fishing for the big prize: The Store Man's bag. Fuck that! This is my show, and I feel I earned this. I yell to my lookout in Spanish to fish out and snag any line going for my catch, and the homeboy starts pulling in any line he can grab. I put stickers around my fishing line like sticky strips, and they help me snatch The Store Man's bag of loot. I hear some *Fuck Yous* and "You ain't shit, Chico" as I pull the bag under my door—winner, winner, chicken dinner! I score some Ramen chicken soup, coffee, a whole mess of candy bars, and around $230 in stamps. Not bad for fishing hot trash off the tier.

I shoot my line over to the lookout and send him some candy bars and a small stack of stamps with a note thanking him for helping the home team score. I tell him I got a birthday in about three weeks, and this caper just turned my birthday bash into a birthday smash. I push all the stolen contraband up under the bed and lay back to see what happens next. Some risks are worth the payoff, and I got paid big. The worst that can happen is I go to the hole. But with the prison on lockdown, we only get a shower every three days. In the hole, there's a shower in the cell. So I win either way.

The Gestapo returns and gets back to their job cleaning out cells. They don't even notice they've been clipped or that I've secured all the goods that are no longer in there for them to take for the homies down the way. Yep, they are this stupid. I can't make this shit up.

JANUARY 11TH, THIRD DAY OF LOCKDOWN, 11:30 A.M.

The homeboy shoots his line over to me with a kite from The Store Man. I think I know what it will be about, but I'm surprised by what I read.

> *Chico, w/ respects to you. I understand that you fished in my store bag that them cops fucked me out of. I know that you took a big risk and, by rights, you got that. I know you're a real convict, and I respect your style, as do the men in here who know the real from the fake haters. I just wanted to tell you that I'm glad you got that shit instead of these bastard pigs. If anyone had it coming, you did, with all that shit you been through.*
>
> *With respects, Big Chop*

Now, after reading that kite, I think I'm looking at it all wrong. Yeah, by rights, that shit is all mine, but convict-to-convict, he touched the right chords, and I want to bring him into the fold with Bomber and Snake. I flip over the kite and write the following to send back to him:

> *With all due respect to you, homie, I'm humbled by your words and the respect you showed me. I know that you hustle hard to live in here, and your money comes as no easy task. Eye to eye, on a level of what I expect of other men, it just don't show up much in this prison. You, on the other hand,*

have shown your worth in dealing with this and have earned my respect. Here is one-half of your loss back. I'm glad to help you recover some of your lost loot.

With respect, Chico

P.S. If you need me, whistle, homie!

After getting my kite, Big Chop yells down the tier so that everyone can hear, "Chico! I know you don't trust a lot of these fake-ass convicts in here, but I got your back no matter what pops off! That was big, what you did for me, homie, you hear me?"

"I hear you, *carnal*," I say back, using the word "brother" reserved for only a chosen few. "Make sure you come over here when we unlock. 'Till then, respects, *carnal. A ti* (to you)."

I hear Snake call Chop and send his respects, and Bomber does the same. I now have three solid convicts who stand with me and want to live up to a very high standard of self-respect, group respect, outsider respect, and rules and programming to better oneself.

This is not a gang, it's a lifestyle.

CHAPTER 38
ARRIVALS AND DEPARTURES

2018

This promised to be another breathless year in politics. I stayed on top of it all, including the non-splashy stories, by doom-scrolling news on my phone and listening to my trusty, outraged cable news anchors.

Just a few days into the new year, The Orange Man quietly disbanded a commission he'd formed last year to prove there was voter fraud in the 2016 election. Because Hillary Clinton had gotten 3 million more popular votes than he had, the election must have been "rigged." However, because the Presidential Advisory Commission on Election Integrity found zero evidence of fraud, it was dissolved without fanfare after a giant waste of taxpayer dollars.

Trump was on track to get his symbolic border wall with Mexico because enough Democrats were on board with a sweeping immigration package that included a pathway to citizenship for the so-called Dreamers—young, undocumented immigrants who were brought to the country as children. But then, in a closed-door meeting, Trump called Haiti, El Salvador, and a handful of African nations "shithole countries" and asked why the U.S. would let those people in and why couldn't we have more immigrants from, say, Norway? His asinine comments sabotaged the votes he needed for his immigration deal, and his wall that Mexico was supposed to pay for landed back in the joke pile.

Just like last summer was marked by themes of violent white supremacy, this one was the summer of immigration and Trump's desire to severely curb the number of foreigners (brown and black) allowed into the country. In June, his administration started separating children from their parents at the southern border, locking up kids in cages while their parents were detained and prosecuted for illegal entry. News coverage was filled with images of sick, crying children packed into holding cells, pregnant women sleeping on concrete floors, and mothers trying to warm their babies with aluminum blankets.

The national outcry from this "zero-tolerance policy" was deafening. So, in a brilliant public relations move, First Lady Melania was rushed off to the Mexican border to tour one of the children's shelters in an olive green jacket with words emblazoned on the back expressing her and Trump world's true feelings—"I REALLY DON'T CARE. DO U?"

———

Another one of my Google alerts led me to a new damning report on Lewisburg prison conditions. This one was released by the D.C. Corrections Information Council (CIC), an independent monitoring body mandated by the U.S. Congress and D.C. Council to inspect, monitor, and report on facilities where Washington D.C. residents were incarcerated. It cited the prison's harsh 23-hour-a-day lockdown policy, continued use of excessive restraints, and violent environment, noting that one inmate recently lost an eye after a CO fired a pepper ball into his cell. The report also described a lack of access to mental health services and prison officials' retaliatory tactics of destroying legal mail and throwing away prisoner-filed administrative grievances.

This CIC report—released 18 months after the joint NPR-The Marshall Project exposé into Lewisburg's horrific conditions—received more attention than its previous reports on Lewisburg and added to the growing national awareness of Lewisburg's wayward Special Management Unit.

The Bureau of Prisons, plagued by continued civil rights lawsuits over Lewisburg conditions and inmate treatment, had course-corrected slightly. The SMU program was reduced to one year, and the amount of time an inmate could remain in the program trying to complete it was limited to 18 months. Four-pointing had been prohibited, but not the ambulatory restraints that were only supposed to be used to keep an inmate from harming himself or others; those restraints were just the last vestiges of punitive shackling that officers could get away with.

In June, the BOP announced, without explanation, that Lewisburg's SMU program would close by the end of the year. The prison would revert to a medium-security facility, and its 950 inmates would transfer to a new SMU program at Thomson, Illinois, housed in a more updated building. A spokesperson from The Lewisburg Prison Project told a state news outlet that the move was bittersweet because the LPP had hoped the program would be eliminated entirely.

—

I shared this news with Scott. We hadn't talked much since Jack died, and this was a great reason to reach out. I texted him a link to the story and was surprised to hear he was now discouraged with his job in Pittsburgh. He'd been in the position almost three years and said, "I still haven't been promoted. And I can't muster the organizational skills the bureaucracy requires." I wondered if that second statement had any bearing on the first but didn't probe.

"So I just keep winning cases through briefs with no adult supervision," he added. "I'm not 'experienced enough' to try my own cases in court. I'm not even experienced enough to help new lawyers try juvenile cases."

Oh, and by the way, he said, his 20-year-old daughter, Ashley, just came out as a lesbian. "I told her I didn't care, that I loved her just the same."

"Congratulations for saying exactly the right thing," I said. "Did you ever suspect?"

"I pretty much picked it up from her Facebook posts and photos. She told her mother quite a while ago … I'm always the last one to hear important things."

And yes, he replied to my standard question, he was dating someone, but he still longed for Lucy.

—

I also shared the news of Lewisburg's SMU closing with Kevin in a late spring phone call. But he had an even bigger news bomb for me—T-Rex had just transferred from Florence ADX to Coleman II.

"Oh my God!" I said.

"I know. I wonder if he came to finish the job on me," he said. We rehashed the letter I'd gotten from Jack's office written by Kevin's inmate friend, who said T-Rex had called the hit order on him five years ago in Florence.

Kevin said he wasn't 100 percent sure that T-Rex had ordered his killing, but even if he did, word had it that T-Rex remained a gang dropout and was still programming. I was skeptical.

"I think you need to stay way clear of that guy, Kevin. Shouldn't you tell your counselor or someone that he tried to have you killed?"

Kevin said they were assigned to separate units, and he couldn't interact with T-Rex even if he wanted to, so I shouldn't worry.

"I think he don't want to get caught up in no more drama ... and I think that incident with Snow getting his head cut off scared him straight."

"What! Who got his head cut off?"

"An AB dude named Snow. They decapitated him in Victorville and then left the knife stabbed in his eyes sticking out."

"When was that?"

"Oh man, this happened right around the time I got stabbed in Florence. Two dudes went in there and killed him, fucking cut his head off. It was crazy."

"Why did they do it?"

Just then, I heard the *beep beep* that signaled the end of our 15-minute call, and so I was left trying to look up online whatever I could find out about this decapitated Aryan Brotherhood associate.

I found some articles from November 2013 about a David Snow, who served as president of the Aryan Brotherhood in Ohio and was killed in the Victorville federal prison. The manner of his death was not revealed, although one story said he suffered "a serious assault," quoting from a Bureau of Prison news release. Snow was 53 and would have been released this year. His latest conviction had been for possessing 50 tablets of oxycodone and being a felon in possession of a firearm—he'd been convicted of robbery in 1979 and aggravated assault in 1988.

I was still curious about the motive for the beheading and made a note to follow up with Kevin the next time we spoke. However, Kevin soon lost his phone and email privileges for three months for acting out after learning his move to an FCI medium-security prison was denied, again.

He told me this in a letter and said that to make matters worse, prison officers moved him to a different unit (not

T-Rex's) and away from the household he'd formed with Bomber, Snake, and Chop. COs broke them up because they were suspicious of anyone congregating in a group even that small.

I emailed him a reply, knowing he wouldn't see it for a couple of months. "You WILL be getting out. I would like to believe you'll do the last part of your sentence somewhere else, but regardless, you will still get out and begin the new life you've been working so hard for. I know it's difficult but try not to despair. You and I are going to be shining a big bright light on dark places, so I need you to stay strong and help me with our project."

When he could email again, he replied, "Gela, I want u to know that u being here for me helps me out more than u could ever think. And one day it will all be worth it when my freedom comes and I can put my talent to use."

—

The same month that Trump's henchmen started locking up migrant kids in cages, the president commuted the prison sentence of a woman named Alice Marie Johnson. Johnson, a 63-year-old great-grandmother, was sentenced to life in prison without parole in 1996 for her non-violent participation in a Memphis cocaine trafficking ring. It was Johnson's first offense, and her overly harsh sentence, combined with her model-prisoner profile during 21 years in prison, made her an excellent candidate for clemency. However, she was denied a pardon by Obama in the last days of his administration.

Enter celebrity and social media influencer Kim Kardashian and Trump's son-in-law Jared Kushner. Kushner, a senior presidential advisor married to Trump's daughter, Ivanka, introduced Kardashian to his father-in-law. Both Kushner and Kardashian were champions of criminal justice and sentencing reform, and Kardashian personally brought Alice Johnson's story to the Oval Office. For the cameras, the *Keeping Up with the Kardashians* TV star posed—glamorous, even in business attire—beside a smiling Trump, seated behind the Resolute desk.

Kushner seized on the growing support for criminal justice reform by both political parties and led the charge for the passage of The First Step Act. The legislation built upon a 2015 bipartisan Senate bill, the Sentencing Reform and Corrections Act (SRCA), which sought to reduce mandatory minimum sentences, among other reforms. An addition to the First Step Act was the recalculation of Good Conduct Time (GCT), which could shave months off of a well-behaved inmate's sentence. Another addition was allowing inmates to get "earned time credits" by participating in more vocational and rehabilitative programs.

While far from solving the country's mass incarceration problem, the sweeping legislation that became law by year's end was a step in the right direction, as its name indicated. The First Step Act tackled a host of other reforms, including retroactive fair sentencing, improved rehabilitation and re-entry programs, changes related to juvenile justice, and compassionate release for elderly and dying prisoners.

Interestingly, Kushner had a personal reason for his advocacy. His father, Charles Kushner, had previously served time in federal prison for charges related to tax evasion, illegal campaign contributions, and witness tampering. The experience likely influenced his understanding of the challenges faced by incarcerated individuals and their families.

—

At the end of September, Scott was fired from his Pittsburgh law firm. He posted it on Facebook but told me about it a few days before. He gave a vague reason for it—something about not maintaining his client list—and I didn't press for details. He'd dropped enough hints that he wasn't conforming to office politics, required processes, or both. I helped with his resume, and after a few months of job searching and interviews, he declared he was a victim of ageism. He said no one wanted to hire a 55-year-old criminal defense lawyer, and he was thinking of suing the firm that let him go for age discrimination.

My life, by comparison, was peachy. I still doom-scrolled everything on the upside-down world, but I was surviving the Trumpocalypse. For a new distraction, I'd thrown myself into the Airbnb craze by turning our historic Philadelphia "Trinity" townhouse rental into a tourist destination. I reveled in shopping for antiques, staging for photos, and earning five-star reviews for superhost status. For pure, non-productive enjoyment, I explored the fun, snack-sized state of Rhode Island with Jim, played tennis with my ladies three times a week, and hosted dinner parties with our liberal friends. Jim once joked that I was a Democrat living the life of a Republican, but I never understood what that meant.

—

Late in the summer, Coleman II made national news for receiving another high-profile inmate: the Olympic gymnastics sports doctor Larry Nassar, who sexually abused hundreds of female athletes and received a total of 175 years in prison for multiple convictions. His arrival was not welcomed by a convict culture that despised molesters, child killers, and rapists, and Nassar was soon stabbed but survived the attack.

And there was even more drama surrounding Coleman's highest profile inmate, Whitey Bulger. The wheelchair-bound 89-year-old complained of chest pains in the spring. A prison nurse, knowing he suffered half a dozen heart attacks over the years, determined he needed to see a heart specialist at the local hospital. When she tried to get him on board with the treatment, Whitey lashed out, telling her point blank, "I know people. I still have connections back home," according to a statement Warden Charles Lockett made to NBC News.

Prison officials couldn't force the geriatric mobster to receive medical treatment, but they did put him in solitary confinement for threatening the staff nurse. Whitey's chest pains subsided, but after he still refused outside medical treatment as a precaution, the warden sought to transfer him. Whitey's transfer was approved in October, and he was moved to USP Hazelton in West Virginia, a Medical Care Level II facility.

Hazelton, known as *Misery Mountain* by its prisoners, was considered one of the more violent high-security penitentiaries in the country; two inmates had been killed there in the previous six months. Like almost every federal facility, Hazelton was chronically understaffed, which got worse during the Trump administration's federal hiring freeze. This meant that prison staff who left their jobs due to retirement or other reasons weren't being replaced and that sometimes staff teachers, administrators, and maintenance workers were forced to fill in the gaps.

Whitey arrived at Hazelton the day before Halloween. Records showed he was placed in his cell at 9:53 p.m. He didn't show up for breakfast the next morning, and officers discovered him wrapped in a bloody blanket and unresponsive. He had been beaten unrecognizable with a padlock-in-a-sock, and the killer or killers had rested his head on his pillow and covered him to make it look like he was sleeping. The murder had occurred sometime between 6 a.m., when cell doors were unlocked for breakfast, and 8 a.m. when COs made their rounds.

A New England mafia hitman was the prime suspect. And the motive was quite possibly the convict code elimination of an FBI snitch, as he'd been labeled. Whitey Bulger, who spent 16 years on the FBI's most wanted list (at one point in the Number 2 spot behind 9/11 terror mastermind Osama bin Laden), always denied being an FBI informant, claiming he only fed agents misinformation to best his enemies.

The night before his murder, Whitey asked to be placed in general population versus protective custody. The man who once reigned over Boston's underworld had just spent the last eight months in solitary confinement for threatening a Florida prison nurse, so that choice was understandable. But Coleman II's Warden Lockett thought Whitey chose gen pop for a different reason.

"Quite frankly, I think he wanted to die," Lockett told NBC News. "I think whatever issues he had, he had come to peace with them."

CHAPTER 39
REPARATIONS

2019

E arly in the year, our Diners Club received unbearable news about our most esteemed and celestial member. Pam had been diagnosed with late-stage pancreatic cancer.

Scott texted me the news, and I was grateful he hadn't called because I wouldn't have made it through that conversation. He said the cancer had already metastasized to her liver, and she had blood clots in her lungs. She was getting chemo and trying to keep her spirits up, relying on her family, friends, and devout faith. There was no need to state the obvious: that pancreatic cancer, an aggressive disease with no cure, was a death sentence.

"I've never known anyone who has survived more than six months," he said. "So that's all I expect. We don't talk about it. She's a firm Christian but has tossed off the Catholic Church."

Like her parents, Pam had always been a supremely faithful Catholic, but I wasn't at all surprised—given what I'd heard about Scott's Catholic School abuse—that she turned her back on that particular church. I felt this was even more anecdotal evidence that what Brad had told me was true.

Soon after that exchange, I got another one of my Google alerts that was eerily prescient and apropos. Douglasville's regional Catholic diocese had just opened up a reparations fund for victims of sexual abuse by its Catholic clergy and lay people. It was a monetary fund to compensate adults like Scott who were abused as children by church and institutional pedophiles.

The move to own up to decades of church abuse and cover-ups had been years in the making. Inarguably, the groundswell for truth and reform followed a 2002 series of investigative reports by *The Boston Globe's* "Spotlight" team that uncovered the widespread child molestation scandal within Boston's Catholic Church. The series earned *The Globe* a Pulitzer Prize for Public Service and was dramatized in the 2015 film *Spotlight*.

The State of Pennsylvania investigated two of the commonwealth's eight Catholic dioceses on similar charges in 2005 and again in the early to mid-2010s. The remaining six dioceses were the focus of a recent two-year investigation into sexual abuse charges that had just concluded last August.

Dozens of abuse victims testified before a secret grand jury and helped produce a landmark 885-page report that identified 300 Catholic predator priests and over 1,000 victims. Senior church officials knew about the abuse and routinely covered it up by shuttling the molesters to other parishes.

The victims were both male and female; some were older teens, and others were prepubescent, but mostly, they were young boys between the ages of 11 and 14. Some were manipulated with alcohol or pornography, others were made to masturbate their assailants, and others were groped and raped. Nearly all the cases were too old to be prosecuted.

Victims who testified before the state grand jury—and later told their stories to newspapers—said they suffered lifelong problems as a result of the abuse, including drug and alcohol dependency, PTSD, anxiety, panic attacks, depression, and social withdrawal. Many also lost their faith and trust in the church and other institutions.

The grand jury recommended the state eliminate the statute of limitations for childhood sexual abuse crimes so that previously barred victims could now sue. The PA legislature agreed and signaled its willingness to adopt the measure. And rather than wait for the inevitable lawsuits that might bankrupt their coffers, dioceses across the state started offering reparations programs.

I found an article from a county news publication that profiled sexual abuse cases by two teachers at Scott's Catholic school in the mid-1970s. The article featured a woman, now 55, who said she was abused by a teacher there when she was 12-13 years old. At least one other former student had come forward to accuse this same teacher, and the woman said she was gratified to know that her abuser's name was on the Diocese public disclosure list of those credibly accused, even though he was now deceased.

A second teacher at Scott's Catholic school was accused of sexual abuse by two former unnamed students during the same timeframe. This teacher was also on the public disclosure list with a notation that his current whereabouts were unknown.

I assumed Scott's abuser was one of these two teachers mentioned in the article. But did Scott know about this victim compensation fund and that it would only be open for seven months? Scott had been out of work for half a year, and I knew he could use the money. Anyone wanting to apply for remuneration had to file before October. I agonized over what to do because I'd never told him I knew his secret.

And then, sadly, my problem was solved. On a chilly spring morning, Bill Powell's more-than-a-housekeeper let herself into the mid-century ranch home where Scott and Pam grew up. She was devastated to find their father had passed away overnight in his favorite stuffed recliner chair. On the carpet, next to the 85-year-old retired professor, was his oxygen mask and a full tank of O2.

Scott was convinced his dad went to sleep without putting on the mask, hoping he would not wake up in the morning. "I know he didn't want to live to see my sister wither away and die," he told me.

—

Gordo and I both drove to Douglasville for the funeral. And I suspected Gordo's gesture, like mine, was twofold—there was no telling when we'd next see Pam. As I drove those familiar roads to the town of my youth, Jack's words about life not being fair echoed from his grave. Though I wasn't as close with her as I was to her brother, I knew Pam to be an unpretentious soul who never had an unkind word for anyone or anything. She was a devoted wife, mother, sister, teacher, and volunteer, and far and away the very best of us among our Diners Club crew.

But I had a third reason for coming to Douglasville, and I agonized over how to proceed.

Gordo and I mingled with the funeral attendees. Scott introduced us to Ashley, who had some piercings and a young woman by her side, and we shook hands with his ex-wife and her husband. We hugged Russ and Pam, who was frail with thinning hair, and we left unsaid among our sympathies the more tragic circumstance of her diagnosis.

Bill Powell's life was celebrated with a Christian Mass that included a sermon, gospel readings, hymns, and Holy Communion. A U.S. Army Veteran and later history professor at our local college, he was beloved in the community and had been an active church and choir member. The officiating priest conducted a *name reading* to honor and remember Bill's loved ones who passed away before him. The priest spoke the names of Joanne Powell, his wife of 56 years, and a brother and sister from Cincinnati. He paused for a moment of silence after each name, and I was sure there wasn't one person in those church pews who didn't grimly wonder when Bill's daughter would join the family roll call.

It wasn't lost on me that this funeral service, held at Douglasville's only Catholic church, was right next door to its parish school, where Pam and Scott attended, and their mother worked as a part-time secretary. This is where I'd chosen to rip off the Band-Aid, but only because the stars had aligned so I could do it in person.

I asked Scott if I could speak to him alone and felt guilty, leading him down a hall and into a Sunday school classroom. He hugged me again, this time with red eyes, and thanked me for coming, but I told him to "Hold that thought" as I motioned for us to sit at a kids' craft table outfitted with construction paper and scissors. I pulled a copy of the diocese announcement about the reparations fund from my purse and handed it to him.

He only needed to read the headline to understand the moment, and as soon as he looked at me, I released my well-rehearsed explanation.

"I'm so sorry to give you this—here, now. But I couldn't email it to you, Scott. And the fund is only open for six more months."

"It's okay, Carla, but how did you ..."

"It was Brad," I said, and I told him the story of how our dead friend slurred a few details and betrayed his confidence almost five years ago.

And then, to my surprise, he said, "Well, I've already started a file with the diocese. One of their attorneys contacted me, and I decided to file a case."

"That's amazing," I said.

After Scott confirmed his abuser's name, I said, "Well, the diocese thinks he's still alive."

He could tell I wanted to know more, and he shared that he never told anyone about the abuse until he was married. His ex-wife's father had connections in law enforcement, and Scott gave the go-ahead for a nationwide search for the pedophile science teacher. They discovered the teacher had moved to a school in Virginia, and Scott called the school and wrote a letter outlining the abuse.

"Maybe he's still in Virginia," Scott shrugged. He said he was aware there was a second middle school teacher on the diocese's public disclosure list but that he didn't know anything about that individual.

"You know," I said, "my brother Tony went to that school for one year as a third-grader right before we moved to Florida."

"Huh. So he would have been too young for science class."

"Yeah."

"But you guys aren't Catholic, so why did your folks send him there?"

"Oh, Marilyn was so pissed off at the public elementary school because they threatened to use corporal punishment on Tony. I guess he was a rambunctious kid, you know, acted out, talked when he wasn't supposed to, and they called my mom and said they were going to have to paddle him. She typed up a letter saying she did *not* agree to her seven-year-old baby boy getting spanked in the principal's office and would sue them if they so much as touched one little curl on his pretty head. She had the letter notarized and everything, which put them on notice, but I guess she thought he'd do better at the Catholic school."

"Wow, quite the story," he said. We sat there in silence until he told me he knew what I was thinking. "Carla, I know you want details, what things happened to me, how it all played out ... and all I'm going to say is that anything and everything that can be done to a child sexually was done to me."

I swallowed hard from embarrassment because he was right, of course, and also to keep from crying.

"And I don't even care if you put this in your book. But I never want to talk about it again."

I bounced my head up and down in the affirmative and quickly caught a tear before it made its way down my cheek.

"You can ask Gordo about it if you want."

"Gordo?"

He nodded. "Yeah. I told him the summer we went sky diving. He's going to write a letter to the diocese, confirming I told him and a bunch of other life-impact shit that would be good for my case file. Pam's writing a letter too. Would you ..."

"I'd be happy to ..."

We smiled after talking over each other.

"Of course, I will," I said.

On my way home, I decided I would not ask Gordo about it. Ever. I didn't need to know more. I didn't want to know more. I already had enough images of prison abuse etched into my brain that no Jedi Mind Trick could ever erase.

—

In the summer, I flew to Orlando to see my mom and Tony. I picked a week that Jim had to go to Germany for work, and I also arranged to see Kevin at Coleman II.

On the Saturday I was there, I joined my mother at Tony's office to volunteer with the weekly food drive he and his wife had started last year. His growing real estate business meant expanding into bigger quarters, which came with a large attached covered pavilion. The outdoor space with rows of picnic tables was the perfect location to spread produce, canned goods, and other items donated by local grocery stores.

A camera crew from a local TV station was there that day filming for a profile on the entrepreneurial couple who helped over 100 food-insecure families a week. Marilyn was a friendly fixture among volunteers and chatted it up with some of the regulars. She and my niece and nephew even got some camera time.

Later that night, we all watched the TV news segment live at my brother's house. It was a heartwarming, feel-good story about giving back and community involvement. The viewing turned into a pool party with some of their friends and volunteers, and we all ate grilled burgers and hot dogs and kicked around their saltwater pool. I was so proud of my brother and sister-in-law and told them so while floating on a foam noodle.

I said I'd never be able to repay them for the love, time, and attention they showed Marilyn. Everything from her finances to healthcare to car repairs fell on Tony's shoulders. "All I do is swoop into town once a year and take her out to lunch," I said. Tony disagreed, but it was largely true. He did all the heavy sibling lifting, and I didn't know what Marilyn or I would do without him.

Bobbing up and down in the water on our colorful foam noodles, I asked him if he still had good memories from his one year of Catholic school in Douglasville before we moved.

"In the third grade? Oh yeah, I had the best teacher, Mr. Doran. He lived near us, you know, and some of us used to go over and play football in his yard ... why do you ask?"

"No reason," I smiled and kissed the top of my little brother's head.

—

I saw Kevin in Coleman II's general visitation room, and we were allowed to hug briefly. Physical contact was severely restricted because girlfriends or partners had ways of passing along small packets of drugs, usually wrapped in latex and concealed in a mouth or vagina.

Kevin presented me with two whimsical drawings, mostly in black and white but with touches of aqua and yellow that he added by rubbing off the color from magazine pages. One was of a woman's hand holding a rose, and the other was a giant eyeball with a spider crawling into it. A small creepy skull reflected off the eye's pupil.

Kevin was "on one," meaning he was in the last year of his prison sentence before being assigned to a halfway house. The First Step Act, with its good time recalculation rule, had shaved five weeks off his prison term. If he stayed out of trouble, he'd be released in April 2021.

He caught me up on the latest prison gossip. An inmate had been strangled to death on Superbowl Sunday, and no one still knew why or who had done it. Also, T-Rex had been abruptly transferred out of Coleman II. T-Rex had been importing through an outside network "legal" documents with corners dipped in Suboxone, which he turned into a highly profitable hustle during his six-month stay. The former AB leader was eventually busted after ordering the killing of a fellow inmate who couldn't pay his drug debt (and who had survived the stabbing). So T-Rex was shipped back to Florence ADX to serve out his life sentence, except now he had a lot of money on his books to ease the monotony of his confinement.

I shook my head at this gruesome tale and asked Kevin, again, if he thought a tell-all book about these gangsters would be worth it when he finally left prison.

"What if you have a family someday?" I said.

He took a long while to answer and said, "I don't think they're a threat no more. The AB in Lewisburg is gone, T-Rex is dropped out and he never tried nothing against me, never sent anyone after me."

"Still, I don't think it's wise to use anyone's real name or even nickname in the book," I said.

"Does it worry you? Personally?"

"Yeah, it does … And it concerns my husband. He worries about it."

Kevin said he didn't think the remaining white power gang members in other prisons had the interest or capability to retaliate over a true story about themselves. And if they did find out about the book, they'd probably like the notoriety.

—

I dealt with that angst by ignoring that aspect of the book, at least for now. I'd written some chapters concerning Scott's and my backstory and about our Diner's Club and showed them to two of my liberal dinner party friends. These two *beta readers*—an English professor/published author/poet, and a well-known niche filmmaker—knew my journey with this story from the start. Their feedback was positive and encouraging, and they loved the prose. But when I showed the chapters to Jim, he said, "Where's all the good stuff about Kevin? I thought this was a story about him?"

It had been a busy year, and I hadn't carved out much time for writing. I'd gone to Europe twice with Jim on his business trips, and I was helping to plan a wedding.

My 2019 ended on two perfect notes. The first was The Orange Man's impeachment over a summertime "perfect call" he'd made to Ukraine's president, in which Trump threatened to withhold foreign aid unless that leader investigated his 2020 Democratic election challenger, Joe Biden.

The second was a perfect wedding. We witnessed the splendid marriage of our oldest son and his beautiful bride, the phenomenal girlfriend we hadn't dared to hope would become family.

The ceremony was held on a crisp late afternoon at the edge of a harvested cornfield. My Florida family and Jim's larger extended brood were all there, seated in folding chairs surrounded by picturesque farmland, pumpkins, and cornstalks. The event also marked our first formal gathering with the parents of our younger son's fiancé. We were thrilled to bring both of these incredible, strong partners our sons had chosen, plus their loved ones, into our fold.

The bride's mother and I took turns at the podium with prepared remarks for the glowing couple. Though I was not religious, I chose to read a famous passage from the New Testament, from 1st Corinthians Chapter 13, that was often heard at weddings. I told the audience it had been recited at Jim's and my wedding 32 years ago, and that one line in particular was regularly quoted in my marriage. I asked everyone to guess which line it was.

The passage came from a letter the Apostle Paul wrote to the church and people of Corinth on *The Gift of Love*:

> *Love is patient, love is kind*
> *Love is not jealous or boastful*
> *It is not arrogant or rude*
> *Love does not insist on its own way*
> *It is not easily angered or resentful*
> *Love does not rejoice in the wrong but rejoices in the right*

"I have to pause here to mention that this 'not rejoicing in the wrong' business can be really hard," I said. "Especially for those of us who are frequently right. Yes, this is the line Jim and I so often quote, and usually, this is how it goes:

"'Are YOU rejoicing in the wrong?' Or 'You're rejoicing in the wrong! You're rejoicing in the wrong!' And someone is pointing a finger.'

"So, yes, absolutely, Jim and I rejoice in the wrong. But somehow, calling it out and laughing about it eases the infraction, so remember that."

I blew a kiss to my son and soon-to-be daughter-in-law and returned to the first row of chairs to hear their vows. They wrote touching affirmations of their love for one another and how they saw their lives play out. And, when they talked of future children and which of their vehicles would be "the French fry car," I felt a lump in my throat and reached for Jim's hand.

The food was divine, and the 10-piece band was outstanding. Jim gave an exceptional toast without notes, and we ended the evening eating Philly cheesesteaks around an outdoor firepit. Two of Jim's nephews whisked Marilyn away to a smoker's corner; she had the time of her life. My mother later declared it was the best wedding she had ever attended.

"No," she corrected herself. "It was the most *perfect* wedding ever."

For non-spiritual people, Jim and I felt blessed beyond reason to be immersed in this much love, happiness, and good fortune. We weren't just surviving the Dark Ages, we were thriving. And so were our people.

—

On the last day of the year, Reuters, The Associated Press, and the German public broadcaster Deutsche Welle all reported that Chinese health authorities were investigating 27 cases of "unexplained pneumonia" in the city of Wuhan. Most people who'd fallen ill had visited the same seafood market, and an assessment and cleanup were underway. All three news outlets mentioned the online speculation that the mysterious viral pneumonia was similar to the 2002-2003 SARS (Severe Acute Respiratory Syndrome) outbreak in southern China. Chinese officials were accused of covering up the SARS outbreak for weeks until the highly contagious disease spread to several other countries and the death toll grew. That epidemic killed 775 people after infecting more than 8,000 and was eventually brought under control through quarantines and shutdowns.

The Chinese health commission said the cause of the recent outbreak was still unclear and called on its citizens not to panic.

PART III

CHAPTER 40
PANDEMIC

To: Kevin Sanders
From: Angela Lansbury
Date: January 11, 2020 1:36 p.m.
Subject: What's New?

How's it going Kevin? I'm packing up our New England apartment, now that my hubs' assignment is over. Movers are coming in two days. After this, I need to get back to the other biz of our project—I'm looking forward to diving back in where I left off before last fall's wedding events detoured me …

You have a birthday coming up! Have you read Devil in the White City by Erik Larson? It's a fantastic true crime story about the 1893 World's Fair/Columbian Exposition in Chicago AND a simultaneous chronicle of a ghastly serial killer who lived nearby. I just finished the audio version and thought you might like it.

Let me know what you're up to, and if you know anything yet on your out-placement date to a halfway house … should be in about four months, right? G

To: Angela Lansbury
From: Kevin Sanders
Date: January 25, 2020 8:21 a.m.
Subject: Re: What's New?

Gela, I love the book, I'm almost finished with it. Good read and lots of facts that make it a learner. :) I'm told I can put in a relocation to go to live with Scott in Pittsburgh and sit here for six more months as it all gets approved or go to California and get out in the next four months. I'm on my case worker to file the paperwork. I'm sending u some records and drawings and photos and things for safe keeping as I get ready to go. K :)

—

To: Kevin Sanders
From: Angela Lansbury
Date: February 23, 2020 5:48 p.m.
Subject: Re: Hey

Hi K - I talked to S last night for almost an hour. He totally gets (as do I) the decision to head out to California if that is your quickest option. And he assured me he will be waiting in Pittsburgh when the time comes that you can make your way there :-)

He finally decided to set up his own practice there. He quit a temp job looking over documents for some law firm. He'll try representing defendants again and is setting up shop near a courthouse. I said his business move was inspiring me to return to our writing project :-)

I got a fancy new scanner that is proving instrumental in scanning in all the wonderful material I have received from you over the years. You know I can never get enough, though, and I always look forward to my mail from you :-)

Take care in there! G

—

To: Kevin Sanders
From: Angela Lansbury
Date: March 9, 2020 6:06 p.m.
Subject: Re: Hey

Hey Kevin — how are you doing and what's going on at Coleman II? Do you have any new info on your halfway house?

Is anyone panicking there over Coronavirus? I traveled with hubs to Atlanta this week but almost didn't. He's at an industry trade show, and a lot of the vendors have pulled out. He's supposed to go to Paris for work next week, and as of now, I'm planning to tag along too, but that trip might get canceled.

Our Philly Airbnb is now suffering along with the mainstream hotel and tourism industry. We lost most of our March bookings in the last two days. There is panic spreading ... Hope you are well, my friend :-) G

—

To: Angela Lansbury
From: Kevin Sanders
Date: March 10, 2020 6:50 a.m.
Subject: Re: Hey

Gela, the halfway house date is not popped up yet :(But soon, I hope. The sickness out there is so crazy and all I think about is the staff bring that stuff in here to mess up the prison. We are all like a little hub that would fall apart in here with something like that, and then getting help in here would be so bad. When u do get sick they don't want to help u, they act like it's too much of a problem to get u the help u need when ur down. So I don't touch nothing and I stay out the way. :) All is good and I'm working, thinking of all I got to do for this release. I hope that ur safe and ur hubs is safe also on this trip. DONT TOUCH NOTHING and wash ur hands. It would kill me after all this time that something would happen to u just before I got out. Can't even think of it Gela. STAY SAFE. K

—

To: Kevin Sanders
From: Angela Lansbury
Date: March 18, 2020 11:51 a.m.
Subject: Hope you are well

K, I just want you to know I'm thinking about you and everyone at Coleman II. What's the status there?

My peeps and I are pretty much riding it out at home. Hubs is working from home. My brother is a real estate agent and is taking a big hit with the housing market tanking. My daughter-in-law is a nurse and is picking up extra shifts—sort of experiencing a calm before the storm, she thinks. It's not as bad (yet) in Philly like it is in NYC. Stay safe and well :-) G

—

To: Angela Lansbury
From: Kevin Sanders
Date: March 19, 2020 11:07 a.m.
Subject: Re: Hope you are well

Gela, the prison has stopped all visits and contact from the outside world, but the staff still work and have to keep a 6-foot space. We only go to the mess hall one unit at a time and really don't have interaction with one another. The other day we was on lock down 'cause some kid got gang raped. :(So crazy with all the crap in here. But I stay safe and in my cell so I don't get in to nothing, not even a chance to be at the wrong spot at a bad time. Never know what can pop off and I don't want to get set up. Haven't heard yet of the date but the issues of the covid19 are slowing things down. I can't lie and say I don't stress over u and ur fam bam with this sickness going around. I pray for all of u and hope that nothing goes wrong out there for u and ur loved ones. I just want to get out and get going. It's all I think of. Take care Gela. K. :)

—

To: Carla, Gordo, Leroy and Eric
From: Scott
Date: March 18, 2020 11:46 a.m.
Subject: Good Luck! Love you guys.

During our first plague-type pandemic, just wanted to wish you all the best. Love all of you.

Scott Powell, JD

To: Kevin Sanders
From: Angela Lansbury
Date: April 5, 2020 12:06 p.m.
Subject: Re: Hope you are well

Hi Kevin—We're all still good here ... I'm curious about the infection rate at your location, including staff and inmates. What can you tell me? My nurse daughter-in-law is being re-deployed to hospital units as the need arises. They are expecting their surge in mid-May. So that is disconcerting to us, of course. She will move into our empty Airbnb in order to keep our son safe and free of Covid. I am thankful that she personally does not intubate patients (doesn't have to put them on ventilators or breathing tubes) or work with others who do, as that seems to be where the greatest risk to healthcare providers is.

So shit's getting real now, and I'm trying not to worry excessively. Stay safe as you can. Talk soon :-) G

—

To: Carla
From: Scott
Date: April 15, 2020 12:43 p.m.
Subject: Happy Pandemic. Just checking in.

Just making sure you and Jim and your boys are still well. Ashley is fine at her mother's. Russ and Pam's kids have moved back in with them, and they're all staying away from other people. Pam is unable to take chemo or radiation treatments. She's up for a trial at Penn with a drug that has had success with ovarian and uterine cancer, but fingers crossed on metastasized pancreatic cancer.

With the courthouses closed, I can't pick up any clients. And my Dad died a year ago today, so I'm a little off …

Scott

—

To: Scott
From: Carla
Date: April 15, 2020 3:05 p.m.
Subject: Re: Happy Pandemic. Just checking in.

Oh gosh Scott, has it been a year? Geeze … And Pam's situation. It's so horribly depressing. As if there isn't enough to be down about right now.

I emailed with Kevin last week. He and all inmates finally got a surgical-grade mask—one—and are locked down except for three showers a week. I think he's kind of resigned to not being able to get into a halfway house during this pandemic. Who knows if he'll get to go to one at all. His out-date is listed as 4-20-21. He's pretty cheerful about being "short" in his sentence now.

All of us Contis are doing as well as can be expected. Jim had to return to the workplace to cover for his plant manager, who can't get back into the country. So he's overseeing about 150 production line workers, engineers, etc. They don't have enough masks and there is no way to operate the line and stay six feet away from each other. They've staggered shifts, but two of the line workers have died from Covid already. The business will remain open because it's "essential," in that they provide parts and equipment for crucial supply-chain customers like UPS, Amazon, and others. I am heartsick each time he leaves for work in the morning.

I call Marilyn almost every day. I know how lonely it is for people living by themselves. I'm not being productive on the book or anything other than keeping food in the house, Jim and me fed, and staying in touch with family and friends.

Hugs

CHAPTER 41
ARMAGEDDON

THE SHITTY REMAINS OF THE YEAR OF OUR LORD 2020

After downplaying the severity of COVID-19 and turning over press conferences to his health experts, The Orange Man had been missing the spotlight. So, in late April, he joined a presser—quickly tagged as "the bleach press conference"—where he rambled on about bleach and spitballed that sunlight and disinfectant could be COVID miracle cures.

Later that night, author and comedian Sarah Cooper posted a homemade video to TikTok and Twitter that spoofed the imbecilic stream-of-consciousness performance. She pantomimed and lip-synced a 49-second video clip titled "How to Medical" using The Orange Man's own words:

> *"... we hit the body with a tremendous—whether it's ultraviolet or just very powerful light—and I think you said that that hasn't been checked, but you're going to test it. And then I said, supposing you brought the light inside the body, which you can do either through the skin or in some other way, and I think you said you're going to test that,*

*too. It sounds interesting. And then I see
the disinfectant, where it knocks it out in
a minute. One minute. And is there a way
we can do something like that, by injection
inside or almost a cleaning? Because
you see it gets in the lungs, and it does a
tremendous number on the lungs. So it would
be interesting to check that. So, that, you're
going to have to use medical doctors, right?
But it sounds interesting to me."*

Cooper's video went viral, and a new comedy hero was born. *Praise be* for her and all the other comedians helping me and my kind survive this inconceivable crisis amid what would hopefully be the last year of the *Dumpster Fire* presidency.

After that press conference, a few Biden election signs popped up in my neighborhood that said, "He Won't Inject You With Bleach." Hilarious? Unfortunately, yes. Impactful? Probably not. Polls showed voters were nearly evenly split between Trump and Biden, and there weren't many undecideds in the upcoming November election. That approximately half the country was willing to return The Orange Man to the presidency was as confounding as it was infuriating. How could that many people hate America so much? Or did they just want to "own the libs" no matter the cost?

—

Two months into the pandemic, Jim's plant manager was able to re-enter the U.S. and return to his duties. So Jim resumed working from our townhouse and growing out his hair and beard again. I now had to keep the fridge stocked for his lunch as well as dinner and had to give up an office bedroom. I set up shop in the kitchen, and it seemed he was constantly invading my space by coming down for another coffee or an apple. "How many Nespressos have you had today?" I barked once, trying to look around him at a crucial cable news story he was blocking. He looked at me and the TV disapprovingly and replied, "How many chapters of your book have you written?"

Book? What book? How could I work on a book when people were dying left and right of COVID, and I had to wipe off my groceries and procure toilet paper and keep tabs on virus surges and stay on top of the Trump shitshow and tune into New York Governor Andrew Cuomo's press conferences for a daily dose of sanity?

"I'm working on something else," I said.

"Oh?"

"It's an escape plan. In case The Dumpster wins again. I WILL NOT do another four years of The Orange Man," I declared, with no other explanation. Jim didn't even ask what I was up to but just rolled his eyes and walked back upstairs with his cappuccino.

I couldn't write with the TV on, but I could certainly work on my family tree to the steady beat of television news in the background. In recent weeks, I'd immersed myself in my Ancestry.com account to fill in the gaps on my father's Italian side of the family. I traced his relatives back to my 6th great-grandparents, to one Domenico Parello, born in 1695. I connected to newfound third and fourth cousins as determined by our DNA tests and linked family trees, and then I got an idea. Or rather, I revisited an old idea with new possibilities.

I'd previously explored gaining dual U.S.-Italian citizenship through my grandparents, who came to this country in the 1910s. Italy was among just a handful of countries that offered the right to claim citizenship based on *Jure Sanguinis*, Latin for "right of blood," i.e., by descent. Typically, this was done through a father or grandfather who had not become a naturalized U.S. Citizen. But because my father's father served in World War I and renounced his allegiance to the King of Italy, that door was closed for me. However, a new pathway was being forged in Italian courts based on a mother's or grandmother's lineage that had previously been blocked.

The Italian courts were starting to recognize that Italian women married to Italian spouses who became naturalized elsewhere were being *subjugated* if they were labeled naturalized just because their husbands were. This was a loophole in a complex web of legalities, and pursuing this option meant hiring an Italian lawyer and gathering many documents. The biggest paperwork hurdle was getting written proof that my grandmother had not, on her own, become a naturalized U.S. citizen. So, I started the process and wrote to the Immigration and Naturalization Services for essentially "no proof" of her citizenship, hoping to get a letter of "no records" in return. I'd read this was a tedious quest that could take up to a year or two, but if my case prevailed, my boys and I, plus any grandchildren, would have immediate citizenship and could get Italian passports. This, in turn, meant automatic entry into the European Union. Our non-Italian spouses could gain the same status after passing an intermediate-level Italian language test.

This whole fantastical pursuit was the only thing that kept me from losing my mind while the world imploded.

—

As summer approached, COVID cases surged in the sunbelt, including Florida and its retirement hub, The Villages. Once the pools and rec centers—with Fox News blaring—reopened, Marilyn was increasingly confronted by her mask-shunning, Trump-loving neighbors. "They're getting really aggressive," she told me. "Biden supporters are getting their cars keyed and their flags ripped off their flagpoles." She said the MAGA faithful paraded around in their Trump-decorated golf carts and continued to gather in groups, defying social distancing restrictions. And after she attended a small Black Lives Matter memorial for George Floyd—the black man murdered by a white cop in Minnesota who knelt on his neck until he suffocated to death—she had to drop out of her regular golf foursome because the discourse got so heated.

"I hate to say it, but I'm living among a bunch of racists," she said of her 98-percent white community. "I guess they were always here, but they never wore it on their sleeves until he (Trump) came along."

The Orange Man derided Joe Biden for running his campaign from his Delaware home, claiming Biden was hiding out in his basement. So, in a show of strength, Trump rejoined the campaign trail in June, kicking off a season of superspreader events that sickened and killed off untold numbers of his worshipers.

The earliest example of this was the tragic case of Herman Cain, an African American politician who co-chaired the Black Voices for Trump coalition. An accomplished businessman, mathematician, and computer systems analyst, Cain was once CEO of Godfather's Pizza and ran unsuccessfully for president twice. (His 2011 White House bid ended abruptly after claims of sexual harassment and evidence of a love child—which he'd denied and kept hidden from his wife—surfaced.) He was perhaps best known for quipping that if a reporter asked him a "gotcha" question like who the president of "Ubeki-beki-beki-beki-stan-stan" was, he would have to say he didn't know.

The Orange Man's team flew Cain to Tulsa, Oklahoma, for Trump's indoor mask-optional June 20 rally as the pandemic raged throughout the city. About 6,000 people attended and sat randomly in clusters in an arena that held 19,000. Cain, who voiced contempt for face coverings on social media, was photographed with about a dozen black rally-goers, all smiling and unmasked except for one. Two days later, it was reported that eight Trump staffers tested positive for coronavirus. And Cain, a 74-year-old stage-four cancer survivor, tested positive a week later. He was quickly hospitalized and, after a month, died of complications from the virus.

Charles Darwin, history's most famous biologist who said that only the species that adapt to change will survive, was having his moment.

—

One hot summer afternoon, Jim decided to wash and vacuum our cars. But I had forgotten to discard the evidence, in the rear of my SUV, of my secret mission that accompanied nearly every one of my rare outings to stock our fridge and pantry. Jim stormed into the kitchen, waving a political lawn banner, and said, "Carla, you have to stop stealing Trump signs. What if you get caught?"

I just stared at him and offered no explanation.

"People have those video doorbells, you know, and if you're not recognizable on them, your license plate probably is."

"You're right," I said. "Good point about those video doorbells. I'm going to have to wear a disguise, park down the street, and go shopping at night."

We stared at each other, and he shook his head. Then, I watched him from the window dispose of the evidence in a black plastic garbage bag before dumping it in the trash bin.

A week or so later, he accused me of trying to pick a fight with one of our neighbors, who started parking his red Ford F-150 along the side corner of our townhouse. Jim saw me remove two of the truck's bumper stickers and slide them into my purse.

"What are you doing, Carla? You are losing it!"

"Why are you spying on me?" I countered. "I don't need to walk out here every day and see this hateful bullshit!"

In my defense, the stickers weren't just normal pro-Trump slogans, they were obscene anti-Biden stickers—one showed a cartoon Trump figure pissing on a Biden-Harris sign, and the other said "Biden for Prison." Also, they were easy to peel off.

"This guy's an asshole, and you know it ... I'd slit his throat for a home COVID test kit."

This rendered Jim speechless for a brief moment until he turned sympathetic and suggested, ever so gently, that maybe I ought to see a therapist.

I did not go see a shrink. I bought another domain name, *TheVileTurd.com*, and started a new political blog. It was the only theft and vandalism-free way I had to combat this never-ending clusterfuck.

My first story for my new blog concerned a recent poll that gave Biden a slight edge over Trump among likely voters and Trump's excuse for his polling plunge. The Orange Man blamed his son-in-law Jared Kushner's "woke shit" reforms like The First Step Act. The party of law and order wasn't a fan of releasing people early from prison, Trump reasoned.

The one—ONE—decent thing to come out of his shitstorm administration, and he wouldn't even recognize it. *That's the president I know and hate*, I thought, and I wrote in so many words on my blog.

I even got Kevin on board with drawing some funny sketches to go with my posts, including different versions of a diapered baby Trump.

—

By August, Coleman II had slowly opened up to more pre-pandemic routines. Kevin was still hoping to hear about a halfway house program, but I think we both felt he would finish out his last eight months exactly where he was. I tapped Marilyn's English class syllabus for book ideas for his last full year behind bars and sent him titles I remembered reading and loving in high school: *To Kill a Mockingbird* by Harper Lee; *Fahrenheit 451* by Ray Bradbury; and *1984* and *Animal Farm* by George Orwell.

As the election and year's end drew closer, Kevin learned definitively that he would get no halfway house time. COVID-19 had upended the program and rendered too many residential reentry centers (RRCs) unavailable or shut down due to virus cases on-site. But even worse than that, the Bureau of Prisons was intent on returning him to his hometown despite Scott offering to sponsor him in Pittsburgh. Kevin had no family or support system in Central California, which meant he'd be released to a *homeless shelter. During Covid.* In addition, the area the BOP wanted to send him back to was a known hotbed for the Aryan Brotherhood and other racial gang activity.

So Scott and I launched a letter-writing campaign reiterating Scott's willingness to help Kevin in Pittsburgh and pleading with prison officials to release Kevin into Scott's care. We sent copies to the warden, Kevin's case worker, and his counselor and then waited for a response.

Scott continued getting "barber shop referral" clients and spent much of the year filing briefs and motions pro bono from his house, assuming the money would flow later when the courts reopened. But I no longer needed to worry about how he was making ends meet. His Catholic diocese settlement had come in, and between that windfall and his half of his father's estate, Scott was now worth nearly $1 million. I was relieved when he told me, and I offered to set him up with the financial advisor Jim and I used, but he said he was following the investment advice of a fraternity brother who operated a hedge fund.

Jim and I braced for election night with mild trepidation and cautious optimism. And we tried to shrug off the four-day wait for some very close vote counts in battleground states. Finally, on November 7, more than half the nation's long nightmare was over when TV networks called the race for Biden. It had come down to a handful of states, including mine. In addition to Pennsylvania, Biden had flipped Arizona, Michigan, Wisconsin, and Georgia from red to blue, mostly by razor-thin margins. The final electoral college count was 306 for Biden and 232 for Trump, making Trump the first incumbent president to lose reelection since George H. W. Bush in 1992. Across the country, Biden won 7 million more popular votes than The Orange Man.

A win was a win, despite the anticipated snot-nosed temper tantrum oozing out of MAGA Country. Trump had already telegraphed that the election would be "rigged" if he lost, so we expected nothing less of this skidmark on America's underpants.

The day after the election was called, the beloved TV quiz show host Alex Trebek lost his battle with pancreatic cancer. The iconic television personality, who hosted "Jeopardy" for over three decades, was an inspiration to millions after revealing his stage-four diagnosis in March of 2019—the same month Scott's sister Pam received her diagnosis.

This made me want to check in with Scott to learn how she was doing and to find out how he was handling the election loss—if he wanted to bring it up, which he did so immediately. He said he was still proudly flying his Trump flag in front of his bungalow, but "I'm getting tired of people driving by yelling *Fuck Trump*.

"I do have my 12-gauge semi-automatic shotgun with a 20-round clip and another one in the chamber, in case they want to do anything about it," he added.

He said he'd keep his Trump flag flying until the U.S. Supreme Court decided that our Pennsylvania legislature erred in extending the deadline for counting some mailed ballots by three days due to the pandemic and postal delays.

For fuck's sake. "You are far too smart to be that delusional, Scott," I said. "The math just isn't there to make a difference with whatever minuscule irregularities might get presented in court. Certainly, you know this is the expected backlash against the vile, reprehensible, radioactive turd who defiled the Oval Office these last four years. The pendulum swings. Math is math. I know you understand this."

"Well, at least it's on the table," he said of the PA court challenge. "There is nothing delusional about my support of Trump. I don't blame you or make any judgment of you. But all of your information comes from institutional sources. And you and everyone you know listen to the same information. I gave up on major media at least five years ago."

He extolled The Orange Man's virtues, as he saw them, including Trump's pulling out of the Paris Climate Accords, dissolving NAFTA, and killing the Trans-Pacific Trade Agreement, all of which were "shitty deals for U.S. Workers but great for International corporations," he said.

Then he texted me an image of an American Flag above the definition of *Patriot: a person who vigorously supports their country and is prepared to defend it against enemies or detractors.* Synonyms included *Proud American* and *True American.* "We're the Resistance," he said.

I didn't have the time or interest to list The Orange Man's failings and vices, so I just texted Scott a link to a CNN story: *The results are in: The stock market likes Joe Biden.*

"I couldn't be a more *Proud American* today," I said. "Waaahhh, waahhh, waahhh—you guys are a bunch of goddamn crybabies. Welcome to my world four fucking years ago."

Then I took a breath and said, "This is NOT why I reached out to you today." I told him I'd read the news about Alex Trebek and wanted to know how Pam was.

"She called me two weeks ago. She's on pain meds. She restarted chemo. And she's still dying."

I asked about his daughter Ashley, and he said they hadn't talked in months. "Not since she gave me an ultimatum that I had to vote for Biden. Which I would never do." He said he texted or tried to call her a couple of times each month but that Ashley had cut him out of her life.

"Oh, Scott, this is all so heartbreaking, I'm so sorry. I know it's hard with young people who are so entrenched in their politics. Our youngest is way far left of center and doesn't think Jim and I are progressive enough. We know many families torn apart by these last four years, but we all have to try and get past it. My brother Tony … a handful of our in-laws … we've basically all agreed to disagree, and we don't talk about it. I hope you can find an opening and patch that wound with her. I think you and Ashley need each other."

"At least you and I can stay friends regardless of political affiliations," he said. I replied with an emoji of a smiley face with heart-shaped eyes.

CHAPTER 42
INSURRECTION

JANUARY 2021

W ednesday, January 6, 2021, I was up at my desk early for what I knew would be a busy day of blogging. All eyes were on Washington D.C. and that day's ceremonial tally of each state's electoral votes in a joint session of Congress. This Electoral College Vote Count certification was the final step, mandated by the Constitution, to confirm Joe Biden as the presidential election winner. But the deranged, narcissistic Orange Man, who claimed victory despite all evidence to the contrary, was stirring the pot.

Trump had invited all his rabid followers to protest the certification, and a growing army of cultists—including white supremacists and far-right groups like Proud Boys and Oath Keepers—had descended upon the nation's capital for the *Save America March, Stop the Steal* rally, etc.

In preparation for the day, Team Trump had been illegally assembling fake slates of electors from battleground states. And their fervent hope was that Vice President Mike Pence would not certify the real electors and buy them time to bring those fake electors in. That Pence would break the Constitution, invalidate an election, and keep a dictator in office was a ludicrous scheme that no one in their right mind thought could succeed. *This was America, for Christ's sake!* And yet, as cable news showed, crowds of protestors continued to grow at the Ellipse near the White House, on the National Mall, and in front of the Capitol building.

I'd been having fun with my new website, *TheVileTurd. com*, especially after Trump's embarrassing loss. I'd written about his attempt to brainwash the country about a stolen election and the sycophantic inner circle that propped him up with nefarious plots to keep him in power. I posted stories about the Orange Man's idiot band of lawyers who'd lost *five dozen court cases* trying to prove the election fraud that didn't exist. I wrote pieces about Trump's comic relief advisors like Mike Lindell, the conspiratorial My Pillow guy, and the once-heralded former NYC mayor Rudy Giuliani and his dripping "hair dye" press conference. I paired these articles with hilarious political cartoons, and one of my favorites was drawn by Kevin. He sketched for me a Trump caricature in diapers, who scrawled in red pen "Stop the Vote" and "No Mail," as a tattooed Uncle Sam figure stood over him, pointing, yelling, "You're Fired!"

My frenetic blogging was all seemingly leading up to this day, and I hoped that once Biden was sworn in as the 46th president on January 20, I'd feel like killing my therapy project.

—

It was the fourth anniversary of Brad's death from alcoholism. A little after 10:00 a.m., Leroy started a Diner's Club text chain (minus Pam and Russ) to mark the occasion. "Happy New Year everyone," he said. "Hope you and your families are all well. Was just missing Brad, four years now …"

I replied, "Happy New Year, all. It's hard to believe four years have gone by. Does anyone stay in touch with his family? Scott, do you still talk to Brad's brother?"

Scott replied with a photo of a crowd of people outdoors in winter jackets carrying Trump signs and American flags. I recognized the grassy location and overcast sky from TV news and said, "Holy shit, Scott! Are you at the MAGAturd rally in DC????!!!! Amazing for a schooled lawyer like yourself to check your critical thinking skills at the door and cling to disillusion. So sad (crying emoji)"

Then I added, "Send my thanks to your POS president for handing over Georgia to the Democrats (laughing/crying emoji)." This was a reference to the day before's Georgia senate runoff race, in which two Democrats beat their Trump-backed Republican opponents.

An hour or so went by with no commentary from anyone on the text thread, so I piled on, "Hey Scott, I hear the stupid My Pillow Guy is at your MAGAturd rally! Why don't you get his autograph?"

Two hours later, around 2:00 p.m., Scott replied, "We will have to agree to disagree." Then I felt bad for being so mean, so I texted back, "Honestly, I don't know why you keep me as a friend (smiley face with heart-shaped eyes emoji).

"Because I like you," he texted back.

"Please tell me you're not trying to rush the Capitol and getting pepper-sprayed," I said.

"They are tear-gassing us. But we are not rushing anything," he said.

I replied only with "(sigh)."

No one else from the text thread—Leroy, Gordo, Eric— was weighing in, but I forgot about them for the next two hours anyway because I was glued to the horror show unfolding on live TV.

Angry protestors started climbing the walls of the Capitol and flooding onto its balconies. Windows were being smashed. Officers in riot gear were being overrun. Trump tweeted some bullshit about VP Pence not having the courage to, essentially, break the law, and then suddenly, the House of Representatives adjourned, and lawmakers were whisked out of the Senate chamber. TV cameras captured rioters surging into the Capitol, and reports surfaced that Pence had been evacuated to a secure location and that the Secret Service had shot someone.

What the fuck is happening? Are these people trying to overthrow the government? I was asking myself, in real-time, what all the stunned news reporters and anchors were also wondering: Was this an insurrection?

At 3:44 p.m., my phone buzzed with another text, and it was from Scott. "Sorry, they were jamming our phones. I came for a peaceful protest. When things started to go sideways I left. Had to walk two miles to the car. The D.C. mayor didn't make it easy for us. We had to walk a long way just to get to the rally. We all know this election was fraudulent. But I understand that major media is telling everyone it was fine. Heading back home. And I still like you, Carla."

Oh my God! I exhaled, weary and shaken, and couldn't stop my flood of angry tears any more than the tirade I started typing. "You are so deep into the MAGA cult that you will believe anything they tell you. It is beyond pathetic that you think the election was stolen. Do you really think that, or do you just want to believe it? Sixty court cases say no. Not enough "evidence" to make a difference in the vote count. Even frickin' Bill Barr says so. WAKE UP! Someone was shot today, probably a protester. YOU may have gone for a peaceful protest, but not the rest of your cult. And yet you will be proud to be part of this failed disgusting coup attempt. I am ashamed FOR you because you obviously have no shame."

I heaved big sobs and wiped my messy face on my sweatshirt, unable to move from my swivel chair.

Then Leroy chimed in. "I'm sorry I sent the message about Brad today ..."

I grabbed my phone and typed, "Aren't we all."

Scott replied, "Brad would have been here with me. Love you guys. I'm going home to enjoy my white privilege."

And that's when I knew my friendship with Scott was over. "Fuck you Scott," I typed and slid off my chair onto the floor, where I curled up and bawled like a baby.

—

My plan to rid Scott from my life was disrupted two weeks later. Toward the end of January, my mother called to tell me that Scott's sister Pam had died. My mother had seen it on Facebook, a platform I no longer participated on. I deactivated my account during the 2016 election after getting into a public feud with a cousin over Hillary's emails, which seemed like such a quaint tiff in hindsight. I wasn't sure if Gordo, Leroy, or Eric knew the news about Pam, and I was almost too embarrassed over the January 6 text stream to find out. But I did send a brief email letting them know, and I apologized for my profane text meltdown. Only Eric responded and said he didn't know what I was talking about—it turned out Leroy used an incorrect phone number for him in the thread, and Eric had missed all the drama.

"I don't know what's going on with you and Scott," Eric said, "but whatever it is, I hope you two can patch it up."

Sigh. I texted Scott my condolences and asked about the funeral plans because I wanted to send flowers. "It's going to be a small private service," he told me. "And I'm not going. Everyone has to wear a COVID mask, and since I won't, I'm not invited."

I screamed at my phone, *What the fuck is wrong with you!* before I threw it across the couch.

Kevin's release date of April 20 was fast approaching. And Scott's and my letter-writing campaign to allow Scott to sponsor Kevin in Pittsburgh made no difference to prison officials. We were told the Bureau of Prison's policy was to return an inmate to their place of origin, full-stop. So, Kevin would be sent to a homeless shelter in Valleyview, California, where he'd have to check in with a parole officer.

One month before his release, Kevin's counselor showed him a two-day, 40-hour bus schedule that would take him across the country to Central California. I told him I'd been gathering some travel items for him, like a phone with a pre-paid calling plan, some clothing, toiletry basics, COVID masks, hand sanitizer, etc., but I didn't know how to deliver them. So, somehow, Kevin arranged to extend his bus trip by 10 hours and take a route that included a layover in Pittsburgh, only four-and-a-half hours away from me. I said I'd happily make the drive to hand-deliver the care package and give him a big hug. I planned to make it a three-day trip by staying two nights there with one of my favorite cousins.

All of our last emails and phone calls centered on Kevin's upcoming release. In the event there was resistance or delay in transferring Kevin's parole to Pittsburgh—as I believed Scott still intended to sponsor him there—I wanted to know what kind of re-entry assistance would flow from that California parole office. Would they help him find a job or secure housing? Kevin scoffed and said, "I'm expecting nothing.

"And I know I got to do this and get it done. You know, I got to put one foot in front of the other 'cause they ain't going to do it for me. They're not going to help me. No way. They ain't helped me not one time yet."

On our last phone call from Coleman II, a week before his release, Kevin expressed a range of emotions. This

46-year-old man I'd known for almost a decade and who had spent practically all his adult life behind bars—17 years in this last stretch—could hardly sleep at night because his mind ran wild. Not just with excitement at finally being free, but also from an awful sense of foreboding related to his journey that he couldn't shake.

"I'm a little worried about active gang members waiting for me in Valleyview," he told me. "I think these cops might be in touch with the gang bangers out there who want some revenge. This bus trip was planned out by the same people who sent Whitey Bulger to his death."

"Wait, what? I thought you said the Aryan Brotherhood was no longer a threat, that they were disbanded and didn't care about you!"

"I'm not talking about the AB, Gela. I'm talking about the Montañistas."

"What on Earth for?"

"That cage hit with Rey. When me and Arson went at him. Before the Tremblay rec cage thing."

"Ohhhhh, that ... " I'd forgotten about Kevin's first rec cage incident. But that had been nine years ago, and today was the first time I heard that Kevin's Hispanic prison gang might still pose a problem for him.

"I'm just putting myself in their heads and how it would be smart to get me right off the bus in Valleyview."

"I don't know what to say, Kevin. How is this even a possibility? Can't you tell someone?"

"Not if the cops are in on this."

I asked him for proof of this plot or something beyond a strange gut feeling, and when he didn't have any, I wondered aloud if this was his nervous imagination at play. He said it was possible he was just feeling paranoid, and we both agreed there was no alternative method for his release. I told him to try not to dwell on the negative and said I would see him next week at the Pittsburgh bus depot.

"I can't wait to see you and Scott," he said, ending our call. *Of course,* Kevin expected Scott to be there because Scott lived in Pittsburgh, and Scott and I were supposed to be friends. Only I hadn't told Scott a thing about this bus layover because I was cutting Scott out of my life. No emails, phone calls, or texts—my condolence message about Pam's death notwithstanding.

When I complained to Jim that I probably had no choice but to tell Scott about Kevin's bus layover, he said, "Carla, why don't you give the guy a break?"

"What?" I snapped.

"Did he break into the Capitol? Did he assault any police officers?"

"Well, he was close enough to get pepper-sprayed," I protested.

"Did he ever steal election signs or bumper stickers?"

"Oh my God, Jim! That's hardly the same thing!" I glared at the husband I didn't recognize because Jim almost always sided with me.

"Didn't his sister just die? And didn't his dad die recently, too?"

"So?"

"I'm just saying the guy's been through *a lot,*" he added, giving me the same look he used to give our boys on rare occasions of disappointment, like when they raided the good wine from the liquor cabinet or ran out of gas on the highway.

"I can't believe you're defending him," I said and stormed off in a huff.

CHAPTER 43
NEW CHAPTERS

APRIL 2021

I got to the Greyhound station well ahead of Kevin's bus arrival and parked in the underground garage. I made my way up to the outside terminal with Kevin's duffle bag of goodies and waited on a wooden bench. It was a warm spring afternoon, and I read the news on my phone and looked up a restaurant we could walk to. Jim and I had gotten our COVID-19 vaccines two weeks previously, and I felt like a million bucks. I was even willing to sit inside an eatery, but I found a nearby burger place with patio seating that I thought would be perfect.

Kevin's mammoth blue bus with large picture windows pulled into its stall relatively on time. He disembarked with a white prison laundry bag containing all his belongings and lit up when he saw me. We hugged for a long time, and he asked where Scott was. I said he was running late and would meet us at a restaurant. We didn't want to waste a second of his 75-minute layover, so we left immediately for the burger joint, talking the whole way.

I asked how his trip had been so far, and he told me about some of the characters he'd met. He went on about two ladies who spoke Spanish and said he'd gotten "some offers" from them on this first bus segment (I didn't ask for details). But he wasn't interested in finding a partner yet, adding, "I gotta get my life straight first."

He explained, "I'm going to go to church, and I'm gonna find the right woman. And I'm telling you, Gela, she has to be with your integrity, your self-respect, your loyalty, and your intelligence. If she don't reach those qualities, she ain't got a fighting chance."

"Oh stop, Kevin, you're making me blush," I laughed.

We sat at a table with an umbrella, and he opened the duffle bag while I pointed out the contents. Aside from what he was expecting, I pulled out a flat shoulder-strap pouch to be worn under his clothing and showed him a $500 prepaid credit card. I instructed him to keep the card and his new phone with charger in the security pouch so they wouldn't get stolen at the shelter. He said he'd add the $56 remaining that prison officials had given him to cover his food on the four-day journey.

"Gela, I can't tell you how much love I got for you, for everything you do for me," he said, and I thought he might cry. I had to swallow hard to prevent my own floodgates from opening, and I distracted us both by showing him how to operate his new Android phone. I'd put both Scott's and my contact info on it. We were each listed under our first initial only, with an email address and phone number—no mailing address noted. I'd given him a burner email address I'd made, but Scott didn't want to go through those motions.

As Kevin practiced texting with me, Scott, carrying a black backpack, found our table. He and Kevin embraced and I didn't get up. "Gela," Scott said, and I smiled back for Kevin's benefit. I don't think Kevin registered my tension toward Scott, which was admittedly a notch lower after I'd broken the ice and we coordinated today's meetup by text.

We ordered our food, and I showed Kevin a photo file on his phone that contained all the drawings and artwork he'd made for me over the years. "So now you have a portfolio for job hunting," I said. "Like if you want to try to get a job at a tattoo place or an auto body shop and do the airbrush work you used to do."

"I probably won't try no tattoo shops 'cause where I'm going, they got a lot of Hells Angels—they're a little bit embedded with the Aryan Brotherhood—and Montañistas. Both groups get lots of tattoos," Kevin explained. "And the bikers. They get them Harleys detailed all the time."

"Oh, right," I said. "I didn't think about that."

"I'm still going to talk to your parole department and see if we can get your case moved here," Scott told Kevin. But none of us expected that would happen quickly, if at all.

Scott and I listened to Kevin while we ate. He kept interrupting himself to say how juicy and delicious his burger was, and I discreetly asked the waiter to bring another one and box it up for his bus ride. Kevin said he thought he would try to find his little stepbrother, who was in his mid-20s now, and his mom, who would have been in her late 60s. The last he heard, his mom was living in Montana. But he knew nothing of his half-brother's or stepmother's whereabouts, and he'd be happy if he never saw his stepmother again anyway, he said.

Kevin had an idea for moving beyond the homeless shelter by aligning himself with a church, the way his now-deceased younger brother had once done after serving prison time on drug charges. This was the brother, two years younger than Kevin, who died of a stroke six years ago after a lifetime of battling drugs and alcohol. According to Kevin, his brother found a church group willing to rent him a subsidized apartment in exchange for cleaning the church and doing handyman chores there.

Kevin also told us about an idea he had for giving talks to at-risk youth groups about perilous behavior and lifestyle choices that could lead to prison. He would tell them things like, "I'm giving it to you straight from the top. I've been around. This ain't the lifestyle you want. This is what goes on in prison. You want to be out there working, not doing no garbage. And if you want to be in a gang, go join the Marines."

When our plates were cleared, Kevin pulled some things out of the duffle bag to show Scott, including the shoulder-strap security pouch. Scott then placed his backpack on the table and said he'd brought it for Kevin. He also said there was something inside that Kevin should keep in the security pouch.

Kevin pulled out a worn brown leather wallet that was thick and stuffed with what you'd expect. Kevin's eyes widened as he opened the billfold and counted ten $100 bills. "This was my dad's," Scott said. "I can't think of a better use for it." When Kevin got up and hugged Scott, it was the second time I'd fought back tears that hour.

"I love this wallet, Scott, not just what's inside. And I love this phone, Gela. I love everything in my world right now—just being free, and then all this stuff on top of it? You two, being here? It's like, wow ..." He choked up, and I could feel my throat close.

To prevent my waterworks, I made Kevin promise he wouldn't use his real name or post pictures of himself—and not let others do so—on any social media. By the time he got to Valleyview, I figured he would have mastered Facebook, Instagram, and Twitter, and I said safety started with anonymity. I had asked him a while ago to come up with an alias, and I'd made a free email account for him using the name he'd chosen and showed it to him on his phone.

He saw the worried look on my face and said, "I'm gonna make it, Gela. The Aryan Brotherhood, they don't have the power to just reach out and grab you. You got to be in their community and around them, and I ain't gonna be nowhere near them."

He added, "The same with the Montañistas—that's a little bit more of a possibility if they really wanted to ... but they only know me by my gang name, *Chico Blanco*. And Chico's dead. He died in the pen two days ago, you know?"

Scott and I shared a look that told me I didn't even need to explain Kevin's sense of dread over his first gang affiliation.

"Now I'm *Mr. Flash Tattoo*," Kevin beamed, referencing his new alias and email name. "I been telling everyone on the bus to call me *Flash*," and we all laughed.

Scott looked at his watch and said, "Well, Flash, we better get you back."

—

Kevin turned philosophical while we waited at the terminal for his boarding time. "I don't know what it is, but God's got me going home for a reason," he said. "There's something out there I got to do. So, we'll see what happens."

"I'm not religious," I said, "but I believe the universe works in mysterious ways. In my own life, things tend to happen for a reason."

"God put us together for a purpose, and everything's working out," Kevin added. "There's still big hurdles, but we're gonna jump and make things happen." He smiled and gave us one last hug before he got in line with the other travelers.

"I'll text you, Gela, and then call when I get to Valleyview in two days." I smiled through quivering lips, holding a tissue in my hand.

Scott and I waved as the bus pulled away, and I walked over to the bench I sat on earlier, dabbing my eyes. He looked toward the street and said, "Feels like we've just sent our 46-year-old son off to college, doesn't it?"

I nodded and wanted to hug Scott, but instead, I said, "I'm still mad at you," and another tear fell.

"I know," he said.

He sat down next to me while I sniffed and used my tissue. Then he said, "Carla, you know I love you like the only sister I have left."

"I know," I said, but I couldn't look at him. I stood, picked up my purse, and offered a half smile before heading to the parking garage. "Have a nice day," I called out over my shoulder.

On my way to my cousin's house, navigating Pittsburgh's curvy, hilly terrain, I decided today's reunion would be the penultimate episode of the limited streaming series based on my book *Under Duress* if I ever bothered to write the source material first. It could even hint at two Hollywood endings: the first was Kevin's, finally a free man, even if it was unclear how he'd stick the landing. The second was a friendship on the mend between two people—one an unapologetic liberal and the other a brainwashed fascist—whose joint custody of a federal prisoner brought them together for the greater good.

CHAPTER 44
OMENS

T wo days later, after Kevin's bus trip had ended, I knew something was wrong because he hadn't called and wasn't responding to my texts. I reached out to Scott, who hadn't heard from Kevin either.

"I'm trying to give him some space and not be a mother-hen," I told Scott. "But he said he'd call, and we've been texting nonstop since he got his phone."

"I'm sure he's okay. He's probably sleeping. He spent a long, long time on a bus," Scott said. I wanted to believe that, but my gut told me otherwise. One week later, Scott called and confirmed my suspicions.

"Kevin's fucked," he said. "He's in the Sacramento County Jail."

"What?"

"When did you talk to him last?" Scott asked me.

"We texted right before his bus was supposed to get in, and that's the last time I heard from him. I knew something was wrong."

"Well, there were Mexicans waiting for him at the bus station and Mexicans waiting for him at the halfway house … the Montañistas."

"Oh my God! He knew this would happen!" I said.

"He called me from jail—on a recorded phone line, so he had to be careful what he said. But he told me he went to a motel to get away from them, and that they followed him, and that there was some kind of bloody standoff in the motel room. He said they were gonna slice him into all kinds of different pieces, so he grabbed the daughter of the big guy and threatened to hurt her to get them to let him go …"

"Oh my God! Who's the big guy?"

"I don't know, some Montañista … and the police were called. Kevin wasn't the only one taken into custody."

"This poor guy."

"It gets worse. He had a weapon on him."

"Oh, no."

"Yeah. A knife. He's been charged with being a felon in possession of a dangerous weapon by the feds and disorderly conduct and possession of a weapon by a *restricted person* by local police."

Unbelievable, I thought, and then I posed some unthinkable questions. "How did the Montañistas know his bus schedule, Scott? How did they know where and when to find him? You know, a few weeks ago, Kevin said he was worried that Coleman cops were in cahoots with outside gang members who might want revenge for that rec cage hit on Rey. The one where he and Arson gave Rey a beatdown. But I thought he was just being paranoid."

"No shit."

"Kevin specifically told me that the same people who sent Whitey Bulger to his death also planned out his bus trip."

"We're dealing with some bad people here, Carla," Scott said, and we left the definition of *bad people* loosely interpreted.

"Do you have a copy of that cage fight video?" he asked me.

"No, but I have the incident report and other supporting documentation. I also have a recording and transcript of Kevin telling me he was worried about going back to Valleyview because he thought the Montañistas might want revenge for that cage hit."

"Good, because there's a detective Kevin wants me to talk to, someone in their gang squad, and I want him to know this is the third time now we're just trying to keep our client alive."

"Does he have an attorney?"

"He should get two public defenders. One from the state and one from the feds."

"Will you be able to coordinate and give them information? I'll pass on all the relevant stuff I have."

"Fuck yeah. I'm not licensed to practice in California, but I'll help however I can … And there's another thing, Carla."

"What?"

"Kevin lost his phone. We need you to turn it off."

Oh my God.

"He doesn't know who has the phone, which is why he wants it cut off right away, 'cause he doesn't want the Montañistas …"

"To have our information!" I said, horrified.

"Right. But also, try to make a backup of any data first because there might be exculpatory evidence on there."

"Well, the phone is password protected, so whoever has it can't get into it."

"Uhm, they either *can* get into it, or they *can* get the password out of Kevin," Scott warned.

"But they've had this phone for a week," I said, swallowing hard with a dry throat.

"Yeah."

"Okay, I'll do that as soon as we hang up … Oh, Scott, I just want to cry."

"I know, Carla. I know."

I went to my computer and pulled up Kevin's prepaid calling plan, which did not provide call or text logs. I used a "Find my Phone" feature to try and track his device, but it yielded no results as if the phone had been turned off or had run out of battery. Then, I suspended the service. I logged into his *Flash* email account and changed that password. I found some contacts he added from his bus journey and downloaded them before deleting everything. I did not see any emails sent or received, and I reported all of this to Scott.

"But if someone did hack his phone," I said, "the only info they would have gotten about us are our phone numbers and email addresses—no physical addresses or even names, just our first initials."

"Great job, Gela. I'll call you after I reach the detective." Of course, many reverse-lookup services online could match us to our phone numbers and pair Scott to his real email address. But I said none of that out loud.

"Scott, you and I wouldn't be of interest to the Montañistas anyway, would we?"

"Nope," he assured me, but I think he was just saying what I wanted to hear.

—

I didn't want to burden Jim with this latest Kevin shitstorm, especially since we didn't have all the answers about what had actually happened. By my count, Kevin had been a free man on the ground for less than a few hours before he landed back in jail. Every time I thought about it, I got sick to my stomach, and I couldn't stand the thought of regurgitating it all for my husband.

Jim was weeks away from ending his successful career in the manufacturing and automation industry. He always joked that no one would ever make a TV show out of what he did for a living, and over the years, the boys and I sometimes struggled to define his job. One of my favorite job titles of his was *product line manager for molded case circuit breakers*—a mouthful that the boys turned into "manager" whenever they were asked. (I'd sometimes crack that I wondered who was managing the *unmolded* case circuit breakers.)

However, serving as his company's president of U.S. Operations this last year had been anything but lighthearted. Trying to keep hundreds of workers safe in offices and on production lines during the pandemic had taken its toll, and the deaths of some workers from COVID-19 hit him tremendously hard. While the new vaccines promised to bring the Pandemic to an end, the worldwide supply chain for parts and components remained unstable and broken. Jim's stress never leveled off, and he was tired of being unable to fulfill orders and constantly disappointing customers.

When he told me he wanted to retire early—three years before his corporate contract would be up—we consulted with our investment advisor. Our wise-cracking certified financial planner (whom we adored despite his affinity for Trump), ran his algorithms and told us that, yes, indeed, Jim could retire early. So, my husband arranged for a genial early departure with a nice exit package, and we wondered what our next chapter should be. I quit my nasty political blog and started browsing for real estate online. Everything from a house at the Jersey Shore to a Poconos cabin to a condo in Florida was on the table.

—

In June, we kicked off Jim's retirement with a road trip to see friends in Rhode Island. We'd just come back from a day trip on the ferry to Block Island and were enjoying mint juleps on our friends' patio overlooking Narragansett Bay when my phone rang. I flashed the caller ID—Sacramento County Jail—to Jim and excused myself to our guest room to take the call. I hadn't talked to Kevin at all since his latest ordeal.

I followed the instructions from the robo-announcer, which said, "Hello, this call is from an inmate at the Sacramento County Jail. To accept this free call, press zero. This call is from a correction facility and is subject to monitoring and recording. Thank you for using Global Tel Link."

"Hey, Kevin, how are you?"

"I'm good. Listen. This is bad. This is very bad. I've been in my cell pacing for 48 hours, trying to get to this point to call you, okay? Your life is in danger."

"Wait, what?"

"Yeah, they have all my information ..."

"Woah, woah, Jesus! What are you talking about?"

"All my stuff that was in that motel room—my address book—they have it. The Montañistas. You're in danger. Scott's in danger. Nobody's listening to me."

"I ... I ... I hear what you're saying, but, I mean, why would they want to reach out to Scott or me?"

"Let me explain something to you. They would try to kill two California prosecutors, and you don't think they would try to kill you guys to get a message to me?"

What the fuck? I didn't get the reference to the prosecutors, but I was processing the horror story just the same.

"So, what do you suggest we do?"

I zoned out at that point, and it was only later, when I played that phone recording, that I attempted to understand a very convoluted story Kevin told me about a staged crime scene at the motel that involved swapped door numbers and incorrect room keys. He insisted that he'd checked into room 401 but that the bloody showdown happened in room 104. He said someone brought his items into 104 to "stage" it like 104 had been his room. He even said someone transposed the 104 room numbers on the door to make it look like room 401. Then he gave me the names and phone numbers of his federal public defender and state defender and asked me to contact them. After five minutes, as the call was coming to an end, Kevin said he would call right back.

I rummaged through my computer bag, found a notebook, and brought it to the guest bed, where I waited for *The Shining Part II* to unfold. I stared at the vase of pink Garden Phlox our hostess had placed on a nightstand until my phone rang again.

Kevin launched into a re-telling of the staged motel crime scene with swapped room numbers. Then he said something about a Montañista at Coleman II who pretended to be a drop-out but really wasn't and alluded to that person being involved.

"So, you need to call somebody in your area and explain what's going on so they can verify and keep you protected because these people ain't no joke, Gela. You understand?"

"I ... I ... I just don't see how that's possible. I mean ..."

"What do you mean?"

"What am I supposed to do? Hire a 24/7 security detail?"

"Listen, Gela, I'm gonna explain something to you. I can't go into detail, but it's bad, Gela. In that motel room— you know the people that were coming to get me?"

"Yeah?"

"Two of them completely ... Uh, they're on the other side."

"I don't understand. I'm sorry."

"They're on the *other side*."

"I, I'm still not following you. I'm sorry. I, maybe it's something you can't say."

"I can't say it, but, um, uh, okay. I, I can tell you, you know Scott's mom?"

"Scott's mom? Yeah."

"They're over there with her."

Oh my God, did Kevin just tell me on a recorded jailhouse phone call that two Montañistas who tried to kill him at a motel are *dead*?

"Ohhhhhhhhh …."

"Okay. You see what I'm saying? You see what I mean? This is big, man. This is, this is bad."

So where are the bodies, and why weren't you charged with murder? How could I ask this on a recorded line?

Then, he cryptically told me that the Montañistas had disposed of the evidence because it had been in their best interest.

"To be clear, when I talk to your public defenders, do you want them to know about the two *on the other side?*"

"No. No. I'm gonna tell them that on my own … I don't want 'em to try to pull you in and make you testify on something—even though the evidence has been destroyed. You understand what I'm saying?"

I was losing my focus and couldn't process anymore until he told me, "And one other thing I'm worried about is, they know that there's gonna be that book that we're writing. You know what I'm saying?"

"They know that because ... ?"

"Of course, everybody, everybody knows that," he said matter-of-factly. I pictured him boasting to a bus full of people, including a Montañista spy, that someone was writing a book about him and he would be famous.

Mercifully, the 15-minute call time was up, and I ran into the well-appointed marble guest bathroom and heaved into the toilet.

CHAPTER 45
LIES

SUMMER 2021

I tried to think about this logically. I told myself that the events Kevin described had happened two months ago. If the Montañistas really did have his address book, they'd had it for two months. I was still here. Scott was still here. We were unimportant nobodies, 2,800 miles removed from that West Coast butchery.

I relayed everything to Scott, who had heard some of it from Kevin already. "But Scott, he told me, cryptically, that he killed two people in that Motel California room."

"Well, *that's* disturbing."

Scott did not think there was any mix-up in the motel room crime scene that police processed because the detective he spoke to said there was a lot of blood in the room, particularly the bathroom.

"You know, maybe the two gangsters weren't really dead, but Kevin thought they were?" I said. "He said he ran outside with only his boxer shorts and boots on … what if the gangsters dragged their injured buddies out of there and they weren't corpses?"

"Very possible," Scott said. "And it makes sense that the Montañistas wouldn't leave anything behind to tie them to the crime scene. They don't want to testify about anything."

"Speaking of which—am I an *accessory after the fact* now or some bullshit because of what he told me?"

Scott said prison officials had access to the recorded call and could give it to the police, and it wasn't my responsibility to share the information. In fact, "Carla, you're still bound by the attorney-client privilege," he said. "And if you have your own recording, I would destroy it if I were you."

"Right." This sounded reasonable, but I wanted a second opinion, and I cursed Jack for being dead because he'd know exactly what to do.

"And our client—because he is still our client—needs to shut the fuck up and stop talking about this. If he calls me, that's what I'll say. And if he calls you, give him that message."

"Okay … Oh, Scotty, about the book. Kevin says the Montañistas know about it, and this is a problem. I think he blabbed about it on the bus. And I tell you what. I'm out. I'm done. I am so over this soul-sucking, gruesome story of torture and murder. I just, I can't …"

"I get it, Carla, I get it."

I took a breath and asked him, "Are you worried about them coming after us?"

"I'm not worried about it, and I've represented a lot of bad people."

"Okay, alright, I'm not going to worry about it," I said.

"What does Jim say?"

I hesitated and then told the truth. "He knows Kevin's in jail, but not about the address book and what went down in that motel room. I haven't found a way to tell him that part yet."

—

I had a new mission. After deleting all my author accounts and social media profiles tied to my now-defunct pen name, I fast-tracked the search for Jim's and my new location. I found a rustic cabin in a gated Pocono golf and tennis resort and told Jim it was the perfect place to begin his retirement. I convinced him to pay cash for the cabin and put the deed into the name of a newly formed holding company. I said I could see us wanting to rent out the cabin someday, and the holding company was a good business move. (I was hoping he'd forget I had tired of managing our historic Airbnb Trinity that we sold last year.) And bless his heart, Jim didn't even blink when I installed a security system in the townhouse we were selling because I said it would add value and that most of our neighbors had one. "Buyers will expect it," I smiled. This was hardly a foolproof plan, but it was the best I could come up with.

The night before our open house, Jim and I cleaned and staged for the three-hour event that our real estate agent said would likely produce multiple offers. I ran the vacuum under our bed until it clanged into something hard. I turned it off, bent down, and pulled out a heavy yellow iron crowbar. This puzzled me, and I yelled for Jim down the hall. When he appeared, I held it up with a scrunched face and said, "What the hell?"

He started laughing. "I see you've found my secret weapon."

"What do you mean?"

"To protect m'lady from the intruders," he chuckled.

"What intruders? Has someone tried to break in?"

"Carla …"

"No, seriously, Jim, have you heard noises or thought someone was skulking about?"

"Skulking?" He didn't understand why I wasn't laughing at the absurdity. Then, when my eyes brimmed with tears, he asked, "What's wrong?"

But his wheels were already turning, and he cocked his head with recognition. Jim was used to my scheming, but he was not obtuse.

"Carla? What's going on?"

I put my hands over my face and folded like the Adirondack chairs I'd just bought for the cabin. I plopped down on the bed and ugly-cried everything I'd held back about Kevin's arrest. Everything from the lost address book to Kevin's dire warning about the Montañistas to what I knew about the Motel California massacre—or not a massacre, Scott and I weren't sure.

"I want to talk to Scott," he said.

I pulled up Scott's number on my phone, and Jim disappeared into another room for about 10 minutes. I didn't know how that conversation went because Jim used his phone, not mine, which was still automatically recording all calls.

When he returned, he hugged me and wasn't nearly as mad as I thought he'd be. He still liked the idea of our Pocono cabin and was still glad we were selling the townhouse. "But no more secrets," he said.

"No more secrets," I repeated, burrowing into warm, steady arms that embraced me despite my shenanigans.

—

I spent the summer fixing up our retreat in the woods and learning how to play pickleball, which quickly became an obsession. Jim golfed, stuck to tennis, and figured out how to restore some of our cabin's ancient windows. He fixed the outdoor shower and even tinkered with replacing sections of rotted cedar shingles—nothing too involved, but just mechanical enough to balance out a life now filled with hiking, sports, reading, and napping in a hammock.

I stayed in regular touch with Kevin's lawyers in California. His tax-payer-funded state attorney, Charlie, was preparing a defense case on a state weapons charge and for disorderly conduct over the destruction of a room inside what I had dubbed the Motel California. His federal public defender, Valerie, was preparing a defense case for violating his parole by possessing the knife. And, in a strange world of coincidence, Valerie was the same public defender who represented Kevin in 2004. That was the case when Kevin's father—who had set Kevin up in a meth-cooking lab in a camper—turned his son in to the Bureau of Alcohol Tobacco and Firearms (ATF) for owning a sawed-off shotgun.

Stranger still was that Kevin's federal case on this weapons charge had landed before the same judge who sentenced Kevin to 10 years in 2004. All those years ago, Kevin had told the judge he wanted to serve his prison time as far away as possible from Valleyview, his family, and street gang connections. The judge honored Kevin's request by sending him to USP Allenwood in Pennsylvania, where ten years turned into 17 years because of Kevin's association with Montañista gang leader Rey. It was Kevin's refusal to carry out Rey's assault order that necessitated Kevin's transfer to Lewisburg, where the rec cage fight with Arson against Steven Tremblay earned him those extra seven years. And, of course, now, Kevin was paying the price for not just disobeying Rey but giving Rey a beatdown in a Lewisburg rec cage that preceded that fight.

These intertwined events and how everything had come full circle made my head spin.

—

I sent the same emails and attachments to the lawyers, Charlie and Valerie, because everything I knew was relevant to both cases. I introduced them to Scott and said it was

Scott's and my opinion that Kevin's charges stemmed from his self-defense of a Montañista gang retribution hit. I gave them evidence of Kevin's and Arson's assault against Rey in the Lewisburg rec cage. I gave them a phone recording and transcript of Kevin telling me he worried about Montañistas coming after him and possibly colluding with prison officials. I said I'd been Kevin's friend and advocate for nine years and explained the many ways he'd been screwed by the system and the Bureau of Prisons. I covered the Steven Tremblay rec cage assault and described how the BOP had sent Kevin to Florence to get stabbed despite having intelligence reports that he faced danger there. I said Kevin had gotten no halfway house time and laid out another case of BOP negligence with prison officials sending Kevin back to Valleyview—to a hub of gang activity—despite knowing an attorney in Pittsburgh offered to sponsor Kevin. Scott's willingness to support Kevin had gone a long way as a character reference.

The attorneys thanked me for the background and documentation, and Charlie put me in touch with his investigator, who needed to gather more information. His investigator, a young, compassionate public servant, was particularly eager to help Kevin's case, telling me, "Kevin must be very special to have such devoted friends." I said that he *was* special and was working hard to start a new life outside prison, away from drugs and criminal elements, and that what had happened to him was no fault of his own.

—

I wasn't writing Kevin's story anymore, but I was predictably curious about what had happened to him after he got off that Greyhound bus. I did some digging while I waited for his state and federal cases to inch along in California courts. I found a brief article from an online publication that covered

Valleyview news, which confirmed a "disturbance" at Motel California. Police had been called, and two people who fled were arrested. It was a vague report with no names listed besides the detective Scott had spoken to, and the date matched perfectly.

I toured the outside of the motel on Google Earth's "street view" and could zoom in close enough to see some room numbers. Rooms 401 and 104 were on far opposite ends of the motel's layout. It was a two-story motel where all rooms were accessed from the outside, and it looked old and rundown. This made sense after I found several articles stating the motel was a well-known epicenter for drugs, prostitution, and gang activity. Turf wars and related crimes kept the local police very busy, and for years, community leaders had been calling for the seedy Motel California to be torn down.

I gathered more puzzle pieces in August and September after talking to Kevin in the Sacramento County Jail. He'd somehow gotten enough money on his books to call me (or he'd bartered to use another inmate's phone time), and he unintentionally leaked more details in frenzied bits and pieces buried within that wider conspiracy of a staged crime scene in the wrong motel room.

Kevin said that before he was released, a Montañista named "Nacho" at Coleman II told him about Motel California. Kevin believed Nacho called California gang associates about Kevin's upcoming release and travel plans and that "Nacho set me up to die."

He said that when he got off the bus, he checked into the shelter with his "property" and claimed people could eat and warm up there during the day but not shower. So he decided to go to the Motel California for a shower, and he checked into room 401 with some of his belongings. (By then, I already knew that the Catholic-run community shelter *did* offer shower, laundry, and storage facilities, plus case management resources for seeking employment and benefits.) He told me, with no hint of surprise in his voice, that a Mexican he knew from Lewisburg happened to be driving by outside of the shelter. The former inmate, "Wino," and a woman "Adrianna," pulled up next to him and offered to give him a ride to the motel. This fell under the *Montañistas-were-waiting-for-me* portion of the story.

The trio parked at the motel and Wino checked into room 104. The three walked to a nearby 7-11 for, among other things, condoms because Adrianna was "coming onto me hotter than fire," he explained. Kevin said he tipped the 7-11 check-out girl $20 and gave Wino $20 to buy some beer and disappear for a little while. Then Kevin returned to motel room 104 with just Adrianna. Different things in different story versions set off his Spidey sense that something was amiss. In one rendition, he saw a hardwood handle fixed blade knife in Adrianna's purse while she showered. Kevin said he tried to call 9-1-1, but the call was routed to a gang member who pretended to be police, meaning the Montañistas had somehow "hijacked" his cellphone. The same thing happened when he tried to call his parole officer.

At some point, he said he opened the window curtain to see Wino and a Mexican in a black shirt and black hat walking toward room 104. He let Wino into the room first, and Wino pulled a knife on him. The Mexican outside had a gun. That's when Kevin used Adrianna as a shield between him and the door while also managing to disarm Wino. Both Kevin and Wino got sliced in that altercation.

"Now, I'm not going to go into no more detail about what went on up in that room," Kevin said, now seeming to care that we were on a recorded line. He jumped ahead in the story to his fleeing the motel in his boxer shorts and boots for a Pizza Hut across the street. The number of his pursuers changed in each retelling. That a Hispanic guy chased him in a white truck was consistent, but sometimes it was one or two others who also pursued him on foot, including a black kid in a hoodie.

Kevin said he ran from Pizza Hut to a Jiffy Lube but hollered at a mailman along the way to call the police. At the Jiffy Lube, he told a young employee to call the police. He said he placed his hijacked phone down at the Jiffy Lube to grab the kid's phone and tell the police directly who he was, where he was, and that gang members were chasing him and trying to kill him. "They're trying to kill me. I'm not on drugs, you need to listen to me," he said he told police.

Kevin then handed the kid's phone back to him but forgot to pick up his phone before running across the street to a donut shop (that's how he lost his phone, he said). The donut shop manager, watching the hot pursuit unfold on the block, locked the donut shop doors and wouldn't let Kevin in. So Kevin ran to the back of the building and jumped up onto the roof. Police eventually arrived, spotted Kevin, and told him to drop the knife in his hand, a knife he had wrested away from Wino, who had also escaped the motel massacre.

"That's my story," he said. "That's what I'm sticking to."

—

Kevin later said that the "things that went on up in that room, I won't disclose, I won't even talk about unless I get full immunity."

He said he was interviewed by a police gang investigator who wanted to know about the girl he went to the motel room with. He said police found her clothes—a green shirt and denim overalls—and the detective asked what happened to her. "Did she walk out of that motel room naked? Whose blood is all over the place?"

Kevin said police charged him with disorderly conduct and being a restricted person with a knife "so they could figure out what went down in that motel room. They ain't got no victims. They ain't got nothing … There's blood all over.

There's a trail all the way to the motel office." He said it was Wino's blood, which, if true, left an unknown Mexican in a black shirt and black hat and the woman named Adrianna unaccounted for.

Aside from all the blood and the woman's clothing, Kevin's discovery material (for his state trial on the two charges) listed all the other things police found in that motel room: Kevin's clothing; the black backpack from Scott containing his parole papers, Coleman II letters, and his artwork; the leather security pouch with $1,000 cash and $500 prepaid Visa card—which Scott told the detective were gifts and not stolen; empty beer cans; a syringe and other drug materials.

Kevin said both his tax-payer-funded lawyers asked him why he disputed that motel room 104 was his. "Because there's drug paraphernalia, and there's alcohol in that room. Why would I take that and give myself a violation in the Bureau of Prisons? Because that's going to ruin everything …"

And there it was. Without that elaborate conspiracy where Montañistas had moved his possessions from his *real* motel room 401 into the bloody motel room 104, Kevin would have violated his parole by consuming alcohol and drugs. And that was an automatic ticket back to federal prison.

—

Jack had been a proponent of Occam's Razor. The principle, attributed to a 14th-century Friar, William of Ockham, stated that if you had two competing theories to explain something, the simplest solution was probably correct.

I didn't challenge Kevin's story in real-time—even though I was sure parts were incredibly dubious—because I hadn't done my research yet nor played back our conversations and studied their transcripts. When I finally pieced together the fullest picture of what had happened that I could assemble, I applied Occam's Razor to it all.

Had Montañistas been waiting for Kevin at the Valleyview bus station? I didn't think so. Kevin learned about Motel California from an inmate at Coleman named Nacho, whom Kevin said sent him there to die. But had Nacho conspired to have Kevin killed, or had he merely passed on what he knew about the motel's easy drug sales?

How Kevin conveniently ended up in the car of a Mexican he knew from Lewisburg (Wino) along with a woman was unclear, and Occam's Razor didn't help me figure that out. But Kevin willingly went to that motel to party and have sex.

Were Wino and Adrianna part of a Montañista hit squad that wanted revenge for a nine-year-old rec cage beatdown of a gang leader? Unfortunately, I couldn't rule that out.

But did Kevin—who loved to brag and had $1,000 on him—flash his cash and blab about his gifts a little too much in order to impress? Could robbery have been a motive for the motel massacre?

That was a simpler explanation that still accounted for two dead bodies and why Kevin's cash was found at the scene. But it didn't explain his lost address book. Who would take an address book but not $1,000 or a $500 Visa gift card? Was the address book truly lost?

—

Some of Kevin's storytelling made me think about the time six years ago when he'd been sent to the hole at Coleman II for a dirty urinalysis. That was at the end of 2015, right before the Third Circuit Court denied our appeal. When Kevin was released, he told me two different stories of how he ended up in the segregated/punitive housing unit.

One story was that his cellmate had set him up by placing Suboxone in his shoes, and COs had found it. The other was that prison officials must have known the appeal denial was coming in and had preemptively put him in the hole because they were worried about his reaction.

Or, Occam's Razor said that Kevin was simply using Suboxone (plentiful at Coleman II), was drug tested, and failed his urinalysis. Then I realized that my monthly stipends to his account no doubt kept him in ample supply.

CHAPTER 46
CROSSROADS

In the second half of 2021, Jim and I experienced a great deal of heartache within our family. The merging of COVID and politics into an anti-vaxxer and pandemic denial campaign was peaking and found followers among our relatives.

I had a tearful phone call with my brother Tony, who had the audacity to state that COVID was overblown and that the vaccines that were readily available in our country weren't just worthless but harmful.

I spouted off the statistics I kept handy, saying that since the pandemic started, our country alone had more than 600,000 *excess deaths* than usual, and those were attributed to COVID-19 or related issues. But Tony wasn't interested in facts and repeated that the numbers were inflated to benefit the vaccine manufacturers. "I don't know why you would put that untested stuff in your bodies," he said.

"You should have a conversation with my daughter-in-law," I spat out. "Every day, she holds the hands of patients dying from COVID and then has to go out in a waiting room and tell their families that they've died. I'm *grateful* she's vaccinated, and the rest of us are too."

I ended our angry call with, "You all will contribute to herd immunity one way or another," and it was the first time I could remember hanging up on my brother.

I started texting Tony links to what I called *the Darwin stories*— news articles or video clips of COVID-denying or vaccine-shunning patients, giving dire warnings as they lay dying in a hospital. *If they'd only listened and gotten a vaccine*, was the refrain. And because Scott was in this disillusionment camp, too, I texted him the same stories.

Midway through the summer, one of Jim's older sisters died suddenly of a heart attack. She was only 70 and seemed in good health despite some medical issues, so her death came out of nowhere and shocked everyone. Before long, there were whispers that some right-leaning family members felt her COVID-19 vaccine might have played a role. For weeks and months afterward, I found Jim crying at random times. He wasn't used to bursting into tears like I was, and I didn't know how to help him cope with his wearying emotions.

—

Jim and I hadn't traveled on a plane since the pandemic started, and it had been over a year since I'd seen my mother, Marilyn. That was the longest I'd ever gone without hugging her. She and I made plans for me to visit in late August, and just to be safe—even though we were both vaccinated—I booked a hotel room. We decided we would be together outdoors even in the extreme heat and humidity.

Two weeks before this trip, Tony called me. "Guess who has COVID?" he asked sheepishly. He told me that he and the kids started showing symptoms after the whole family came back from a vacation in Indianapolis, where I knew they roamed unvaccinated and unmasked. COVID's Delta variant was surging, and their doctor guessed that was the strain they'd all picked up. His wife remained symptom-free, and their two teenagers—whose worst symptom was that their eyes hurt—seemed to be faring better than he was but were still confined to bed. He sounded raspy, and I asked him if he thought he should be hospitalized. He said he didn't think so but admitted, "I'm a little bit scared."

I told him I would have an oximeter sent to him overnight—one of those gadgets people wore on their fingers to measure their oxygen saturation level. I had three at my cabin but Amazon could get him one faster than I could ship one of my spares. I told him to keep that thing on his finger all goddamn day, and if his oxygen level dropped below 90 percent, he needed to go to the hospital immediately. I gave these same instructions to my sister-in-law and asked her to keep me updated.

I was about to have a good cryfest over this news when, right on cue, my mother called. "Oh Carla, why? Why didn't Tony get vaccinated?" she asked, sobbing into the phone. I wanted to say something like, *I don't know, Mom. Why do you smoke?* But that wouldn't have been helpful, so instead, I said, "Because he's an idiot, Mom." This was also not helpful, but it's all I had, and it produced louder crying on the other end until we were both bawling and cursing the anti-vaxxer movement. As much as she wanted to see me, she insisted I cancel my trip to the Sunshine State that was swimming in Delta COVID infections.

A day after his oximeter arrived, my brother agreed to go to the hospital. Marilyn was a wreck. But she was comforted by one of the nurses she happened to know, who told her, "Try not to worry. We'll get him through this. This is what we do." My mother and I both clung to that advice while we hoped and prayed Tony would not need a ventilator.

Tony spent his 50th birthday in the hospital and struggled to breathe for most of a week. He couldn't talk on the phone, so my sister-in-law galvanized all the family she could—including our jovial Pittsburgh cousins—to text him stories, photos, well-wishes, and jokes to help him pass the time. Finally, after eight days, Tony was released—not necessarily a changed man, but as someone who thought vaccines might indeed have benefits.

I texted Scott every day throughout my brother's ordeal and begged him, "Please, please, please get vaccinated. COVID is culling the herd of the stupid and stubborn, and you don't need to be culled. It is your choice." Scott replied only that he would pray for Tony, and I don't know why I thought my scare tactic would work. Around that same time, Scott came down with a virus, and by fall, his sense of taste and smell were still out of whack. He told me this in a text exchange about an update on Kevin, and I replied that his sensory loss was a classic COVID symptom and that he was now contributing to the herd immunity. He was nonplused, except that he missed beer, which he didn't drink anymore because it tasted like swill.

—

By the end of October, Kevin's federal parole violation case started falling apart. This was based on evidence provided by his state defender, Charlie, that Kevin's use of that knife was in self-defense. Supporting this theory were two 9-1-1 phone calls that Kevin made from his phone (even while he thought his cellphone had been "hijacked"). Kevin made one call in the motel room and told a 9-1-1 operator that he was in a "hostage situation" and that "they're trying to shoot me." Kevin made another 9-1-1 call as he ran into the Pizza Hut, saying, "They're trying to kill me." There was also evidence of a third call Kevin had placed to his parole officer amid the chaos.

Even in the face of this evidence, the State of California stubbornly refused to drop its charges against Kevin of weapons possession by a restricted person and disorderly conduct. That case was set to go to trial in January and was possibly just a strategy to learn if there were any victims from the Motel California incident and who they were.

The federal government formally withdrew its petition alleging Kevin violated his parole, and he called me from the Sacramento County Jail in early November, the night before his release.

He explained that his federal defender, Valerie, had put him in touch with a local residential self-help program called The Crossroads Academy (CA). The program provided an alternative to incarceration for people struggling with addiction, criminal behavior, and homelessness. Kevin had written to CA, and a representative had interviewed Kevin in jail and determined he was a good fit for their program. The idea was that CA was a safe place for Kevin to live and work on his addiction—an issue neither of us acknowledged—while he waited for his state case to resolve. I was relieved to hear this and told him, on that five-minute phone call, that I would figure out how to send him a new cellphone to replace the one he lost.

Before we hung up, Kevin basked in beating the first of his two court cases and looked back on the Motel California episode almost in awe. "Hey, Gela," he chuckled. "That's a wild chapter for the book, ain't it?"

"Oh my God. Oh my God," I said. "I can't even ...," and then we were interrupted by the prison robocall voice thanking us for using Global Tel Link.

If I could have finished my thought, I would have used nicer words to say there was no *fucking* way I was writing that *fucking* book. But I had all kinds of time and would break that news to him some other day.

—

I emailed the federal defender, Valerie, and asked if she knew how I could mail Kevin a cellphone. She replied, "He is not allowed to have a phone while he is at CA."

That was curious, so I tried to find out why. I emailed and left a voice message for the Crossroads Academy, and the program director returned my call.

After he determined I was one of Kevin's trusted friends who wanted to ensure he was okay, he explained how the program worked. He said their residents lived and worked together in a structured environment to learn accountability, responsibility, and life skills. If they completed the program, which could run from 18 months to two years, they would successfully reintegrate into society. The director was the one who interviewed Kevin in the Sacramento County Jail for program placement.

He asked if there was a message I wanted to pass on to Kevin. I said I wanted to know how to send him a new cellphone to replace the one he'd lost, maybe a backpack and some other things—for when he got out of the program. I said I understood he couldn't have a phone or contact with outsiders currently.

"Did you already buy that stuff?"

"Some of it," I said.

"Return it. I'll tell you why. Kevin is a grown adult—he's in his forties. When he graduates from the Crossroads Academy, he'll learn to do everything for himself and not need anything from anybody. Our goal is to get Kevin to a place where, when he graduates, he's able to buy his own phone, backpack, car, and place—something he's never been able to do.

"The last thing he needs is anybody enabling him in any way. Take yourself out of the equation. Kevin needs to learn to stand on his own two feet. We will teach him how to do that as long as he stays. And at the end of his two years, he won't need a phone or a backpack from anybody. He'll have a job, he'll make his own money, he'll buy his own car. That's our goal with him."

"Two years …" I said out loud.

The director said, "That's if he finishes the program," and he acknowledged that Kevin could leave at any time.

Then, he asked me for more background on how I knew Kevin. I gave a short version of his Lewisburg rec cage assault case that I worked on with Scott. I explained that Scott was willing to sponsor Kevin's supervision in Pittsburgh, assuming Kevin beat his state charges.

"I'm going to share something with you," the director said. "I'm a guy who was a drug addict for 27 years. I did a two-year prison term, a five-year prison term, a six-year prison term, and a 10-year prison term. I promise you if he goes to Pittsburgh and all he has is a sponsor, he'll be back in jail. A sponsor in and of itself is not what Kevin needs."

He continued, "Kevin has a shit ton of stuff to work on and needs behavior modification. He's had decades and decades of criminal thinking and criminal issues. A sponsor is not going to fix that."

I was on the verge of crying but composed myself enough to say that the Montañista gang might have wanted revenge against Kevin, and that was partly what led to the charges from the motel.

"Here's what you don't understand," he said. "He went to that motel room to get high."

I knew this, but for some reason, hearing him say it opened my floodgate of tears.

The director continued, "I don't care about the Montañistas or whether he says he was defending himself. When was the last time you needed a weapon to defend yourself? Probably never, because normal people who make good decisions and put themselves in healthy situations don't need to defend themselves. As soon as you start getting high, you're starting to make bad decisions again. None of that would have happened if he'd come straight here."

I told him Scott and I were impressed with the Crossroads Academy website, their reviews, and online videos, and I wish we had known about CA to advocate for Kevin's placement there.

I asked if Kevin would be safe there from the Montañistas, and he said, "Well, I've never had anybody come into this house looking for anybody. I've had people show up on the property looking for a woman, you know, the disgruntled boyfriend who's also a drug addict. And I've chased them off. But we've never had an act of violence here."

I thanked him for his honesty and said I would share this information with Scott. I asked if I could check in with him from time to time about how Kevin was doing, and the director said he'd be more than happy to give me those reports personally.

"He's been here for a week," he said, "and so far so good. He's starting to see the value in the change process. But believe me, if he goes to another state, nothing's changed. He's still the same Kevin who got himself in all that trouble. Please understand that no matter where he goes, nothing's changed. He's still the same Kevin."

He ended the call by saying, "If you guys care about him, let him change his life. Cut the umbilical cord and let Kevin figure out how to become the 2.0 version of himself."

—

That call drained me, and I thought about it for a long time. I summarized it for Jim, and we both agreed I needed to recap it for Scott. Scott felt as I did, that this Crossroads Academy might be Kevin's only salvation, regardless of how his state court case played out. And because Scott wanted to hear some things for himself, he and the director had their own conversation. After their call, Scott said he was withdrawing his sponsorship of Kevin's federal supervision until Kevin completed the CA program.

CHAPTER 47
BECK AND CALL

EARLY 2022

Kevin lasted almost six weeks at the Crossroads Academy—far longer than Scott thought he would. I learned about his departure from his state defense lawyer, Charlie, who emailed Scott and me wondering if we'd heard from him. When Kevin missed a meeting about his upcoming trial, Charlie called the Academy and was told that Kevin had left the program.

That winter, Kevin called me six times from a cheap flip phone he'd bought with the remaining gift money from Scott and me. On that first post-academy call, he admitted that his setup there had been good. He'd shared a clean, warm bunk bedroom with five other men in a nice house and been well-fed. But he also had to clean toilets, do everyone's laundry, move furniture for free, shave his beard, and attend meetings and programs—"cold brainwashing stuff," he called it—and he couldn't reach Scott or me. He also admitted to butting heads with the director. "And finally, I was just like, you know what, I got bigger things to do in the world."

When I asked him, well into the call, if anything in particular made him leave, he said, "Yeah. One of the

Montañistas showed up. And after I had a confrontation with him, he left."

"A Montañista showed up at the Academy?"

"Yep. He knew who I was. And when I told the Academy people about it, they tried to turn it around on me like I'm stupid. I was like, whatever."

"Hmmm," I said skeptically.

All I knew for sure was that after 17 years in prison, Kevin was tired of structure and following orders and wanted his freedom.

—

Kevin couldn't venture too far from his federal parole office because he had to check in on Mondays, Wednesdays, and Fridays and turn in urine samples to be drug tested. So he said he hung out in south Valleyview—away from where the Montañistas congregated—and bought a mountain bike at a pawn shop to see his parole officer. He refused to go to a shelter and instead slept on benches and the porches of some businesses while enjoying his daytime freedom on the streets. On sunny days, he soaked up the warmth on the sidewalk and enjoyed knowing his schedule was completely free.

However, he said, the Montañistas sometimes waited for him at his parole office, but they couldn't catch him on his bike. One time recently, though, they had him cornered in a 7-11, and he had to call the police—he could never fight back, or he would be charged with a crime, he said

"They're getting sneaky," he said, explaining how a young woman lured him into a trap by giving him a suitcase full of nice shoes, shirts, and other items. When Kevin rolled the suitcase to a nearby 7-11, a bunch of Montañistas drove up to the store so they could get him.

"I called the cops so quick. They showed up and started getting IDs of certain ones and all that. The same individuals that was involved with the gang thing."

"Huh? Goodness," I said. "Well, I guess the moral of the story is that if it seems too good to be true, then it is, right? No one's going to give you a suitcase full of goodies for free."

Around the time Kevin ran out of money, the weather turned, and he decided "homeless life is terrible."

"Oh really? How long did it take you to come to that conclusion?" I asked.

"One snowstorm," he said. But don't worry, he told me. He befriended a man in a wheelchair who lived in subsidized housing. The man, Peter, let him sleep on his couch in exchange for helping him get around and doing household chores. In the housing unit, "there's no gangs, there's no drugs, there's no swearing, there's no bad stuff," he said. "It's an excellent environment for me."

—

The State of California dropped its disorderly conduct charge against Kevin but was still going to trial on his charge of weapons possession by a restricted person. A new prosecutor had taken over the case for the state, and Kevin's lawyer, Charlie, was hoping to convince his office to let the case go in light of all the self-defense evidence and the fact that the federal government had dropped its weapons charge against Kevin.

Earlier in the process, Charlie tried to convince Kevin to allow him to put on a defense that included mental health extenuating circumstances. He showed Kevin police body camera video of his arrest and told him he thought he was suffering from post-traumatic stress. Kevin protested vehemently—he even told me he thought his attorney was plotting against him—until Charlie backed off. Not coincidentally, the jail's psychologist also suggested Kevin had PTSD.

Charlie told me that in the two months since Kevin had left the Crossroads Academy, Kevin had had 17 non-arrest run-ins with police. I repeated Kevin's story that the Montañistas kept trailing him and that he couldn't use any weapons to defend himself, so calling the police was his only option.

When the new prosecutor refused to drop Kevin's case, Charlie prepared his subpoenas and emailed Scott and me, asking if we would testify on Kevin's behalf. I was blindsided and hoped that the documentation I sent could stand on its own or be admitted in court without me.

"Regarding testifying, I will NOT be able to do so," I told Charlie, "and I'm sure you can guess why … I cannot allow myself to be publicly linked to Kevin and discovered by the same people who tried to kill him. Kevin has already warned me about my safety back when he said the Montañistas had taken his address book. I hope you can understand and appreciate this."

Scott, however, said he would do it.

—

I planned to explain this the next time Kevin called me. I'd been trying to keep our calls brief and still be supportive even though he knew Scott and I both thought he belonged at Crossroads Academy or someplace that could help him with his addiction. Letting him know this and that I agreed with Scott's decision to withdraw his federal supervision was the extent of the tough love I delivered. At that time, I knew Kevin had no interest in facing his demons. Still, I hoped that under different circumstances, he'd give rehabilitation another try and that somehow I could help.

Kevin called me from Peter's apartment on a snowy January day in the Poconos. He sounded really off, though, and he carried out most of our conversation in a whisper. He said someone had installed a spy virus on his flip phone and that his roommate Peter had "given him up" to the Montañistas. He said he was holding the door handle shut with both hands because Montañistas were in the hallway, on the other side, trying to break in. He begged me to call the police.

I asked him why he couldn't hang up with me and call the police himself, but I got a nonsensical, whispered reply. He gave me the address of the public housing building, and I did as he asked. I looked up the local police phone number and told a dispatcher that my friend thought intruders were attempting to gain entry to the apartment.

I didn't process the surreal event as it unfolded, but later, I realized he must have been high. I'd seen enough *Breaking Bad* TV episodes to understand the paranoia that came with methamphetamine use, which I assumed was his drug of choice, given his history and the syringe found at Motel California.

Were Montañistas really on the other side of that door? Two things could be true—that he was high, and the gangsters had found him. Did he need me to call the police because he thought they'd take the threat more seriously after all his other calls for police help that winter? Or was the drama a ploy to get me to convince Scott to reconsider sponsoring him in Pittsburgh, where it would be safer?

Oh, Friar William of Ockham, help me. Help me.

—

And then, I didn't hear anything from Kevin for three months. Just when I'd begun assuming, as a defense mechanism, that he was dead, his public defender, Charlie, reached out to say that the feds had put Kevin back in prison. But on the bright side, Kevin's state case had finally been dismissed, and there would be no trial.

Kevin was in a medium-security private prison, serving three months on a federal parole violation for a dirty urinalysis. I was hardly shocked. But I was surprised to learn that at the end of those three months, he'd be released with "no papers" and never have to report to a parole office again (assuming he did not rack up a new state or federal conviction). Kevin had written the federal judge overseeing his case and asked for a prison sentence that would "expirate him." He'd already served eight months in the Sacramento County Jail, which counted toward this parole violation, and he asked the judge for an "expirated" term of not more than one year. He told the judge he needed to be free of the Valleyview parole supervision so he could go to another state far away from the Montañistas.

So, as he'd done before, the judge granted Kevin's request. And in late May, Kevin was released with no money and just the clothes on his back. Also released that day was a young black kid, Javon, who invited Kevin to join him at his uncle's house in another state. Kevin was grateful for the offer and stayed in the back room of a rundown house in a not-so-very-nice part of town. Kevin did some tattooing for Javon and his friends but soon realized Javon and his uncle were active members of a local black gang that ran their turf out of a car wash. Out of respect for his housemates and the Black Lives Matter movement, Kevin joined them in a street fight against a rival gang.

Kevin told me all this in a phone call a month after his release. He had borrowed Javon's phone, whose name and number I didn't recognize, and I almost blocked the call. Kevin said he had contacted his lawyer, Charlie, to get my phone number.

I was glad to hear that Kevin was safe and had a roof over his head, and he told me, "I'm free. I'm clean. I get up in the morning, and I'm training. I'm gettin' it done."

I was on the computer when he called. As he told me that crazy story of the street gang fight with his newfound black associates, I looked them up and was amazed to find they had a Wikipedia page listing them as one of the oldest criminal street gangs in his new location.

"Holy shit, Kevin," I said. "You have now officially associated with three race-based gangs! Who thought you could have added a black gang to your resume?"

"I know. You can't make this stuff up, can you, Gela?"

Then, for the first time in a long while, he asked me about the book. It had been a year since he told me my life was in danger and that story of the bloody motel room. Why either of us thought I was still on board with the project was insanity. Yet, enough time had passed that I was mulling over writing a safer, fictionalized version of the story. I explained this and said, "I was even thinking of killing you off to help you out with the Montañistas," and we both laughed.

"You already know you have creative license to do whatever you want to do," he added.

He ended our call by telling me not to worry about him, that he was going job hunting and always did what it took to survive. "I'm free, you know? I'm happy I'm just free," he said, promising to call again soon to let me know how he was.

—

Two weeks later, in early July, he called me from the same number that showed up as Javon on my caller ID. He said he left Javon's after a drive-by shooting tore up the house and that he was holding onto his friend's phone because Javon was back in jail. Kevin said he made his way to a different part of town and applied for a job as an exterior building painter, which the receptionist, a pretty brunette, helped him get.

In fact, he and the receptionist, Maria, hit it off immediately, and he was calling me from Maria's house, where he now lived with her and her two cats. He introduced me to Maria on the phone, and the two of them recounted their exceedingly fast courtship.

The painting company owner wasn't interested in hiring Kevin because of his tattoos, lack of ID, and recent release from prison. But Maria had been checking him out and convinced the owner to give him a chance. Maria approached him on his first day on the job, "And the chemistry, it just come," Kevin said. He got her number and called her the following day, Sunday, as she was leaving church. "I'd like to get to know you better," he told her. And from there, they clicked. "We've got a special bond, you know?" he said.

"I did think he was cute," Maria giggled, and said she saw him as a "breath of fresh air." She was divorced without children and in her early 50s—only a few years older than Kevin—and she was saving up for a tummy tuck as she'd recently lost a lot of weight. When they'd met two weeks ago, Maria was on the rebound from a failed relationship.

"She's very sophisticated. You're going to like her a lot," he said. "She's real special, real cool." He described Maria as "tech-savvy" and said she was helping him get his birth certificate so he could get an ID. They both asked if I would email her copies of Kevin's artwork so she could post it on a website.

I gambled big and cautioned them both about not using Kevin's real name on the artwork and not using his name or photo on social media—not knowing what, if anything, she knew about his backstory. "Kevin, I hope you told her why," I said in my mother-hen voice.

"Oh, I know all about the Montañistas," Maria said immediately. *Hmmm. So far, so good*, I thought.

"Everything's good, Gela, and I'm slowly making it," Kevin said. He described himself now as a "homebody," saying he does normal things like "go to work, live, be happy, take your girl out every Friday ... just enjoy life. All the free things in life." He said they attended her church on the weekends and Wednesdays.

Maria and I chatted some more, and she asked about my college major, journalism, and told me she was working toward a B.A. in Sociology with the idea of getting licensed as a case manager for the county housing authority or maybe working in a prison environment.

I told her I appreciated this delightful phone call because Kevin knew I worried about him, and I said maybe now I'd worry a little less.

"You don't have to worry about Kevin," she said.

I gambled again and asked the two of them if Kevin was staying "clean," and he replied "yes," except for smoking pot sometimes. He said he had anxiety from being in prison for so long and that even a trip to the grocery store made him nervous. Same with church, he added, saying, "I make her hold my hand."

He repeated, "So a little pot sometimes. I keep myself real calm and cool."

"No judging on pot," I assured him. "My husband and I have our edibles," and we all laughed until I said in my mother-hen tone, "As long as you don't do anything more than that."

"She's making it very clear—cut and dried—you do anything beyond that, and you're history," he said.

"Excellent. I approve. I like her even more," I said.

Then he said, "She's not street-wise, she's square, like you ...," which made me howl. "Ha! Excuse me? I'm square?" I asked. "No, I am totally square," I conceded, still laughing.

"She's what I need, Gela, to keep myself centered and get everything going. I have a place now. I'm not out there being stalked or homeless. That was wild, Gela."

"I wish you nothing but boringness and happiness," I said. Maria worried aloud that Kevin might get bored now, to which he replied, "How am I going to get bored? This is a mansion—I can walk to my kitchen and make something to eat, play with the fur babies ..."

We all made plans to talk soon, and Kevin, once again, expressed his appreciation for everything I did for him while he was in prison. "I am going to get on my feet. I am going to make it," he said.

"Oh, I know you are," I agreed. "You have help now."

CHAPTER 48
DESTINY

LATE 2022

On the last day of July, Kevin called me with another update. In the three weeks since we'd last spoken, he had gotten a job at a body shop airbrushing designs on motorcycle rims and muscle car hoods that paid much more than the painting job. He worked regular hours Monday through Friday and usually picked up extra work on Saturdays. He and Maria still attended church on Sundays and Bible study on Wednesdays.

"I don't mess with nobody. I stay out of the way. I'm living the life that most women want me to live—I don't drink, I don't do nothing," he explained. He said he got up at 4:30 a.m. every day, even when he wasn't working, and always had Maria's coffee waiting for her. He usually worked out at a park across the street, enjoyed watching TV, and sometimes chased the cats with a remote-controlled toy car.

He said he and Maria had a fight yesterday but didn't elaborate and said that the men in her past life were "slimeballs." He explained, "So now, when she gets into a really good relationship, she don't know how to take it … She thinks I'm going to go out there and run around and make up for lost time. I tell her I'm past all that. I'm way past that. I ain't got nothing to make up for—I'm making it all up right now."

He said they reconciled quickly when she came to the autobody shop to have lunch with him.

I reminded him about all the stability Maria was providing in his life, and he said, "That's what I tell her every day. I tell her, 'You don't even know—you opening that door for me—how big that is. You just inherited a pitbull for life.' She knows."

He added, "She knows in her heart that I'm really trying to stay out of trouble. I'm a good guy now. No problems, no fighting, no drinking, no drugs. I don't do nothing."

Later that day, Maria texted me some pictures. One was of Kevin, in shorts and a long-sleeve shirt, posing in front of an aquarium with sunglasses on top of his head. Five were selfies of the couple, heads touching, sometimes kissing. Another was of Kevin curled up with a white cat on top of a bed.

"You two are adorable," I texted back.

I got a similar, happy report in August, and Maria and I texted about plans to have a FaceTime video call on Kevin's new iPhone. "Thank you, Carla. I truly love Kevin. He's an amazing man!" she told me.

"I'm so glad you two found each other (smiley-face)," I said.

—

Three weeks later, in mid-September, Maria texted and asked if I could call her. She stepped outside her office into the summer heat to take my call, and the first thing she asked me was, "Am I in danger from this gang that's been after him?"

I gulped and said I didn't think there was a Montañista gang presence where she lived, and I hoped Kevin would confirm this.

"I just want to let you know that I care a lot about Kevin, but I'm starting to question things ... he's starting to say things that scare me."

I asked what she meant, and she said she found him pacing in her living room back and forth one day, looking out a window, saying, "They're out there. They're watching me." She asked him if he'd been taking drugs because she had never seen him act that way before, and he said no, he wasn't on drugs.

"I told him, 'No, they're not watching you. There's no one there,' but he said if the gang ever found him, they'd kill both of us. He said, 'They're brutal. They will ask no questions. They don't care that you're a woman. They will kill you.' ... So now I'm asking, what did I get myself into?"

"Oh, goodness," was all I could say.

Maria asked me how well I knew Kevin, and I said I'd known him for ten years but not intimately the way she did. I gave her a frank assessment of his probable PTSD and his addiction issue, which she was aware of.

"He could be using again," I cautioned her, saying Kevin's pacing and peering out the window sounded very much like the paranoid phone call I'd gotten in January where he said gangsters were trying to break into an apartment. "I thought he was probably on meth," I said. "And then he went right back to prison after a dirty urinalysis."

I told her that at one time, the Montañistas had a hit order out on Kevin for things that happened in prison 10 years ago. "Do they still want this revenge? I can't say for certain, but I think Kevin *believes* they do," I told her. Again, I said I thought there weren't Montañistas within hundreds of miles of where they lived.

"I live all the way over here in Pennsylvania," I said, "and if you think over the last ten years, something like this hasn't crossed my mind many, many times, it has. It's one of the biggest reasons I've never put this into a book."

"He keeps talking about that book," she said. "I told him that if you wrote that book, that would just be stirring the pot, and it could all come back on him."

"Agree, agree," I said. "The idea haunts me—to think that I could lead people to him, to you. I just can't go there, and I don't want to lead people to me or my family."

"Unfortunately, Kevin has also been very loose with his story," she said. "He tells a lot of people what's happened to him. This has me quite concerned as well."

Maria was honest about her ex-husband being a drug addict and said her most recent boyfriend had been abusive. She said she learned much from both failed relationships and could spot the warning signs but didn't want to accuse Kevin of doing something he wasn't. Yet at the same time, she saw him staring at other women and felt he wasn't attracted to her anymore, and she had a nagging sense that he was just using her for a place to land after prison. She recognized that she had let him into her life far too quickly after falling for him practically at first sight.

She said she and Kevin had been arguing more lately, and one time, he left for a day and a half, riding around on his mountain bike. Just the fact that he could take off like that gave her pause, too.

He had denied using drugs several times and had also been giving her all his paycheck to hold for safekeeping so that he wouldn't do anything stupid with it. She told him he needed to grow up and take some responsibility.

"Honestly, I'm starting to get cold feet here," Maria said. "I don't wish him any harm, but at the same time, I have to look out for myself."

"You absolutely do," I said. "Maybe this is all plenty of reason for you to say to him, 'I think you need to spread your wings. I've enjoyed this ride with you, but I think I'm a little too afraid to be your partner.'"

We had talked for 35 minutes, and Maria had to get back to work, she said, promising to keep me updated on their situation.

Two days later, she told me Kevin moved out.

For almost two months, I'd carried a euphoric belief that Kevin had found the new life with a loving partner he so desperately wanted. He had found it alright, but I should have known better than to think he could keep it.

—

Two weeks later, at the end of September, my phone rang from the Javon caller ID. Kevin wanted to check in and told me, "My life has taken off big. I got my own place. I live at my body shop where I work and paint. I do custom paint jobs, make a lot of money. I'm doing it. I'm doing it big."

I acted surprised that he moved out because I promised Maria I wouldn't tell Kevin we had spoken. He said he now lived in a fifth-wheel camper on the auto body shop compound and that he and Maria were still together, "just doing a monogamous thing until marriage. 'Cause we go to church, and we're really being respectful to all that."

"You're getting married?" I said with genuine surprise.

"Yep."

I said "congrats" on the marital news, which I didn't really believe.

I asked how Maria was, and he said she was "excellent" and that he wanted to buy a Harley to take her for a ride every now and then. He said he was still going to church twice a week and staying out of trouble and that in a week, he'd be talking to school kids in cooperation with the local police gang unit. "I'm gonna tell 'em about prison and the real lifestyle of gangs—just really give it to 'em like they need it."

"That's wonderful," I said. "You have valuable information to share with young people."

And then he said, "Hey, I'm gonna be in a movie."

"What?"

He said movie location scouts had driven by the auto body shop and thought it would be a good place for one of the scenes and talked to the shop bosses. The bosses signed a movie contract, and some employees, including him, were given scripts for their roles.

It was going to be a movie about time travel and people "hiding a whole bunch of Nazi gold ... They can shoot you with this gun and send you back in time, and they're taking money back into the authorities to go fight Hitler and all that."

I was speechless as he continued. "Well, at this spot where we're at, we're the ones designing all the armor and all that. So I'm the one that's making the armor, but I'm a drug dealer ... so there's this guy that comes out the back of the spot where I'm at, that I just treated bad, and I tell him, 'No, you can't do it.' ... It's pretty wild, Gela."

"That sounds crazy," I said. "But now listen. If you're in a movie, your face and your name will be out there. I think you should be concerned about that."

"Nah, I'm not worried about it. Do you know why?"

"Why?"

"'Cause God protects me."

"Oh, Kevin," I sighed. "You gotta protect yourself."

"So, okay. I just wanted to make sure that you know I'm doing alright."

"Well, thanks for the update. I appreciate it."

He said he would send me photos of the airbrush projects he was working on at the shop and take pictures of what his Fifth-Wheel camper looked like inside.

"Sounds good," I said. "We'll talk soon. Take care."

"Bye-bye."

"Bye-bye."

That was the last time I ever talked to Kevin Sanders.

—

Kevin and Maria patched things up, and she let him move back into her tidy house. For two more months, they cohabitated, but as fall transitioned to winter, his behavior changed. He became detached and less loving. He started missing days at work and disappeared again for a day or so at a time. He'd lost weight, had no interest in food, and wasn't sleeping. When Maria asked if he was using drugs again, he denied it, but she persisted and said there were people from their church who could help him.

She discovered photos of voluptuous women on his phone, which they fought over, and he shoved her in the heat of an argument. Maria called her sister, who lived out of state, and they talked about Maria leaving her once charming ex-con and moving in with her sibling.

In November, the week of Maria's birthday, she came home from work and heard someone else's voice in her house. She walked to the bathroom and found Kevin and a homeless man shooting each other up with a shared hypodermic needle. After the yelling and screaming subsided, Kevin admitted he had returned to his first love, meth. But then he said it was all her fault, that she'd had too many rules about things like drinking and church, and that she had pushed him to do it.

And that was it for Maria—it was over. She deserved better. She kicked him out and cut off his cellphone service. Kevin took what few possessions he could carry on his mountain bike and disappeared, but not before calling her a whore and threatening to blind her. As soon as Kevin peddled away, Maria called her sister.

—

A couple of weeks later, Kevin showed up at her door as Maria was packing up her house. He was unshowered, emaciated, and carrying a puppy in a cardboard box. She asked what he wanted, and he said he'd lost his job and was living in a $250 car. He wondered if she'd give him $10 for a mismatched collection of plastic food containers he'd brought.

"I'm not giving you $10 for this dumpster-diving stuff," she said, and then asked him, "Why would you get a dog when you can't even take care of yourself?"

When he saw that she was moving, he asked where she was going. All she said was, "Far away from you," and she told him to leave. Before he walked away, Kevin asked for my phone number. "I accidentally deleted it," she said.

CHAPTER 49
REDUX

2023

A ddicts are made, not born.

Why some people can ride through the horrors of life without turning to substances to dull the pain, while others can't, is a mystery. Environment, social pressures, nature-versus-nurture—they all play a role. And why some can't conquer their addictions—despite having a support network and access to treatment programs—is for psychologists and doctors to explain.

I do know that Kevin had a near-zero chance of not becoming an addict. He was raised by an alcoholic, drug-addicted, abusive single mother who used to move Kevin and his younger brother Martin around constantly. They bounced around between relatives and friends and lived out of her car, and the boys were often hungry. When Kevin met his father, Big Daddy, for the first time at age 11, he begged to be able to live with him and his new wife for some stability.

Big Daddy, who ruled with a bare-knuckled fist, took both boys in. He owned an auto body shop and taught both sons the art of tattooing and airbrush design. But Big Daddy was also a chapter president for the local Hells Angels club, the outlaw motorcycle gang. The brothers spent their formative years hanging out with their father's criminal associates in the auto shop, where they had easy access to alcohol and drugs. At age 11, Kevin had his first beer and experimented with pot. At age 15, he smoked crack and took LSD, then moved on to heroin. As a rebellious teenager, Kevin joined a Hispanic street gang as their "tagger," meaning he was the graffiti artist who marked the gang's territory. He and his low-level gangsters—a substitute family—committed petty robberies and street crimes to support their drug habits. This activity led to several stints in juvenile detention.

When Kevin was 25, Big Daddy taught him how to cook methamphetamine, the Hells Angels' drug of choice for consumption and commerce, and Kevin began injecting it daily. All of these substances were available to Kevin's brother Martin, who also fell in and out of juvie and jail like his older brother. Eventually, when he was 36, Martin died on his lawn from a stroke brought on by years of alcohol and hard drug use.

And just when I thought I knew everything there was to know about Kevin and his backstory, I learned something extraordinary. Beginning when he was 13, his stepmother—who earned her living as a stripper before becoming Big Daddy's second wife—lured Kevin to her bed. She made him do drugs with her and her friends and perform sexually like an adult for their pleasure. It never occurred to Kevin that this was molestation. It never occurred to him that his stepmother was a pedophile who'd abused him as a teenager. His little brother Martin was abused this way as well.

Kevin shared with me, years ago, that his brother Martin was actually the biological father of their little "stepbrother." The stepbrother was 20 years younger than Kevin and 18 years younger than Martin.

Kevin told me this in 2019 and sent me a photo of him, Big Daddy, and his "stepbrother," with Big Daddy standing between them, arms around each "son," a cigarette between two fingers. Big Daddy wore his white hair in a ponytail and a matching white mustache. On the left, Kevin had a similar dark mustache and was shirtless. Kevin's chest was heavily tattooed, and he wore a black ball cap backward. On the right was the young "stepbrother"/ "nephew"/ "grandson" / "son" who also wore a black ball cap backward. The family resemblance among the three was unmistakable, and it occurred to me, after I learned about the stepmother's abuse, that Kevin could just as easily have been that young man's father. The dates Kevin was in and out of prison allowed for this possibility.

The photo had been taken in the auto shop shortly before Big Daddy turned Kevin in to the ATF for owning a sawed-off shotgun. Federal agents had raided Kevin's meth-lab-in-a-camper and found the gun, just as Big Daddy said they would. For reasons I never understood, Kevin was only charged with being a felon in possession of a weapon. Regardless, that was the event that landed Kevin in federal prison, where he stayed for 17 years.

Remarkably, Kevin and Big Daddy reconciled through letter-writing and phone calls before Big Daddy died in his sleep in 2013 at the age of 68. When asked why his father turned him over to the feds, Kevin told Scott and me the same story. Kevin said Big Daddy had been jealous of the money Kevin was making in the auto shop and the meth camper. That never made sense to me, and years later, I wondered if his little stepbrother's parentage had anything to do with it. But that was a wild supposition on my part, as I imagined a dramatic scene where perhaps Big Daddy learned an ugly truth and took out his revenge.

In 2019, Kevin told me his little stepbrother didn't know about his real biological father, "but the truth is the truth, and I don't worry about it," he said, meaning he didn't worry if that revelation came out in the book.

The book. The book I didn't write for ten years.

In early 2023, Jim and I bought a new house. We kept the Pocono cottage as a rental, and between managing that property and our move, I was plenty busy. We found an old Victorian that had been updated, but I could still add my personal touches to, so I was also planning a mini makeover of our historical homestead.

Jim started consulting part-time, mentoring and career-coaching clients over Zoom in his home office. His flexible schedule still allowed time for family gatherings, tennis, golf, volunteering at the local food pantry, and trips with his fraternity brothers. He'd created a fulfilling, purposeful, and fun semi-retirement with a work-life balance that was never possible during his executive years.

By March, I still hadn't unpacked all my boxes labeled "Carla's office." I poured myself a coffee, turned on HGTV, and started digging through, sorting, and tossing what contents I could. I saved all the "Kevin Sanders" boxes for last because I dreaded revisiting what was inside. But I was determined to get through the ordeal because I wanted that feeling of order and serenity that awaited on the other side.

I spent an entire afternoon pulling everything out of those "Kevin Sanders" boxes and laying it out in piles on my office floor. I had duplicates of trial transcripts and the massive appeal file, so I stuffed those into a black trash bag. Ten years of Kevin's artwork was sprinkled throughout, so I organized that by date. And then I started putting everything back in chronological order, all the time wondering why I was bothering and if I'd hang on to these boxes as long as I'd kept some of my by-lined, above-the-fold newspaper stories.

I lingered over some files and notepads as I handled them, trying not to despair over Kevin's state. I couldn't help playing the what-if game. What if Kevin had stayed in good standing with the Montañistas at Allenwood and been released in 2014? Or what if we'd won the trial and he'd been released on time, or we'd won the appeal and a re-trial and he'd been released two years later? Or what if there'd been no COVID and he could have spent a year in a halfway house transitioning into society? Or what if he could have gone to live with Scott in Pittsburgh?

In my heart, I knew he still would have ended up in a bathroom with a homeless guy shooting up meth. And, sadly, I believed he still would have wound up living in a stolen car, skinny and jobless, having squandered his talents and any goodwill he'd built up along the way.

I had done some research and learned something Kevin wouldn't have known about the methamphetamine formula that re-ignited his addiction—it was not his father's meth. It was not the same meth he learned to cook in a camper behind Big Daddy's body shop in the early 2000s. Today's meth was much more addictive and deadly and derived from a compounding method called P2P that used new chemicals and solvents (as featured in a plot line of TV's *Breaking Bad*).

This altered super meth caused a rapid decline in body and mind, and induced psychosis, hallucinations, paranoia, and isolation. Back when Kevin first became hooked on meth, it was far easier to maintain a job, keep relationships etc., much like a functioning alcoholic or substance abuser who could hide their habit. But that all changed with the new chemistry. And while the country's opioid addiction remained more in the spotlight, the reformulated methamphetamine, on its own, had already sparked a new wave of mental illness and homelessness across the country.

—

In my office, my mountain of Kevin-related legal pads with hand-written notes was more challenging to file because I had to flip through pages to find a date. When I came across the yellow notepad from my 2015 phone interview with Steven Tremblay, the rec cage assault victim, I caught a word I underlined and circled: *snowball*. I hadn't thought about that in years. And then it hit me like I'd just been struck in the face with a packed ball of slush and snow—that fucking snowball. It started everything. What happened to Steven, Kevin, Scott, and me emanated from that single moment.

The sequence of events played out in my mind like a Grade-B horror show, starting with the snowball to MacDonald's face, then a groin kick, then the Captain's humiliation and vow of vengeance, and MacDonald making sure Steven ended up in the rec cage with Kevin and Arson. Those two got indicted and charged, and Scott was appointed Kevin's public defender. Scott wanted a website to raise money for an expert witness that their cranky judge denied them, and he called me. "This'll make a great true crime book, Car," Scott had said to lure me in when I wanted nothing to do with any of it.

I fake-wallowed in bitterness at this incomplete origin story because I was all in on everything pretty damn fast. Sure, I'd wanted to help a friend, but working on the case made me feel important and useful. And it was also a VIP ticket to a true crime story unfolding in real time. Hadn't I always wanted to write this kind of story?

And then another lightbulb went off, this one making me angrier still. *Goddamnit.* That snowball scene? Helluva way to start off the book, right?

—

In late March, I called Scott. We hadn't spoken or even texted since last June when Kevin had been released from that medium-security prison and hitched a ride with his young black friend Javon. Kevin asked me for Scott's phone number, but I told him I could only pass on his new phone number to Scott. Scott wanted to keep his distance, I said.

"I'm done with him," Scott told me then. "I don't trust him anymore." Also, Scott had a new wife.

Scott had met Kelly, a petite paralegal, in Pittsburgh through a dating app. They went to brunch on their first date, and by the end, they each confessed they were ready to delete their app profiles—neither saw the point in dating anymore because they secretly felt they'd just found their new soulmate. The politically aligned couple made it official a few months later, and for a wedding present, I sent them a butcher block cutting board engraved with their names.

A few months before Scott met his wife, he attended the funeral of a cousin in Cincinnati. It was another long Catholic mass and life celebration, where the officiant called out the names of family members who'd already passed away. As the names of Scott's mother, father, and sister were spoken, the recognition that he was all alone washed over him. A floodgate of sorrow, anger, and regret spilled open, and he cried like a lost little boy searching for light. Not long after, he renewed his subscription to the dating app.

—

"Guess what? I'm doing it. I'm writing the book," I told Scott.

"For real?"

"For real."

"I always knew you would," he said, and I wasn't sure I believed him. Or maybe I hadn't thought myself capable until then and was projecting.

We talked for two hours about our families, our lives, and Kevin and the book. He didn't know anything about Kevin's last chapter, which saddened but didn't surprise him. "I always felt he was getting screwed," Scott said, "and that's why I stuck with him ... to a point."

I told Scott that he'd read Kevin's tea leaves far sooner than I had. But I didn't say out loud that I believed there was more to Scott's "zealous advocacy," as Judge Anderson once put it, of Kevin-the-client. I thought Scott saw something of himself in Kevin—a sensitive, intelligent soul who was a survivor despite the odds and what had happened to him. Or someone who *could be* a survivor.

Scott and I talked about how Kevin seemed to fare better in prison than in the outside world—particularly under Montañista rule, where drugs were forbidden and he was presumably clean.

"The irony," I said.

"Yeah, go figure," Scott replied.

I told him I looked up some of the characters, like T-Rex, who'd died in one of the medical prisons a few years ago, and Rey, who was doing life at Victorville. Little Eagle was at USP Beaumont in Texas, closer to his mother and sister, and had 25 more years to serve on his bank robbery charges—he'd be 81 when he got out. Arson had been released long before Kevin but ended up in a Nevada state prison for robbing casinos. The judge had died and had had a courtroom named after him, and the prosecutor had retired. Lewisburg remained a medium-security facility after the SMU was shut down, following that joint 2016 investigation by The Marshall Project and NPR.

Those news outlets, I told Scott, did it again last year, with another joint report on SMU atrocities in Thomson, Illinois. "All those Lewisburg inmates were transferred to Thomson, only to have the whole cycle repeat: murders, gang hits, and torture multiply. Then The Marshall Project and NPR team up again to uncover the brutality, and *that* program gets shut down."

"It's just rinse and repeat. The whole system's fucking broken," he said, and I agreed.

I outlined my vision for the book, telling Scott it was going be a more personal story now and that I needed to know how much I could reveal about him. He told me to write what I wanted and congratulated me before we ended the call. I said *congratulations* were premature, because we should see if I could write the damn thing first. Then I quoted the author Dorothy Parker, who said, "I hate writing, I love having written."

—

Right before Christmas, when I called Scott to tell him I signed a book contract, he said, "Congratulations!" But I told him to hold that thought, that we could celebrate when it came out next fall and was *real*. And, by the way, would he please sign the release form I just emailed him, which my publisher insisted upon?

He mailed me back a signed hard copy with a sticky note that said, "Don't screw me over, Carla" with a smiley face.

CHAPTER 50
CHAINED BIRDS

2024

Scott and his wife Kelly moved down South to be near her family. They sold Scott's Pittsburgh bungalow and paid cash for a mid-century brick ranch near the beach.

Before he knew it, Scott had gone from being single and without a family to becoming a husband, a step-buddy, and a step-grandfather to Kelly's boisterous brood of relatives and add-ons. The in-laws entered the house without knocking, talked over each other at the dinner table, and treated his refrigerator contents like community property. When he got COVID a second time—and gifted it to his wife—the relatives brought soup and mowed his grass. Maybe this new family thing wasn't so bad after all, he thought.

Scott's daughter Ashley, now 25, had gradually resumed texting her father, but their relationship was still strained. Scott was hopeful that the allure of a beach vacation with babies to play with would result in a reunion. Father and daughter texted about the idea, and when Ashley didn't immediately dismiss it, Scott took that as a partial win.

He bought a small fishing boat from his neighbor and set up a workshop in his detached garage to restore and refinish it. While Kelly spent the work week as a legal assistant in a new law firm—because, unlike her husband, she wasn't ready to retire—Scott worked meticulously in the garage while a big shop fan circulated air.

The first thing he did was get help (from the relatives) to move the 143-pound top-heavy engine into his garden tool shed, where it would sit until the end. Then, those handy relatives helped him hoist the boat onto two sawhorses. Scott began by tearing out and cleaning the makeshift steering column, steering wheel, throttle, and steering cables. Then he removed the gas tank and storage bin and cleaned those out, too.

He spent hours and hours with his sander grinding off 24 years of fish guts, gasoline, and paint on the boat's surface. He replaced the disintegrated wood floorboard and filled holes with a guaranteed waterproof adhesive sealant.

The boat came with two life jackets, a good anchor, an old fish finder, and a fire extinguisher, and would hold two adults and a child. Kelly said she could see herself tagging along once in a while, and her two oldest grandkids were already fighting over who would get to go fishing first and catch trout or red snapper.

Scott had grown up fishing in a canoe with his dad on the Susquehanna River in Douglasville and on a pontoon boat on Shawnee Lake at the family cottage. After Scott's divorce, when he lived at the cottage, he never moved the pontoon back into the water. Now, that pontoon boat was part of the lake cottage property sale that Scott was in charge of in the summer of 2024.

A long-time cottage renter had not renewed their lease, and Scott and his brother-in-law, Russ, were ready to sell it. Neither Russ nor his adult children wanted to keep it because it reminded them of their wife and mother, Pam. It had been three years since Scott's twin sister had died from pancreatic cancer, and Scott and Russ had communicated only a handful of times because Scott still found Russ depressing.

When Scott told me he was returning to Pennsylvania to clean out the cottage and get it ready to sell, I said the timing was perfect for us to see each other. I would be at our Pocono cabin, turning it over from the last guests for a summer rental, and so I invited Scott for a politics-free lunch that was an easy drive from Shawnee Lake.

"You look great!" I said, greeting him on my covered rustic porch. "Married life agrees with you, I see." We hugged. "It's so good to see you, Car," he smiled and then took in the cabin's great room with its fieldstone fireplace that reached the vaulted rafters. "This place is incredible," he said.

"Does it remind you of anything?" I asked.

"Jack's cabin."

"Yes," I nodded. I made him a coffee and gave him a tour, and when we got to the laundry room, I moved sheets and towels into the dryer for the next guests. As he admired Jim's and my quaint woodland retreat, I told him it was too "cabiney" for me and that I was glad to live in a real house now with fewer spiders. I said the cabin had served its purpose, and we still liked going there between renters. I added that the community's golf course remained Jim's favorite, and he was on the course's back nine now and would join us for lunch at the clubhouse.

"Come here," I told him. "I have something to show you." Scott joined me at the long Windsor bench in the entryway, which held a cardboard box. I flipped up the lid, and he reached in and grabbed one of a dozen books with my name on it.

"Is this what I think it is?"

"Yes! And, well, no … It's just a galley copy. One of those simple bound versions they send out to get reviews, blurbs, and maybe some podcast spots."

"You're going to be on a podcast?" he gaped.

"I don't know, maybe!" I laughed.

He turned the galley over in his hands and commented on the cover art, which featured Kevin's haunting black-and-white drawing of the eagle with a chain around its foot and a broken chain around the branch the bird sat on. "I do remember this," he said. "This is perfect, Carla."

I agreed and said it was my most cherished piece of Kevin Sanders artwork.

"You still haven't heard from him?"

"Not since he called to tell me he was going to be in that movie about time-traveling Nazi hunters. That was almost two years ago."

"Do you think he's dead?"

I shrugged. "He could be. He was certainly heading in that direction. There's no such thing as setting up a Google alert for a county morgue, so I might never know."

Scott studied the cover again and said, "Wait, why is this *Chained Birds* plural? I thought you were calling it *Chained Bird* after his drawing?"

"Oh, God, that's a story," I said and promised to tell him on a little hike to the Pocono community's hidden gem, a spectacular sight that would have been worth the drive alone.

—

I led Scott down the road, which turned into an asphalt walkway, then a gravel path, and finally became a dirt hiking trail. We meandered through a forest of old-growth birch, hemlock, white pine, oak, and poplar trees that survived the 19th-century timber barons' lumber harvesting. Breezy ferns, purple rhododendrons, and pink mountain azaleas popped up along the way. Other than summer bird songs and the hammering of a woodpecker, the scrape of pebbles under shoes and our voices were the only sounds.

He asked if I'd gotten my Italian passport yet, and I said I was still working on it. "But guess who signed up for Italian classes?" I said and told him I hoped our 45-year-old French lessons would somehow help, that there was a bit of crossover in the romance languages.

I asked how his boat was coming along, and he said a mechanic was tuning up the 25-horsepower engine and that it would be ready for the water soon. He pulled out his phone and showed me pictures of the 14-foot aluminum-sided vessel upside down on sawhorses in his garage. He had primed and painted the inside white, and the outside was coated in the most calming, cheerful shade of cerulean blue.

"Gorgeous," I told him.

"I spent way too much money on it."

"Can you put a price on happiness, though?"

"So, *Chained Birds* ..." he said.

"Right, *Chained Birds* plural. This was my mother's doing. It's entirely Marilyn's fault." I explained that my mother, a retired English teacher (as he knew) and one-time newspaper proofreader extraordinaire (which he didn't know), had read an early book draft with the title *Chained Bird*. After her red pen had done its work—tackling, among other things, my comma-itis and heavy use of the word "pretty"—she said my title was utterly misleading.

"She said I went into great detail about how Kevin was chained from the belly and shackled at the wrist and ankles and that obviously he was the chained bird. But then she said all three of us were chained birds and chained to each other. And I'm, like, *whaaat*?

"She said you were chained to Kevin without probably realizing it because his salvation was your salvation."

"No ..."

"Yes. And that I was chained to Kevin and displayed it more openly than you. She said no matter how many years went by, I couldn't quit the story, that I cried all the time, that I sent him money and bought him stuff, so I was chained to him. And, Marilyn concluded, I freed myself by writing the book."

"No shit? It makes sense …"

"I know! She also said I had my own addiction, that I was addicted to the true crime story. Can you believe that? I told her that was some highbrow ninth-grade literary analysis I wasn't expecting."

"Ohhh, our beloved Mrs. Parello …"

"When we hung up, I was furious because I had to change everything. References on my website, social media profiles, email addresses, mock-up book images, business cards. It was a royal pain in the ass. But, of course, she was right."

—

Our wooded trail slowly widened to a field of tall grass and wildflowers where two deer grazed. They paused to stare at us before returning to their tawny cottongrass, and the not-so-distant rumble of water signaled we were almost there.

"You know, we were in our 40s when this adventure started?" I said.

"Back when some of us had more hair," he said, touching the top of his head.

"And some of us had no grey hair," I added, pointing to my hair's left side and a skunk stripe of white curls that I stopped coloring.

"Yeah, I was going to ask about that …"

"It was too much work trying to keep it covered," I said, "so I decided to let it go and own my shit. I am going to be 60, after all." This was the big birthday year for all our remaining Diners Club members, and I was the baby of the bunch, clinging to my 50s like a toddler to a lollipop.

The edge of the field echoed with the loud rush of water and ended with steps leading to an overlook that faced a two-tiered, Catskill-style, 135-foot-high waterfall. The upper falls tumbled over sandstones and siltstones into a middle plunge pool that was supposed to be off-limits to swimmers, and so, naturally, was a magnet for the resort's teenagers. The lower falls dropped into a bedrock basin that hikers could access from a winding, covered tower of staircases.

We leaned over the guardrail, just looking and listening for a long while. "This is stunning," he said. I led him to the many staircases where we descended to the bottom. A patchwork of grass and dirt opened to the rocky, shallow watershed where the vertical falls ended. Near the water's edge stood a few small cairns—carefully stacked stone towers erected by local wanderers.

"So, you gave this up for a real house?" Scott asked.

"Yep," I nodded. "It's nice to come back to once in a while, but I was missing civilization."

"You know who would love this?" he said, spreading his arms around. "All of this, this day, your book?"

"Jack," we both said at the same time.

"I miss him," Scott said.

"Me too," I said, and then I asked if he remembered the three of us talking about who would play us in the movie version of the book.

"Definitely Vin Diesel for Kevin," Scott said, "and didn't Jack say Sandra Bullock for you, or maybe Marisa Tomei?"

"And I said Clive Owen for you ... and anyone with a department store Santa suit could play Jack," I added, and we laughed.

We closed our eyes, lifted our faces to the sun, and thought about this last chapter in our decade-long, stranger-than-fiction crime saga that united and changed us more than we probably wanted to admit.

"Any regrets?" he asked me.

"You mean writing the book?"

"All of it. Me dragging you into the case …"

"Oh, I think the word *drag* might be some revisionist history," I interrupted and ignored that ephemeral question because I didn't know the answer.

He finally asked, "So, what made you write it?"

"One of my beta readers asked me this, and I didn't have a good answer. Closure. Guilt. Obligation. Therapy. Anger. Take your pick."

"Anger?"

"Oh my God, yes. I was mad at Jack for dying, pissed at Kevin for mistreating Maria and blowing a chance at a nice life outside of prison. And you and all your insurrection bullshit …"

"Hey! I thought this was supposed to be a politics-free afternoon?"

I pointed a finger at his face, daring him to counter-attack, and said, "I basically decided—fuck all of you. This is my story. And you guys can be in it."

This hit Scott like I was a stand-up comic killing it at the mic, and he doubled over, howling, which gave me massive giggles and produced a steady stream of laughing tears. Our bellies hurt from the silliness, and as we composed ourselves, I tried to wipe my eyes on my shirt. Then Scott gave me the biggest bear hug and kissed my still-wet cheek.

"Carla," he smiled, "it's always been your story. You just didn't know it."

EPILOGUE

It's a rare day when I don't think about that pivotal snowball thrown long ago on a prison compound in Central Pennsylvania, which was the launchpad for *Chained Birds*. I still sometimes marvel over the mind-bending convergence of people and events that were necessary for this book to happen.

It's true that a laundry list of emotions and the need for closure are what propelled me to finally write it. But I was also inspired by the journalists who came before me and first shed light on atrocities at Lewisburg prison. I learned much from Bucknell Professor Karen Morin's 2011 journal article, short titled *"Security here is not safe."* That piece was published shortly after Lewisburg's Special Management Unit opened, and Morin's revelations of its inhumane and murderous conditions were the first deep dive I'd seen into the SMU horrors.

Likewise, I was moved by The Marshall Project and NPR's joint 2016 and 2022 exposés into SMU abuses at Lewisburg and Thomson, Ill. Those timely, years-long investigations helped close both SMU prison programs.

The similar stories I tell in *Chained Birds* are my contribution to the canon—more anecdotal evidence of the failed SMU debacle that I hope will add to the conversation.

—

When I was a young reporter in metro Detroit, my gregarious and old-school editor—who printed out our stories to mark them up with a red pencil Marilyn-style—had two signs hanging on the wall behind his desk. The first read: *When in doubt, send them out*, which meant, back in the day, send your reporters out in the field, don't let them phone it in.

The second sign featured a famous quote adapted from the 1902 book *Observations by Mr. Dooley* by journalist and humorist Finley Peter Dunne. The quote comes from Dunne's fictional Irish bartender, Dooley, who mused satirically on the role of newspapers, and it's been the mantra for journalists for over 100 years. The phrase, as it's usually remembered and how it appeared on my editor's placard, is: *Comfort the afflicted, and afflict the comfortable.*

I wonder what this editor, my first professional mentor, would have made of *Chained Birds* had he lived long enough to receive a signed copy in the mail. Would he have thought I'd lived up to the credos painted on his two wooden signs in our 1990s cramped newspaper office?

I hope so. I think so.

ACKNOWLEDGEMENTS

I wish to thank my family for their love and support throughout my decade-plus journey with this story. I'm eternally grateful for my spouse and alpha reader, Jim, who was not only born to make me smile but knows just when to interject some sage advice I didn't ask for. Thank you all for having my back when I didn't want to write this book and then cheering me on when I did.

I owe my high school friend Scott a heartfelt thanks for making me his partner in crime and for always believing in my ability to tell this tale, especially when I doubted it ad nauseam. Scott introduced me to Kevin, who trusted me with his story, and my only regret is its unhappy ending.

I am deeply grateful to my beta-reading besties, who've been with me from the beginning, particularly my mother Marilyn and JH, for their phenomenal early manuscript insight, suggestions, and deft red penmanship. I am also indebted to LG for her eagle eye spotting niggling typos.

I sincerely appreciate each member of the WildBlue Press team whose dedication and enthusiasm made this book available to the masses. Serendipity led me to my incredibly skilled and delightful editor, Rowena Carenen, all because press founders Steve Jackson and Michael Cordova saw merit in my story. In particular, I'd like to thank Steve for convincing this stubborn writer that there's only one proper way to tell a true crime story.

I have immense gratitude for my sound engineer, Jeff King of Baker Sound Studios in Philadelphia, for his exceptional audiobook production. Jeff's inspirational coaching and directing gave me much-needed confidence for my narration duty, and his sound design and mixing expertise are nothing short of magic.

Last but certainly not least, I'd like to thank photographers NK and MC—including his loaner of the red Porsche—for stylish author photo shoots that made me feel infinitely more special than I truly am.

GLOSSARY OF ACRONYMS AND PRISON LINGO

AB — Aryan Brotherhood (also The Brand). The nation's oldest major white supremacist gang, and also considered the most violent and powerful prison gang in the country.

ADX — Stands for Administrative Maximum and is synonymous with "supermax." ADX/supermax is a super-maximum prison control-unit for the long-term housing of inmates classified as a high-security risk and prisoners who pose an extreme threat nationally and globally.

ATF — Bureau of Alcohol, Tobacco, Firearms and Explosives, primarily responsible for the investigation and prevention of federal offenses involving the unlawful use, manufacture, and possession of firearms and explosives; acts of arson and bombings; and illegal trafficking of alcohol and tobacco products.

AUSA — Assistant United States Attorney. AUSAs prosecute all criminal cases brought by the federal government and defend the government in civil cases.

Bid — A sentence or term of imprisonment, a stint in jail.

Boss versus **Hoss** — Boss is a correctional officer (origin: Sorry, Son of a Bitch first letters spelled backward). Hoss is more affectionate than "Boss" and refers to a correctional officer an inmate respects more.

BOP — Bureau of Prisons

Cellie — Cellmate. Also written as celly.

Car — The group an inmate associates with inside prison, typically bonded by geography, crime, race, or race-based gangs (i.e., your homies).

Banger — A shank/shiv or prison knife.

BNL — Stands for Bad News List, a gang-generated list of inmates not in good standing with the group and, therefore, are targets for violence or worse.

CO — Correctional Officer or Corrections Officer.

DCP — Douglas County Prison

DOJ — Department of Justice (Bureau of Prisons is part of the DOJ)

Drama — In prison, it means a fight or an assault.

Fam bam — Family

FBI — Federal Bureau of Investigation

Fishing line — A long strand of fabric or string fashioned from bed sheets or clothing threads that can transport small items from one cell to another underneath cell doors or outside windows.

Hack — Another name for a correctional officer

Hit the deuces — The alarm button that COs press to bring in backup COs due to inmate fighting or other violence.

Hole — Synonymous with the SHU (pronounced "shoe"), which stands for Special Housing Unit. The hole/SHU is solitary confinement housing used for punitive or protective purposes.

Homeboy — An inmate from the same town, gang, or prison as another inmate. Variations include Homie or Homes.

Hustle — A means of income inside prison, such as bartering or selling tattooing, artwork, legal services, or conducting gambling enterprises.

Ink — Another name for tattoos

Keep-aways — Specific prisoners, races, and gangs from which an inmate must be kept away due to incompatibility, which affects housing and recreation, among other things.

Keister — Mainly used as a verb, such as when an inmate has a prohibited item and no place to hide it, they might "keister" it in their read end.

Kite — A contraband note written on a small piece of paper folded or rolled and secretively passed between inmates.

Lifer — Ann inmate serving a life sentence.

Lock in a sock — To literally put a padlock in a sock to use as a weapon against someone.

NLR — Nazi Low Rider, a white supremacist prison gang serving as foot soldiers to the Aryan Brotherhood

PC — Protective custody, as in, "He PC'ed up and is off the yard."

Peckerwood/Wood — A nickname for a white inmate, particularly one belonging to a white race-based gang.

PETA — People for the Ethical Treatment of Animals, an animal rights organization.

Programming — Slang for an inmate's educational and behavioral classes, i.e., efforts to become a better person.

Quay Hearing — A meeting between prison officials and an inmate to determine the inmate's incompatibility with other inmates, races, and gangs for housing, recreation, and other purposes.

SAC — Soldiers of Aryan Culture, another white supremacist prison gang modeled after the Aryan Brotherhood.

Sallyport — A separate, secure, controlled entryway to an enclosure, like a recreational cage.

Short — Means to be "short" on a prison sentence, with one-to-two years or less to go.

Shot-caller — Prison gang leader who calls the shots and must be obeyed. Also, the person who hands down the orders to associates of a lower rank.

SHU — Pronounced "shoe" and stands for Special Housing Unit. Also synonymous with the "Hole." The SHU/hole is solitary confinement housing used for punitive or protective purposes.

SIS — Special Investigative Services. An SIA (Special Investigative Agent) investigates gang-related infractions and other prison rule violations, similar to the role of an FBI agent.

SMU — Special Management Unit: a highly restrictive, nearly 24-hour lockdown, experimental prison program that no longer exists in the federal prison system. Designed with the misguided aim of housing the "worst of the worst" federal inmates to make the other prisons safer, the SMU at Lewisburg, PA (2009-2018) was rocked by high rates of inmate violence, prisoner deaths, and reports of abuse with excessive punitive shackling. An inundation of civil lawsuits and press reports exposing the abuse and violence led to the shutdown of Lewisburg's SMU. But those inmates were merely transferred to a new SMU program at Thomson, IL (2018-2023), where the same austere conditions resulted in similar violence and abuses. As with Lewisburg, civil lawsuits detailing mistreatment by Thomson officers and new press reports of the failed program triggered the closure of that unit.

USP — United States Penitentiary (federal prisons)

X'd out — When there is some drama or beef with rival gangs, shot-callers might put a hit order out on an offending inmate, meaning that inmate is "X'd out" and their days are numbered.

Yard — Prison yard

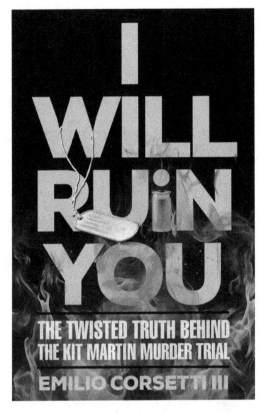

http://mydearpress.com

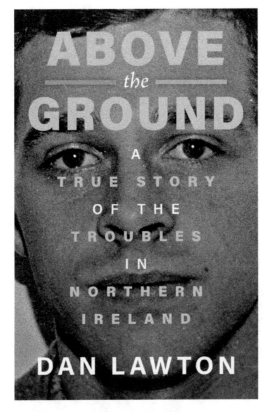